Grace Hartman, a Woman for Her Time

Other books by Susan Crean

WHO'S AFRAID OF CANADIAN CULTURE
NEWSWORTHY: THE LIVES OF MEDIA WOMEN
TWO NATIONS *(with Marcel Rioux)*
IN THE NAME OF THE FATHERS

SUSAN CREAN

Grace Hartman

A Woman for Her Time

NEW STAR BOOKS
VANCOUVER

Published by New Star Books Ltd., 2504 York Avenue, Vancouver, BC, V6K 1E3.
All rights reserved. No part of this work may be reproduced or used in any form or
by any means – graphic, electronic or mechanical – without the prior written
permission of the publisher. Any request for photocopying or other reprographic
copying must be sent in writing to the Canadian Copyright Licensing Agency
(CANCOPY), 6 Adelaide Street East, Suite 900, Toronto, ON M5C 1H6.

Photos on pp. 55, 66, 188 and 200 appear by permission of the Toronto Star Syndicate.
Photo on p. 122 appears by permission of Murray Mosher/Photo Features. Photo on
p. 146 appears courtesy Provincial Archives of Manitoba. Photo on p. 210 appears
by permission of Canada Wide Features.

Every effort has been made to contact copyright holders of material reproduced in this
book. In the event of an omission, please contact New Star Books.

Publication of this book is made possible by grants from the Canada Council
and the Cultural Services Branch, Province of British Columbia.

Cover by Kris Klaasen / Working Design
Printed and bound in Canada by Imprimerie Gagné Ltd
1   2   3   4   5   99   98   97   96   95

Royalties from this book will go to the Grace Hartman Fund to help
finance women's equality projects of CUPE local unions.

Canadian Cataloguing in Publication Data
Crean, Susan, 1945-
Grace Hartman

Includes index.
ISBN 0-921586-47-7
1. Hartman, Grace.   2. Canadian Union of Public Employees – Biography.
3. Trade-unions – Government employees – Canada – Biography.   4. Labor
movement – Canada – Biography.   I. Title.

HD8107.H37C73 1995   331.88'1135471'00092   C95-911020-8

CONTENTS

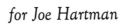

for Joe Hartman

AUTHOR'S NOTE

Grace Hartman was a fixture on the labour scene in Toronto when I came of age politically in the early seventies. I saw her first at the "Strategy for Change" conference in 1972, and quickly became aware of her face and her reputation. I knew Madeleine Parent and Laurell Ritchie, two other union women at the conference, through our involvement with the This Magazine collective, but it was Grace Hartman I saw – we all saw – in the news. However I didn't meet Grace and get to know her until the late eighties, at the SCM Book Room, which she and Joe Hartman supported. They came out to all sorts of our events, book launchings, the "Conversations with Authors" series, solstice pageants. She emceed the launch of my last book, In the Name of the Fathers, which was about child custody and family law reform. A group of men's rights activists had called in, threatening to disrupt the event, and had I known of Grace's experience with the 1979 CUPE convention I might not have been so nervous. Nothing untoward happened, in the event; Grace spoke movingly about single mothers and about the legal system and how it treats women.

I call this book a documentary biography because of the association with radio and film documentaries whose techniques I frankly borrow. I have used Grace Hartman's words wherever possible to describe people and events, and based the narrative of her life on interviews she gave and texts she wrote. The shape of the book thus follows her direction. Like a film documentary, Grace Hartman, a Woman for Her Time *tells a story which is not the whole story but one aspect of a life, one view of the mountain. There are many others. So too are there other stories with which Grace Hartman's own intersects; the history – or, again, histories – of* CUPE, *for example, or of the early organizing days of the women's movement and the birth of the National Action Committee on the Status of Women. I have tried to see and relate these tales with Grace's eyes and sensibilities.*

Throughout the writing of this book I have been aware of Grace every step of the way. Her determination to see this project through, a determination born of her belief in the history of working people and especially working women, has often inspired me.

This book began life as a project of the National Women's Task Force of the Canadian Union of Public Employees in the months following Grace Hartman's retirement as president of the union in 1983. My first thanks must be to those CUPE members – too numerous to list here – who contributed time and money to the book then, and to Debra Lewis who was hired to write it. Lewis kindly passed on her research to me when I took the project over, and granted me access to the two conversations she taped with Grace Hartman in 1985. In the spring of 1989 Gene Errington approached me with the idea of writing the book, and over the next several years I spoke with Grace many times about it. In the fall of 1993, shortly before Grace Hartman died, CUPE's national executive board agreed to fund it and to allow me access to CUPE archives.

The Grace Hartman Biography has now become a reality with the support of Judy Darcy and Geraldine McGuire, the national officers of CUPE, and with the assistance of staff in the National Office (Morna Ballentyne, Shereen Bowditch and Tracy Morey), a grant from the Writers' Reserve Fund of the Ontario Arts Council, legal counsel from Marian Hebb, and administrative miracles courtesy of Louise Leclair in the BC Regional Office of CUPE, who actually made it happen.

Grace Hartman, a Woman for Her Time *is the result of the patient contribution of many people, primarily Grace Hartman's friends, relatives and colleagues who spent time talking to me about her. The Hartman family were* unstinting with their help, their memories and their photographs; Warren Hartman provided genial assistance sorting Grace's papers, and Grace herself was the biographer's dream – a pack rat with legible handwriting. The voice of Grace Hartman in these pages is mainly derived from an extended, wide-ranging interview conducted by Wayne Roberts in 1989 for which I am deeply grateful. A 1993 interview with her by Todd Harris provided valuable background too.

There are several people who helped me with the research, including Patrick Davidson who did the bibliographic search, Rachel Zelechow who helped with media files, and Shereen Legault who provided background research and sage advice throughout. Anne Molgat helped with NAC papers and Shirley Carr with CUPE documents and photographs I could find nowhere else. I owe particular thanks to Gilbert Levine for his editorial advice and historical prompt-ings, to the staff of the National Archives of Canada, especially labour specialist David Fraser, for their indispensable assistance, and to Audrey McClellan and Rolf Maurer of New Star Books for superb work under a tight schedule.

To my editor, Peter E. Wilson, I express eternal gratitude "for all you've done for me." And to Laurie Edwards, my loving thanks for introducing me to Grace in the first place.

SUSAN CREAN
GABRIOLA ISLAND
SEPTEMBER 1995

Grace Hartman, a Woman for Her Time

Grace Fulcher with her mother Frances Pidgeon Fulcher, circa 1920.

1

The Early Years

It was Hallowe'en and a Friday that year, 1930, and as Mary Lennox and Grace Fulcher made their way along the leaf-coated sidewalks towards Palmerston Avenue Public School, Mary's mind was on the fun ahead. That and Grace's startling news that she and her three sisters weren't going to go shelling-out or even to put a jack o'lantern out on the front porch. Though two years apart in age, Mary and Grace were best friends. At school they spent their spare time with each other, at recess and in the schoolyard they stuck together, just talking and talking. When Mary had come down with a strain of bovine TB which blinded her temporarily, Grace had gone round to the house every day to read books to her. Neither of them palled around much with other kids; neither had much opportunity to either, for they were both the eldest of several children – Grace had three sisters, Mary three sisters and a brother – and home life took all their time and attention.

"You mean you're really not going out tonight?" Mary inquired for the umpteenth time. "No, as I said, we have to keep things quiet around the house. Mother is getting sicker." Grace's voice trailed off and Mary sank into silence for a few minutes until finally she suggested that the lot of them, Grace, Velma, Edna and Rae, should

come over to her house that evening for a party. "I think I was
angling for us all to go out together," Mary says, remembering how
the two families of girls often played together. "But they didn't have
costumes, and when I'd reported that to my mother she'd said 'Well
then, we shall have a party for them' and we did. We all had a
wonderful time. My uncle dressed up as a Scottish 'kiltie' and Grace
answered the door when he arrived and was just delighted."

A few months after the Hallowe'en party, Grace's mother, Frances
Fulcher, died at the age of thirty-six of breast cancer. Her youngest
daughter, all of five by then, had been just six months old when the
cancer was diagnosed and only remembers her mother as someone
in bed. "I would have to sit at the foot of the bed and be quiet. I
think she was well enough once to wash my hair, but I wouldn't let
her because her arm felt so heavy on my head. It had been paralyzed
by radium treatments and was like a dead weight. So I called for my
grandmother."

The treatment for breast cancer in the twenties was not pleasant;
what was done was generally cumbersome, ineffective, expensive
and often quite lethal. After Frances had a mastectomy, Ray Fulcher
investigated all sorts of cures, sparing no expense in his search for
something to help his wife. He paid $1,000 for the radium treatment
which was still in experimental stages but like the others, it scarcely
slowed the disease. Frances lived for five years in appalling discomfort, spending most of that time in the hospital or in the upstairs
living room which had been converted into a bedroom so she could
enjoy fresh air from the front balcony, her days and nights cosseted
by morphine. When she died the family was exhausted and Ray, as
they said in those days, was a ruined man. When Frances became
ill in 1926 he was doing well, a successful businessman of modest
means who owned two houses, a car and a cottage which he had
built himself up near Meaford on the shores of Georgian Bay, in
addition to some savings and investments. When she died all the
savings were gone and the houses heavily mortgaged.

The descendants of Frances Pidgeon Fulcher know little about her life beyond the barest detail. Born in Wicklow, on the east coast of Ireland, in the 1890s, she was raised with a sister by a maiden aunt in Dundalk, up north near the border. Around 1916, in her mid-twenties, she emigrated to Canada and took work as a (men's) tiemaker in a shop on Spadina Avenue. Her parents had both died young, leaving five children who grew up apart and then scattered to different parts of the British Isles and Canada – one brother was killed in World War I. The elder sister married out west, another brother settled in Toronto, and Frances met and married Ray Fulcher and had four daughters there in 1918, 1921, 1923 and 1926.

Ray – short for Lawrence Ray rather than Raymond – was an ebullient character who loved to sing and dance and make music, who thrived on his family and children. When his fourth child was born, Frances had such a bad time that the doctor warned there should be no more. "My father said he always wanted a Ray, and looking at me he declared 'this is Rae.' I didn't like the name growing up; people said it was a boy's name. Still I'd only let those I liked call me by my nickname." Rae, who is sixty-nine now, remembers how her father had pet names for his kids, and how "On Saturday nights we'd all have baths, get into our pants and shirts and Dad would wrestle with us, or teach us to dance." There was an open air dance hall in Meaford, and on Saturday nights in the summer, Ray Fulcher would put on a white silk shirt, his white ducks and spectator shoes, and take the whole family out. He always insisted on dancing with each of his daughters whom he would start teaching the foxtrot at age seven or eight.

Then there was the music; the Fulcher house was full of it, and not just the radio or the Victrola. Everybody read music and played the piano or sang, it ran in the family. Ray and his three brothers grew up performing choral music, and all eventually became choirmasters at their churches (Ray at Epworth United at Christie and Yarmouth streets in Toronto). Originally they sang as a quartet, but when children swelled their ranks they formed the famed Fulcher Choir which performed at Easter in churches up around Elmira, St.

Marys and St. Jacobs, the area of southwestern Ontario where the Fulchers had settled in 1785 and where Ray grew up. His three older girls all sang in the choir with their cousins, aunts and uncles. And even after Frances died, the music lived on. As Rae remembers, "Dad was always at the piano, playing for kids who tapdanced or sang, giving lessons to men from the church." Grace also had memories of sitting around the piano while her Dad played; "or three of us sitting on his knee in his big wicker chair, singing and telling stories."

Ray Fulcher did not have much formal education, but he was an enthusiastic reader and kept a library in the house. He encouraged his children to read all sorts of books, recited French poetry to them, bought them the encyclopedia and taught them the value of an education. What he himself lacked in degrees (he had wanted to be an architect, and all his life had plans and blueprints for some project or other – such as the cottage – tacked up along the walls of the garage) he made up for with his natural talent for mathematics and numbers – columns of which, it was said, he could add up at a glance. He was sharp, energetic and enterprising, trying his hand at many things. Shortly after Grace was born he took Frances and the baby to Winnipeg for several months, where he worked in the first Ford sales office opened in the city. By the late twenties, though, he was back in Toronto and had settled into a job as shop supervisor at Berts Paper Company (later Moore Business Forms), which would be considered a senior management position today. His immediate boss was the vice-president of the firm, one level down from the owner. He was working there when the Depression hit and when Frances died, leaving him with four daughters to raise.

In the last years of Frances's life, Ray's mother, Margaret Fulcher, had moved in from Elmira to help out, her own husband having died quite suddenly when she was in her early seventies. Frances could no longer be left alone, and the children needed a mother as well as a father. A housekeeper, Mrs. Shepherd, was hired to do the heavy work Grandma Fulcher was too old to do, and to keep the household operational. Mother and mother-in-law seem to have admired and understood each other. Towards the end when both of them knew Frances was dying, Grandma Fulcher turned to her one day and assured her she would look after Ray and the girls. "I'm not worried about the girls; he'll look after them. I'm worried about *him*," Frances had replied. She knew her children would not be separated from their siblings as she had been when her mother died, because she knew that her husband would raise them – was, in fact, raising them. And she understood that there was family around to help, at least for a while. Still, there was much for her to worry about: the state of her husband's finances, the security of his job, his wellbeing after she died. Perhaps she urged him to remarry.

It must have seemed to Grace that her mother was ill forever, and her dying an odyssey that went on for years – which it did, keeping everything at the house on Palmerston Avenue in limbo. Then following her mother's death everything speeded up, the world went awhirl. Within a couple of years Ray remarried a younger woman named Jean Gibbons, who was working at the grocery store in Meaford when they met. At twenty-six, Jean was closer in age to her eldest stepdaughter than her husband. Grandma Fulcher, who might ordinarily have left at this point, stayed on for the sake of the younger children, and Jean moved in. Moved into the house, maybe, but hardly into the family which would admittedly have been a tough assignment for any stranger.

The four Fulcher sisters were a spirited little band who knew how to make their own fun, and were devoted to their father. Theirs was a tight-knit family and all four kids were very independent. "We were stubborn in our ways and determined about what we wanted to do, having had no mother from a very young age," was the way Grace summed it up. Certainly, Ray Fulcher does not seem to have been the sort of man who needed much help fathering. He tended his children, took them places, took a keen interest in their chums who were given to ringing the front doorbell to ask if Mr. Fulcher would come out to play. Grace would later call him a "good father though probably a frustrated one having four daughters," yet this hadn't held him back from sharing his more rugged enthusiasms with them. "He liked the outdoors so he taught us to use boats and to fish and to do the things he liked to do. We all learned to play poker." Ray Fulcher's methods of discipline were somewhat atypical too, quite understated and egalitarian, relying primarily on admonishment. For example, says Rae, "If we were getting noisy around the house when he was reading his newspaper in the evening his foot would start going – up and down – and we would know to cool it. He'd play with us and take our friends anywhere, but when he said no – that was it. We knew he meant business." Once he caught Edna smoking and instead of punishing her told her if she felt she was old enough to smoke and could afford to, then she should go right ahead and do it. "And the way he said it could make you feel about this big," Rae says, holding her thumb and index fingers an inch apart. "But he never raised his voice with us, he always had a smile and you knew where you stood."

As Rae and Grace describe it, control in the house was based on fairness and respect – qualities grievous illness has a way of bringing out. "He instilled in all of us a sense of responsibility, of the things we had to do, because he could see we were going to be left on our own. He always encouraged us to do what we thought right. We always had his guidance there but he didn't like to keep his thumb on any of us." Corporal punishment was not part of the scheme either. Rae can remember her father spanking any of them only once. It was the evening Velma was heard in the kitchen telling her grandmother to shut up. "I never saw anyone move so fast," Rae recalls with some amusement. "My father was in the living room and he had her over his knee in no time, telling her she must *never* speak to his mother like that again. Edna and I stood at the door crying; we'd never seen him hit anyone before. And after we wouldn't speak to him because he'd hit our sister. He said he felt terrible and told us that it had hurt him a lot more than Velma."

Ray Fulcher was a central figure in his children's lives, and so was tiny five-foot two-inch Grandma Fulcher. Everyone loved her and everyone called her Grandma, including the breadman and the milkman. To the younger three girls, particularly Rae, she was the only mother they had and they all hated the thought of her being upstaged. The arrival of a stepmother was a big upheaval and Grace's response was, in the circumstances, crucial. Not only was she quite a bit older than her sisters and fast reaching adulthood herself, but her reaction would influence the younger ones. There was also the factor of her special bond with her father, tempered by the ordeal they shared when Frances was dying. Grace was something of a confidante and parenting partner to her father, looking after her sisters and helping them deal with the tragedy of their mother's early death. At school and around the neighbourhood Grace got used to "looking out for them all the time."

There was no way round it, Jean's presence in the house was invasive and awkward. She didn't seem to have any good reason for being there save to share Mr. Fulcher's bed and go bowling or dancing of an evening. She didn't go out to work, and she didn't take care of the children. "My father wouldn't allow her to discipline us. We were to go to our rooms and he would handle it when he got home. He didn't want any more friction in the house than there already was," Rae recalls. And the main source of that friction was the animosity between Grace and Jean, who disliked each other from the first day – a deep dislike which on Grace's part evidently extended to Jean's family. "Grace stood up to anything she didn't like and she didn't like Jean's brother. I remember he said something which annoyed her one day and she spat in his face, walked out and never spoke to him again. Her reaction was complete defiance."

But it wasn't only youthful resentment on Grace's part that caused the trouble; there was jealousy and possessiveness on Jean's part as well. "Edna and I were younger and she didn't resent us, but she resented the older two and my father's affection for them." Yet it

The Fulcher family at Little Lake in 1933: (from left) Grandma Fulcher, Ray, Rae, Edna, Uncle George (Ray's brother), Velma and Grace.

could be that the two characters clashed for good reason. "Jean was flighty and flirty and Grace was old enough to see through it, old enough to realize what she was really like whereas we kids weren't," says Rae.

These were difficult times for Grace, and Mary Lennox remembers their long talks. "I guess we were good for each other. We talked about what was happening to us and that must have been therapeutic. Grace had such problems with her father and this Jean who tried to take over." Like Mary, Grace was very attached to her family and devastated by the disruption caused by the remarriage. And, of course, since Frances died things had been a struggle financially. "Father would explain that there were things we could no longer do and we accepted that and, like everyone else, made do with hand-me-down clothes and found ways to entertain ourselves. Mary and I would go to the library and come back with armloads of books and exchange them," Grace remembered.

And then what was already a bad situation suddenly got worse. Ray lost his job when he refused to take the cut in pay his employer demanded. He was fired, and then remained unemployed for the better part of two years. "My father was stubborn. He was third in line in the company and figured he worked hard and earned what he was being paid. The secretary stayed but he didn't," explains Rae. It was happening all over then; older highly paid executives were being laid off in favour of fresh university graduates who could be hired at entry level minimums.

At that point, Grace, aged sixteen, dropped out of Grade 11 at Harbord Collegiate and went to work to support the family. She found a job at the Oriental Carpet Company, an importer of Asian rugs on Wellington Street. Already a skilled needleworker, having learned early from Grandma Fulcher who was an expert, she made $10 a week ($12.50 when the minimum wage for women was raised) repairing and putting borders on the carpets. These were brought in from India and China and would often be damaged when hooks were used to unload the bales from ships. Grace didn't really know how to do the work when she answered the ad, but she quickly learned all the rug weavers' knots and became very adept. It was grueling, on-your-knees work, and dirty; she said the rugs often smelled of camels.

If the Depression changed Grace's life, introducing her to hard times and hard work early, it was not all depressing. As she and her sisters grew into their teens, they laughed and sang, listened to the radio and danced the jitterbug in the living room. When they were finally old enough they went dancing at the Palais Royale Ballroom or the Seabreeze down by Lake Ontario. It was the era of the Big Bands and jazz, and their enthusiasm for music soon carried them to the clubs downtown. But it was open air dancing that captivated them and their group. During the holidays, Edna and Rae would be out five nights a week. Both of them met their husbands at the Palais Royale and that's where, according to Rae, "Grace and Joe became really tight."

*

Joe was Joe Hartman. Grace was sixteen when she met him; Joe was twenty-three. A well-spoken and good-looking young Scotsman, he had arrived with his family (mother, five brothers and sisters) from the Old Country in the late twenties. The Hartmans were known for their allegiance to union politics and progressive causes. They lived in the same neighbourhood as the Fulchers, and Joe first noticed Grace walking past the house on her way to church on Sundays. They met at a party; she was outgoing and talkative and he had never met a girl he liked so much. The summer Grace turned seventeen she went up with her family to the cottage near Meaford, where Joe visited her. You can see from a photo someone snapped as the two of them perched on Joe's newly acquired Ford, that they were already an "item."

"That was a great old 1931 Ford," Joe reminisces fondly. "I had a motorcycle to begin with and Grace's sisters all liked riding on the back, but not Grace. She told me I had to get rid of it. So I did, sold the motorcycle and bought the Ford." Not before a friend of Grace's fell off the back of it one night when Joe was trying to start it up quietly by rolling it down a steep hill and putting it into gear after gaining momentum. Grace's father may have had a point about safety (he wouldn't allow her to ride behind Joe on any major excursion) but once the Ford had arrived, "we'd pile as many as seven or eight people into it, put a gallon of gas in the tank and chip in the seventeen cents, and off we'd go to the beach where we did a lot of tumbling and hand-balancing and gymnastics. We'd swim of course. We used to have a lot of fun down at Sunnyside which was a very popular spot at one time. There was a dance hall there where Bert Niosi played, and the Top Hat Club." (Sunnyside, called the "poor man's Riviera," opened in 1922 along the lakeshore to the west of the city, and with its Ferris Wheel, the merry-go-round and the famous bands performing, was one of Toronto's major attractions through the thirties. As for the gymnastics, Joe Hartman was a serious athlete, good enough to be asked to join the Finnish Gym Team and compete in the Workers' Sports Club.)

Almost from the beginning, everyone knew Grace and Joe were, well, Grace & Joe. Joe was seven years older and serious, just as Grace seems to have been despite her age. Like her, he'd grown up before his time, forced by circumstances to earn a living at fourteen, and he wasn't given to fooling around. Moreover, there was Joe's mother to consider, a most remarkable Scotswoman whose travails began when she married a German. Joe was three when World War I broke out and the British authorities rounded up all "enemy aliens" like his father and shipped them off to internment camps for four years on the Isle of Man. The fact that Peter Hartman was married, had six kids and had been living in Scotland for years meant nothing. Mary Carroll Hartman was left to fend for herself and her children, which she did by taking in sewing and dressmaking. When the war ended, Peter Hartman went back to Germany, to Derne near Dortmund, and tried to start again. His wife and children joined him, but he was shattered and turned to drink. Mary, meanwhile, found she couldn't cope with the language or the life in Derne; pregnant with her eighth child, and with her family disintegrating (three sons had already gone back to Scotland), she picked up her little ones and returned too.

Joe, at the age of twelve, left Germany in 1923 with his ten-year-old brother, Andy. "Like two innocents abroad we made our way through French-occupied territory to get to Hamburg, waiting for patrols to pass so we could sneak across the border. When we got there we had instructions to go to the shipyards and find the *Jon Sauber*, a tramp steamer which plied between Hamburg and Scotland." They found her among a forest of vessels towering seven stories above them, and after two days in heavy seas landed near St. Andrews at seven in the morning. "It was too early even for church." Joe's oldest brother was already back in Blantyre working, and the family regrouped there. But after a time the Hartmans, like the Pidgeon children ten years before, set sail for opportunity in Canada.

Although he was an apprentice stonemason, Joe Hartman left for Toronto expecting to work on a farm near Guelph. Instead, he took a job as a busboy at the new Royal York Hotel on Front Street, after his brother-in-law met him at Union Station with news there was a job all lined up for him right across the street. Eventually he began looking for better paid work in industry – as a stonecutter originally – in and around Toronto. For several years he kept two jobs going, working as a waiter in hotels, restaurants and private clubs (like the Eglinton Hunt Club, the Granite Club and the Primrose Club), and on the Great Lakes steamboat *Cayuga*, which ran between Toronto, Niagara-on-the-Lake and Queenston. "It was the Depression and we took work where we could get it."

The Hartman brothers were a self-reliant, adventurous and athletic crew of men. They had a rough childhood but now there was peace and they were in Canada, more than ready to enjoy life. But never without politics. This had a lot to do with Mary Hartman, and Mary Hartman did not survive the devastation of belonging to both sides in an imperial war without an analysis. "Mother was always aware of what was going on in London with the government and politics. She was always interested in that and I can tell you she didn't have much use for Churchill. Chamberlain, of course, was at the bottom of the list. He went off on a fishing trip while Hitler invaded the Sudetenland." Independent of mind and deed, Mrs. Hartman listened to the news on the radio, read the papers, debated current affairs and raised her children to be conscious and critical of the world around them. Her legacy was working-class consciousness and an inquiring mind.

Like many of his generation, Joe was impressed by the socialist ideas which had become current in Britain at the turn of the century and which circulated through the trade union movement. He was part of the wave of immigrants who brought those new ideas and social ideals with them when they came to Canada to work in the plants and mills the manufacturers were building in record number. The economic boom of the twenties produced record immigration

Joe Hartman and Grace Fulcher with the 1931 Ford at Kiawana Beach near Meaford, Ontario, in July 1935.

along with record profits; it brought industrialization that transformed the workplace and eventually the labour movement too, leading to radicalization of the working class such as hadn't been seen in decades.

The twenties had been a dismal time for the labour movement in Canada. Organizing halted and union membership plummeted "as union after union collapsed before the onslaught of business-sponsored company unions and open shops. Strikes fell into disuse ... conditions and wages were as bad as they had ever been." So writes labour historian Irving Abella, noting that the experience of the 1919 Winnipeg General Strike had left the labour movement depleted. Ten years later there were two rival labour centrals in operation: the Trades and Labour Congress of Canada (TLC) and the All-Canadian Congress of Labour (ACCL) which comprised the unions expelled from the TLC for "advocacy of industrial unions and antagonism to international unionism." The leadership was divided and the movement idling.

In 1930, the Communist Party created its own labour central, the

Workers Unity League (WUL), a militant organization which ambitiously set out to organize not only industrial workers, but the unorganized and the unemployed as well. According to Abella, the WUL provided the leadership for most of the important labour struggles between 1930 and 1935, including the 1931 Estevan miners walkout where police killed three strikers, and the On-to-Ottawa Trek of 1935. By then the WUL had 40,000 members, most of whom were not Party members, and had succeeded in establishing the basis for industrial unionism in Canada. That same year, on orders from Moscow and the Communist International, the WUL was summarily disbanded and members were instructed to work within the mainstream union movement in pursuit of a Common Front. Consequently many of its organizers turned to working for the American Committee for Industrial Organization (CIO) unions in Canada.

At this point, 1935, there were 275,000 union members in Canada, the lowest number since World War I. Canadian workers were restless all the same, eyeing the new industrial organizations in the United States and envying their triumphs against giant American rubber and automobile plants in Akron and Flint, they "desperately begged the CIO to come to Canada." In fact, the CIO never did come to Canada in the sense of sending money or organizers or even encouragement. Yet the CIO had become such a magic name that workers here flocked to its banner almost regardless of who was holding it. The turning point came in 1937 with the strike at General Motors in Oshawa when 4,000 workers walked out for union recognition – as the CIO-affiliated United Auto Workers – and a forty-hour week. The Liberal premier of the day, Mitchell Hepburn, branded the CIO "Communist" and in his determination to keep it out of Canada, raised his own police force – "Hepburn's Hussars" (though in Oshawa they were called "Sons of Mitches") – to back the company. The strikers continued to picket, sometimes 600 strong, and set up their own strike police. Twenty-five thousand people rallied in their support at Queen's Park and two cabinet members resigned, one (David Croll) remarking that he'd "rather walk with the workers than ride with General Motors." In the end, the strike was settled. It was a decisive victory for the workers, and it opened the floodgates. In the months which followed, thousands of workers organized around the country. Says Abella, "A renewed sense of militance and idealism permeated Canadian labour for the first time since the Winnipeg Strike."

When Grace Fulcher met Joe Hartman, she met an experienced man of the world who had survived war, poverty and family collapse; a man who loved her on sight and kept on loving her for the next fifty-nine years. He introduced her to a way of seeing things – including her own situation in a non-unionized workplace – which made some sense of the contradictions surrounding her. Why was it that her mother's illness cost the family its savings? How was it now that she could get work but her father – able-bodied, capable man that he was – could not? She may also have wondered why it made sense for her to leave school while her father's new wife scooted about town in the family car.

By this time Grace was asking about a lot of things. "I grew up in a time when most young people were leaning to the left or the extreme left. It made for lively lectures from my grandmother who thought anything that was good enough for my grandfather was good enough for me, and that included the Conservative Party. I began asking questions at Harbord Collegiate where I was in the minority as a Gentile. I remember the riots at Christie Pits [a park in downtown Toronto which used to be a sandpit] in 1933 – where we used to play – and the anti-semitism and I remember being quite shocked to discover that there were all these people who didn't like Jews. Most of my friends and most of the students at Harbord were Jews. I searched for answers and didn't get many. I think my own family was probably anti-semitic, for I remember the first school dance I went to I went with a Jewish boy and would not let him pick me up or take me home. So I had a sense this was something my family would disapprove of." There were radicals at Harbord Collegiate and though Grace wasn't involved (she joined the Glee Club and played basketball), she was aware of them and some of their activities, such as the May Day they ran a red flag up the school flag pole. It was through the Hartman family that Grace was radicalized.

"Joe and his brothers were all ardent trade unionists and they were all involved in the Workers Educational Association which was an important organization in the thirties. I learned a lot from Drummond Wren, especially about trade unions, and I thought 'this is for me!' I attended schools and lectures and it was a whole new world opening up. But it meant I had to get rid of all the things I'd learned at home." After being around the WEA for a while she also began seeing her father and his work in a different light. In later years she realized that in his role as a manager he had probably either broken a strike or stopped a union organizing Berts. "It's all very vague and I was quite young when it happened, but it fits."

The Workers Education Association was started in Canada in 1918 as an offshoot of the British WEA, which had been set up to offer workers a liberal arts education at the university level. It was meant to provide a "link between labour and learning," and in Canada the motivating forces behind its inception were two prominent educators, Sir Robert Falconer, president of the University of Toronto, and W.L. Grant, headmaster of Upper Canada College (a private Anglican boys school). With funding from the university, and tutors from the university's faculty, classes were offered at night for fifty cents a year. By 1925 the WEA in Ontario was providing sixty courses serving about 3,900 students. Although trade union leaders were involved with the WEA from the beginning, many workers were suspicious of its connection to the university. Their suspicion was mutual. In particular, William Dunlop, the head of the extension department who handled the WEA grant, "deplored the existence of a class consciousness" and in 1926 made a move to clip the WEA's wings by restricting enrollment to organized workers as defined by the Trades and Labour Congress, bringing a rapid decline in membership and activity. Then, out of adversity came Alfred MacGowan and Drummond Wren, who secured outside funding so the WEA could afford to hire Wren as a full-time organizer.

There were two opposing philosophies operating in the WEA then: one which frankly saw the WEA as an instrument for combatting radicalism; the other which sought not "to stifle worker discontent while the cause still exists but to replace irrational condemnation with constructive criticism, enabling working men and women to refashion society to their ideals," as one association member, George Sangster, editorialized in the WEA newsletter, *The Link*, in 1936. In the thirties this view won out as the WEA turned itself into a real workers' association, largely controlled by working-class members who now had representation on the non-partisan board.

In ten years, Wren built the organization from 230 members in two districts in Ontario to 2,100 members in twenty-nine districts across the country. Academics continued to teach WEA courses (Harold Innis, Frederick Banting and Bora Laskin among them) but other teachers and experts like MacGowan (an activist in the Toronto local of the International Typographical Union) were invited too. The WEA program expanded to include summer schools and classes for the unemployed, a weekly program on CBC radio (*Farm Forum* and later *Labour Forum*) and its own research arm, the Industrial Law Research Council. In Toronto the Association also became known for its public forums on current issues such as union security, or wages and prices. The centre on St. George Street was alive with committee meetings, meet-the-tutor nights, Sunday discussions and Friday fireside groups. It provided much more than educational opportunities; it provided a place for working people to build friendships and solidarity.

Like Grace, Joe had had to curtail his schooling early, but he had never let that stop him from reading and learning for himself. This was an inspiration to Grace. "It was a very interesting time for young people and you could easily have lost your way. But by that time I was part of Joe's family and involved with their discussions – which were often heated. They read Jack London and Conrad and Balzac as well as books about history and politics, so I began reading them too."

But it was Mary Hartman who became her mentor and in later years, when asked about her political roots, Hartman always talked about her mother-in-law. "Grace was sixteen or seventeen when they met," says Joe. "She'd come to the house and they'd have long talks. Mother was a political animal too, you see, having been brought up in mining towns in Govan near Glasgow where everyone was a union member. As far as I know the family was always interested in the labour movement. In Scotland we got the labour press, *The Worker*, and supported the Labour Party." She supported her family in all their unions, Grace would recall. "My husband had two brothers who were painters and I remember being at the house one day and Mum [Mrs. Hartman] and I had been having a discussion about something Winston Churchill had said and I'd quickly discovered she knew a lot more than I did. (In fact, she explained more to me about what was happening in the war than anyone else.) So I was trying to back off when the two brothers came in. They'd been out shopping for overalls and the first thing she said to them was, 'Do they have union labels?' That stuck with me."

It's easy to see why young Grace Fulcher was attracted by the older woman, by her knowledge and determination as well as by the heroic stories about hiding conscientious objectors during the war. It is hard, of course, not to conclude that she was also drawn by Mary Hartman's mothering nature, the tea and cookies which came with the ideas, something she'd had precious little of since she was a girl of eight. Her sister Rae believes Mary Hartman was a mother for Grace. "I think at that time she needed what the Hartman's had more than anything she had at home. They were a much better support system for her than we were."

The Hartman house on Yarmouth Gardens soon became Grace's second home. It was an unusual household in more ways than one. "Joe's mother was really a feminist before her time. Even when Joe and I were going together – he would be twenty-five or twenty-six – we didn't go out on a Saturday afternoon until he got his floors polished. Everyone had jobs to do around the house and everyone did them. You pressed your own pants and polished your shoes. Unlike a lot of Scottish miner families where mother did all those chores, the Hartman boys did their own and a lot of other things around the house besides which might be considered women's work." In Mary Hartman, Grace recognized the answers to many questions, both the personal and the political. She was fascinated and perhaps relieved to know there was another way to live as well as another way to think, and for the first time since she began to move beyond her father's orbit, she realized that she was leaving her background behind her.

Grace Fulcher had grown up on the other side of the political divide, in a family with small-town southern Ontario roots and strict allegiance to conservative tradition. She always described her father in the same terms – Protestant Orange and Tory Blue and a Mason who "always went to Lodge." When he returned to work in the mid-thirties it was as an executive accountant on Bay Street at the Trust and Guarantee. It was, in fact, to the world of business and finance that Ray Fulcher aspired and from which he absorbed his values about labour, capital and economics. Yet as Grace often acknowledged, her father wasn't hidebound or rigid. As a parent he was lenient in his relations with people, generally liberal, and when confronted with injustice by his boss, he stood against it on principle. He was also not above revising his opinions and even apologizing, as he actually did about Jean. Says Rae, "Dad had figured she'd be young around us and be good for us that way, but after about two years he admitted to Grace he had made a big mistake and he told her he was sorry."

Predictably, Ray Fulcher was suspicious of Grace's new politics and though he liked Joe very much, he deplored his influence on her. Joe had joined the Communist Party in 1932 and at the time he met Grace was active in efforts like the Workers Unity League, the WEA and the election campaigns of left-wing candidates like Tim Buck and J.B. Salsberg (who ran successfully for Toronto City Council in 1937). Soon Grace became active in the Young Communist League. Her sister remembers the reaction. "When the *Clarion* used to come into the house, my father would pick it up, look at it and tell Grace, 'Your garbage is here.' He wouldn't read it and he never said anything more than that. We knew there was complete disapproval there, but he didn't ride her." It was not Ray Fulcher's way as a father to lay down the law. His response to Grace's association with Communism and left-wing trade unionism was tolerance. He let her discover her own truths and make her own decisions, never putting her on the defensive. Grace simply learned to keep her political opinions and activities to herself. Joe was welcome in the house and that was the main thing.

But the turn of events did create a rift between father and daughter. The big worry from his point of view was her safety, and his concern was not unfounded. There was a history of violence around trade union organizing, and the Communist Party had been outlawed once already. In 1931 seven leaders of the Party were jailed for five years, charged with belonging to an international organization advocating violence, or as Party organizer Sam Carr said, "convicted for Communism." The same year, Fred Rose (who would be elected to Parliament in 1943) and five other members of the Party in Québec were sentenced to a year's hard labour in Bordeaux prison for sedition. The sedition charge was nothing new, but the sentence for holding Communist views was a first in a Western democracy. You didn't have to be paranoid in the early thirties to fear trouble with the authorities.

Grace, of course, didn't see it that way. The Young Communist League "was saying things I wanted to hear. I wanted to see things changed. Other organizations weren't radical enough, I guess." In fact, there wasn't much choice at all at the time for a woman, especially a working-class woman interested in political action. The labour movement was an obvious place to be, but women were scarce as workers, organizers and as leaders. The Communist Party was about the only organization which accepted women in leadership positions at all. Becky Buhay and Annie Buller had both worked in Toronto in the early thirties, Buhay as secretary to the Canadian Labour Defence League and head of the Party's women's department, and Buller as business manager and columnist for the Party newspaper, *The Worker*, and an organizer with the newly formed Industrial Union of Needle Trades Workers. Buller had gone, in her capacity as a union organizer, to join the Estevan strike in 1931, and she led the demonstration in which three miners were killed by the Mounties. Later she was charged with incitement to riot and jailed for a year.

It does not seem that Grace's break with her father was acrimonious. He was hurt by her "defection" but understood it was not an act of defiance or a rejection of him. Grace may have been attracted to radical ideas but she wasn't rebellious by nature. Mary Lennox remembers her as an exceptionally kind and compassionate youngster who thought of others and was loyal to her family. She was rather shy and reserved with people she didn't know. Even within her family she was something of a loner, stranded at the top of the sibling lineup and forced out of her childhood early. To her sisters she was an icon; to her father, the one child he did not nickname. And so, by the time the other girls were entering their teens, Grace was out in the work world and active in the community. In the fundamental sense of making a life for herself, she'd left home.

Then in the late summer of 1936, Ray Fulcher, aged forty-eight, collapsed of a coronary. Grace was with him when he died the following day. Although he had managed to get himself back on his feet financially by this time, virtually none of his assets came to his children. "We'll never know what happened to the house, or the shares," says Rae. "My Dad didn't leave a will." Grandma Fulcher went to live with another son, and Jean stayed on in the house with the girls after her husband died. That experiment was a disaster and by spring Jean was gone, Grandma Fulcher was back "and they lived happily ever after," as Joe jokes. So Grandma was left with the burden of providing for the three youngest girls (which she did as best she could with some relief), and keeping them in school. Despite her efforts and Grace's, Velma left school at fifteen to work, Rae quit at the same age and went to night school ("It was a question of had to," says Rae); only Edna finished Central Commerce by working weekends at Loblaws. During the worst years of the Depression their father had to accept welfare himself, a turn of events which cut deep into his pride. How he must have felt when Grace left school is not hard to imagine; even at eight, Rae could read his face: "To have reached the point, after being so successful, where he had to watch his sixteen year old go out to work to put bread on the table, and all because he lost his job when he refused to take a cut in pay ... ?"

This was the backdrop to Grace's political awakening and while it is true, as Rae points out, that she did not pick up her socialist ideas at home, there was enough in the situation there to ignite a sense of injustice and propel her in that direction. It is ironic, and in a way tragic, that for all his belief in the system and the principles of self-sufficiency, Ray Fulcher ultimately was not able to provide for his children. His legacy was substantial all the same; the legacy of honesty, fairness and independence which, of course, stood them all in better stead than mere money. It's a tribute to him that the four of them stayed together and finished growing up together. Says Rae, "I think we were so lucky. Even though he wasn't around that long he had such a strong influence on us. Four girls age ten to eighteen on their own can get into big trouble and not one of us did."

*

For the next three years, Grace and Joe continued their political work and continued to save money by living at home and postponing marriage. Joe wanted to see his brother and sister through school; Grace wanted to see her sisters similarly launched. She also wanted to get herself out of the deadend job at Oriental Carpets. For two years she went to Shaw Business College at night, where she took typing, shorthand and some bookkeeping. Finally, on June 30, 1939, she and Joe went to City Hall with Andy and Winnie Hartman, Joe's brother and sister-in-law, to get married. There was a wedding luncheon at the house afterwards, and a weekend at Two Oaks Cabins on Wasaga Beach for a honeymoon. Then Joe moved in with Grace, her sisters and her Gram to the house on Hepbourn Street. It was practically a non-event, for Joe was already one of the family. He and Grace had been going together for five years, and even when Ray Fulcher was alive he was often around the house to babysit. To Rae and Edna he was just there, like a brother.

Within a couple of months of their marriage, the war broke out and Joe's plant went out on strike. He was working for the Trane Company of Canada, the branch plant of a big American firm which manufactured air conditioning and heating equipment. "We were trying to organize the place for the Steel Workers and they laid a bunch of us off for trying," says Joe. "The reason they gave was that they could no longer get the aluminium supply they needed from England. So we picketed the place. They locked us out and then what did the company bosses do? They brought in a huge load of fresh cinders to put down on the track where we had to walk. Well, we walked those cinders until they were flat!"

The plant was out for several weeks and Grace helped form a women's auxiliary ("Oh my, she hated that word, though," winces Joe) which provided lunches and solicited food from local merchants for the strikers' families. She was still working at Oriental Carpets then. "I'd do the picket line in the morning and hop the streetcar to work. I'd come back at night, and in all my inexperience and youth, I'd go around to talk to the strikers' wives, trying to convince them this was the right thing to do. Some of them were quite receptive; others would have no part of me and I can't blame them. There was no strike fund and those women had families. Workers were being watched and spied on by management and people had reason to fear reprisals. In one plant Joe was in, I remember an older man who agreed to be president of the local being fired and then blacklisted." That sort of tactic really bothered Grace, but she realized Joe was in a different position from most of the men he worked with at the time; he lived at home and had no other mouths to feed. For him the risks weren't so steep. The company outlasted the strikers; Joe and several others lost their jobs.

Grace began working in small offices as a temporary clerk. Though a vast improvement on Oriental Carpets, it was a conventional job for a woman. "Sure, there was nursing, and teaching and office work. I wanted to be a lawyer. I remember a family moved in next door on Palmerston and the youngest son was just finishing law school. I realized I wanted to study law, but saw the length of time that took and figured out it was not going to be for me. Then I thought about being a teacher, but I didn't stay in school long enough for that. I did want to *do* things and I was frustrated; I always thought I'd go back to school – but you don't go back, at least you didn't in those days." But she soon discovered that her secretarial skills could be put to a progressive purpose; even revolutionaries need steno services.

After taking several ordinary, short-term office jobs, Grace went to work for C.S. Jackson at the United Electrical, Radio and Machine Workers (UE). In July 1941, UE was setting up its first office at Queen and Bay streets, and Joe, who was a big supporter of Jackson's union, contributed $200 to the endeavour by taking out a loan at the bank, using the steady job he had by then at Metallic Roofing as collateral. Following the victorious UAW strike of 1937, Jackson, an ex-WULer, had been one of the first CIO organizers on the scene in Toronto. That same year he was appointed organizer for UE District 5 (Canada), and by the spring of 1941, although the UE was a small union, Jackson had gained a reputation as a leading voice on the left. He was a member of the first executive committee of the Canadian Congress of Labour (CCL) (created through a merger of the CIO unions and the ACCL in 1940) and quickly became the Congress's most acerbic critic. By May of 1941 the rest of the executive was mad enough to vote to suspend him from the committee (in a constitutionally dubious move), but before that could be resolved he was grabbed by the RCMP and interned for anti-war activities.

Jackson was gone six months, during which period Grace Hartman ran the office. She was there all through the crisis, witnessing the political shakedown in the trade union mainstream. She remembered Jackson as "a very shrewd man who knew how to pull a union together. He was a great organizer and he was doing it while fighting against the worst odds, for the UE (it had not been expelled yet) was considered a Communist-led union and was not received anywhere." She helped with organizing drives at General Electric and Westinghouse, and helped produce thousands of leaflets. She left the UE in December 1941 and returned to temporary work. (Over the next seven years, the UE was suspended or threatened with suspension by the Congress no less than six times and though anti-Communism was the primary motive, the C-word was never invoked publicly. Jackson didn't admit membership in the Party, and never, even on the eve of his final suspension, let up on his criticism of CCL policy and leadership.) Around the same time, Grace did a brief stint with another left-wing union, this time the breakaway group from the Steel Workers Organizing Committee (SWOC) which formed after Jackson's one-time fellow CIO organizer, Dick Steele, was fired from SWOC for harbouring "undeclared Communist intentions." Charles Millard, a ubiquitous anti-Communist and Co-operative Commonwealth Federation (CCF) supporter, who had also figured in Jackson's battle with the CCL, was hired to replace him. Four locals in southern Ontario rebelled, forming the so-called Ontario Executive which was run by Harry Hunter, Harry Hambergh and Steele (until *his* internment). They set up shop in a storefront down on Queen at Shaw Street. Grace would go in in the morning and light the coal stove, do the leaflets, the letters and answer the phone. Mornings and evenings she would likely be leafletting at plant gates, which was *the* way to organize in those days, the best means of communicating with workers. "They [Steele and Hunter] were really dedicated people and committed to workers' rights. They were gut trade unionists who could talk to workers and understood their problems because they'd been through them. The workers followed them ... Those men were a great influence. I remember they took great patience talking to me." A woman heading for leadership in the union movement might learn a great deal on a job like that.

During the war years, and after Grace and Joe had moved out on their own to a little apartment on Huron Street, life, love and work revolved around politics. Both were active Communists although Joe was the only Party member. Both worked at a series of jobs. Joe moved from metal plants to the shipyards, where work on minesweepers exempted him from conscription. When Russia joined the war, the Communist Party reversed its previous anti-war position. So too, governments which had always frowned on married women working did a volte-face and began providing subsidized daycare to help lure married women into the workforce. Grace Hartman, for the time being, was headed in the opposite direction. In the fall of 1942 she had her first son, Warren, and for some time she stayed home with him, though "staying home" in her case still meant committee work and occasional jobs for the UE. (Warren would be dropped off at the public nursery school in Jessie Ketchum Junior School.) As the war unfolded there were more political events to attend as well as social events. Warren Hartman remembers those

Joe and Grace Hartman outside the Huron Street apartment in 1944.

days in Toronto's Annex neighbourhood, when the world extended as far as the Royal Ontario Museum at Bloor and Avenue Road, and the Boys and Girls Library down on College Street. From the point of view of a gregarious child, family life was filled with people coming in and out of the house, the camaraderie of group picnics and concerts, and the excitement of trips to the theatre. One of his earliest memories is of going out to dinner on his own for the first time at age four, all the way down the street to supper with Mr. J.B. Salsberg. But from those years he also remembers women like Lil Greene, who worked for Drummond Wren at the WEA, and Mildred Helfand Ryerson, an occupational therapist who set up a shop called Artisans in the Gerrard Street Village to market the work of craftspeople and native artists. Both women were Party activists busy changing the world, who still had the time for children and, in Mildred's case, time to intrigue young Warren with music, art, dance and the joy of his own creativity.

*

When Warren was six, Grace became pregnant with her second son. She was just turning thirty – about the same age her mother was when she had developed cancer. Grace was in her eighth month, baking in the kitchen, when she struck her breast with a cookie sheet; a lump developed and the doctor prescribed a mastectomy. A few days after the operation, labour was induced and Robert was born. It was the family physician, Dr. Moore, who took care of her, delivered her baby and took her breast, and afterwards it was he who advised the couple to keep the story to themselves. People's experience with cancer in those days was brutish: nearly anyone who got cancer died of it. Just knowing that, and knowing about Grace's disfigurement, would cause people to reject Grace and turn away from her. Recovery, he thought, would require silence. Joe remembers, "The doctors were amazed they had done such a good job and got it all. Grace and I were young then, you know, and didn't take illness so seriously. We thought of it as something you get over. Which she did." But for quite some time they kept it to themselves, not even telling Grace's sisters.

Grace Hartman's childhood was overshadowed by the two calamities of her mother's death and the Depression which put her father out of work. These events forced independence on her early, forced her to take responsibility and to think for herself. They set her on the path out of her class and into the trade union movement. Sadly, her mother's legacy was mainly the memory of her horrible illness and lingering death. To that was slowly added the fear that the cancer would return, that her family was blighted. When her own body erupted, Grace began to suspect it might be something in their genes. But she shielded her sisters from the subject for a while, until they began to get married and have babies too. No one in her family on her mother's side had made it through middle age for two generations. Now it became Grace's determination to change the script for her generation. If Frances's death cast a pall over her firstborn daughter's youth and health, it also focused her energies. It was a mature person's insight Grace gleaned, that life is a one-shot deal with no trial runs or guarantees of attaining even half the allotted three score years and ten.

From her father's side of the family, Grace Hartman inherited Grandma Fulcher's small frame and her father's strong features. People said she was the spitting image of him, sharing the Fulcher streak of stubbornness and the stout chin to go with it. Like him, she was blessed with energy, drive and a basically positive nature. By the time Ray Fulcher died, though, Grace was already set on her own course. The experience of the Depression, the poverty and unemployment, the exploitation – especially of women – had taught her something about inequality and injustice and she was deeply affected. Young people who see the world around them in those terms often try to change things, either by becoming delinquent or dissident. Grace eagerly joined the dissidents in search of other ways to organize things so that the world wouldn't be so unfair, and women wouldn't have to endure so much drudgery. But it wasn't until she met Joe Hartman that she found the words for those understandings.

373 REPORTER
SEPTEMBER 1960

"TO GET AN OVER-ALL PICTURE OF OUR BUSINESS,
I SUGGEST WE CALL IN THE SWITCHBOARD OPERATOR"

DON'T FORGET

UNION   MEETING

september 12, 1960

COMMUNITY HALL

The cover of CUPE Local 373's newsletter, 373 REPORTER, September 1960.

2

Local 373 and
the Township of North York

1949 was the year of the big move. For the first ten years of their married life, Grace and Joe Hartman had lived close to the heart of the city. First they lived with her sisters, then with Joe's brothers in a rented duplex on Huron Street just below Casa Loma – Winnie and Andy downstairs; Grace, Joe, young Warren (and latterly infant Bob), along with Joe's brothers Jimmy and John, upstairs. These were working-class neighbourhoods then, parts of Toronto which had been built up for almost a century; communities which had histories as well as a politic. Densely populated and racially mixed, the area abutted the Annex where some of Toronto's wealthiest families lived along St. George Street and Bedford Road to the east. Although Mary Lennox remembers Palmerston as a fairly Anglo-Saxon enclave, the larger community was actually highly diversified. The Chinese were well established along Dundas and Elizabeth streets, as were the Jewish shopkeepers around Kensington Market. Already the area west of Spadina had become a catchment for immigrant populations as they moved into the country and before they moved up to more prosperous sections of town. Advantage and disadvantage lived in closer proximity then, and politics nearer the streets. In the summer of 1933, for example, a baseball game between Jewish and non-Jewish teams, played before a crowd of 10,000 at Christie Pits, became the scene of a violent fight provoked by a local Nazi group which lasted until two in the morning. But if anti-semitism was rife, so were progressive politics and these were the neighbourhoods in Toronto which elected Communists to Toronto City Council and the Provincial Legislature.

The thirties and forties had been years of tremendous public agitation and activity in Toronto; the political and social upheavals of the Depression and the war had demanded that, though not all of the public gatherings were confrontational by any means. There were strikes and protest rallies aiming dissent at unemployment, the work camps and wartime prices, but there were also parades and drives in support of the war effort which, like the Depression, had a salutary side to it: the side which drew people together to organize for themselves. Grace and Joe lived close to the political action in those days, in the thick of the left community which has been described as a counterculture all its own. Socialism was understood, after all, as a challenge to the fundamental values of capitalism; those who followed its lead looked to a future where not only the relationship between wealth and production would be rearranged, but also the relationship between the individual and the state, altering the whole concept and significance of citizenship. The sixties generation was not the only one to invent itself artistically and socially as well as politically; there was political theatre, music and art in the thirties, just as there were communal approaches to living (the summer camps and schools), and always that intense engagement with the ideal of a better world. This was the time of the Progressive Arts Clubs, the Theatre of Action, the West End Community Centre in Vancouver, and ethnic cultural groups of all descriptions. It was a disciplined life, but it was rich with ideas and alive with the commitment to social change. Grace was still wearing bandages and recuperating after breast surgery when, as Joe recalls, the two of them were down at Harbord Collegiate to hear veteran Communist Sam Carr speak.

In 1949 Grace and Joe Hartman left all that and moved out to a brand new housing division on the northern reaches of Toronto in the Township of North York. Right after the war, huge numbers of young people began migrating to newly developed subdivisions above the city, which would later be called the suburbs. They were attracted by cheap land and low taxes – vacant lots were going for a song in North York, some four thousand of them having been abandoned by speculators during the Depression. Many bought serviced lots and built their own houses, which is how the subdivision of Dunview came into being on land above Sheppard Avenue east of Yonge Street, where farmers had been planting crops only a few seasons before. Joe and his older brothers built a bungalow together on Dunforest Avenue, big enough for Joe's family to share with his brother Jimmy and his wife Hilda.

The end of the war and the coming of economic prosperity coincided with a major shift in the Hartmans' lives; it was a period when Grace focussed her attention on her young children and the tiny community she had just moved into, one which the Hartmans and the other couples who met there created from scratch. It started with the effort around getting the houses built – a good deal of which was organized like barn raisings on the prairies. Later on there were the Christmas and Hallowe'en parties for the children, summer outings and winter skating on the nearby creek. Someone gave all the kids pumpkin seeds to plant and then organized a competition for the largest pumpkin in the fall. Someone else organized a bowling league with a difference: ten pairs where six would bowl and four would babysit in rotation each week. Another person, who had been a caller, suggested a square dance group, so the Dunview Square Dance Club was born.

"We'd have our dances in people's empty basements in the beginning (when they started putting in carpets we had to go elsewhere!), and everyone would bring something – coffee or the bread or salad. It was sort of illegal but we sold liquor and made enough to buy a record player and a sound system. Before long we had the kids dancing too. They squared at the Canadian National Exhibition and the Royal Winter Fair and the local plazas." Sybil Bellmore met Grace Hartman on Dunforest Avenue and they became friends on the spot. "We just hit it off; we had the same interest in sewing and knitting and cooking. My husband Ray was quite close with Joe, Jimmy and Andy; he got into the same things."

Sewing and knitting and domestic arts acquired a new importance. In the first place, Sybil and her twin sister Hazel ("You are talking serious dressmakers here," Joe Hartman says of them) shared an exceptional talent for needlework of all kinds with Grace. This was a passion Grace had had since childhood, a skill learned at home with her sisters who were now reaching the age when they too were marrying and dispersing. She had always been adept with her hands and creative in ways which Mary Lennox had found remarkable when they were girls. "She'd do all her own Christmas cards, I remember, and had such talent. I always thought of Grace that way, as artistic, and figured she would do something with that." For a time Grace had an opportunity to let her creativity flow in traditional directions. She baked, cooked and put up preserves; she crocheted, embroidered, mended and sewed all sorts of clothes, costumes and curtains. There were even perfect circle felt skirts with appliqué designs for the square dance club; Grace's was black, decorated with tragedy and comedy masks and a red rose.

Pat Bell, newly arrived from Britain, met Grace in 1949. "We were all back from the war and we started having babies like that. Bang. Dunview was known – tongue-in-cheek – as Hatchery #1. Wedgewood subdivision up the road became Hatchery #2. But we were creating a community from the ground up, and I mean literally building our homes. I had a baby outside in the field in a 'moses basket,' I was expecting the second and I'd be up on the second floor hammering in floor boards." The thing about the Dunview neighbourhood, Pat adds, "what made it so wonderful," was that the personalities were so different. Or as Sybil puts it, "No one matched, really." Indeed, personalities and backgrounds did differ, but the endeavour worked because people decided to keep things social. Few

Grace with son Bob (right) and nephew Richard (Velma's son) on a fishing expedition in Muskoka, Ontario, around 1954.

of the Dunview crowd were of the Hartmans' and Bellmores' political persuasion, for instance, and a lot of them were decidedly anti-union. So for the first time in her adult life, Grace Hartman's social life rested on ground which excluded politics. The connections revolved around children and community work: folding bandages for the cancer society; organizing and typing the index cards for the first permanent library in North York (the Gladys Allison Library, housed in the Memorial Community Hall from 1950 until a new building opened); and setting up a Home and School Association for Finch Avenue Public School – Grace Hartman as founding president.

There was little presiding to do, however, as work in the Home and School was strictly limited. The group organized fundraising dances, but could do nothing with the money raised other than hand it over to the principal. "When they had a raffle to raise money for books, they were told this would only cause the Board to reduce the school's allocation for books – and so on," explains Sybil. "It was frustrating because you couldn't do what you wanted. You could not even go as a delegation to speak with the principal. You could do afternoon tea and bring cookies, or help organize a field day, but you couldn't interfere in *anything*." Occasionally Grace would return to her old causes and help out a bit. Sybil and Hazel love to reminisce about the great collection of dolls the three of them dressed for one event. "It was early on. Grace got us all doing them for a bazaar the *Tribune* [the CP paper] was sponsoring. We bought those little dolls, the equivalent of Barbies at the time, and made costumes for them – Bo-peeps and old-time ladies' fashions – about fifty of them. Grace had a way of getting everyone involved in something like that, and you did it without resenting it or ever feeling forced."

The Dunview years were critical for Grace. Although she did not curtail her activity outside the home, she transformed it so that she was spending most of her time with her family. There was camping in the summer in Algonquin Park, picnics and fishing trips and costume parties galore for the kids. It was as if she were giving her constitution a time to heal, a chance to recharge. It was a good time artistically and spiritually, too, as she put down roots among the friendships and acquaintances she had with other families and their children. Though haphazard in its assembly, there were some aspects of the Dunview community reminiscent of other co-operative experiments of the time, like the kibbutzim in Israel. Certainly the *esprit* and the collective approach to shortages and emergencies were somewhat similar. Dunview became a family by affection and, because of that, a touchstone in Grace's life.

Still, Dunview wasn't without its drawbacks. "Here I was, this big city girl, used to living in a very different kind of community, moving into a brand new one with mud everywhere. I used to work for my sister [Edna] on occasion then, but it was such a long way to go into the city and public transportation was terrible, it made it hard."

Grace felt the isolation and it wasn't strictly about geography or distance. "I really got tired of listening to women griping about husbands or families or the kids. I used to think – there has to be more to life than this, and somehow I've got to get back to it." Grace may have been stranded in the suburbs, but she wasn't stranded in a suburban marriage and she wasn't bored. Hers was isolation of another kind; from the old activism and engagement with people of like mind who were prepared to put serious energy into organizing for change.

In 1954 Grace and Joe Hartman decided on another move, to a home of their own on the west side of Willowdale on Kenton Drive. Warren was twelve, heading into his teens; Bob was in school full time; and after fifteen years of marriage, Grace and Joe were ready and eager to be on their own. They could scrape together the down-payment by borrowing $1,500 from Grace's sister Edna, but even before moving it was clear Grace would have to go to work to help pay for the house, which cost $12,000. Joe's work was in construction and seasonal, but the mortgage payments were due year round, so they would need a steady income from Grace.

In the fifties this was an admission of failure. Sister Velma, for one, didn't think Grace was doing the right thing at all; the other sisters supported her but Velma was a homebody who felt women ought to stay home when they had children. It wasn't a minority opinion. For instance, there was the concept of the family wage, one sufficient for a family to live on, which was prevalent in the labour movement, and one person was supposed to earn it, not two. Everywhere in the popular culture, including the movies and the new American television shows, the message about where women belonged was the same – in the kitchen. It wasn't true, of course, that women deserted the workforce *en masse* after the war. Large numbers of them had to work, with or without children. The participation rates for women in the Canadian workforce stayed relatively constant through the forties, rising from 22 to 27 percent between 1951 and 1961. But there wasn't a lot of public sympathy for women like

Grace who quit hearth and home for the workplace and a second income. "It was not the thing to do among my Dunview friends," she would say. And no doubt there were days when she really doubted the decision herself. A couple of weeks before she reported to her job, Hurricane Hazel roared through Toronto. She and Joe had decided to shop on the way home that day, and the two boys were at home alone. Warren remembers sitting with Bob at the big front window in the living room, "watching the window pane move with the force of the wind, and garbage cans fly down the street, thinking how frightened I was knowing I was in charge until they got home." Grace didn't need any help to prick her sense of guilt; few mothers do. Yet she was better off than most: "The kids had become very independent, you see, and we had the same kind of household as Joe had had, there was no designated work, boys did dishes and everyone pitched in."

Still, going back to work did entail some homemade arrangements in the childcare department – leaving Warren in charge of his six-year-old brother at times. The boys would go to and from school on the bus, and Grace would rush home in her aging car to get them lunch, but often they were alone in the afternoons until one of their parents returned. They were latch-key kids in the days when the only official term for that was neglect. Grace and Joe had long since moved beyond the reaches of their extended families and they hadn't other options. There were certainly no public daycare centres to turn to. One of the features of suburban life at the time was just this sort of ad hoc arrangement.

When Grace Hartman left Dunview she was leaving more than a neighbourhood and a milieu behind. She was leaving a whole way of life and a group of friends who did not, in the final analysis, share her basic beliefs. There was more than economics driving her. "I had to get a job, but in a way I was glad to get into this wider world. I had all kinds of friends in the other, but I was looking for something more."

In 1954 it was not hard for someone like Grace Hartman, with good secretarial skills, to land a job at the North York civic offices. North York was one of the fastest growing municipalities in Canada. Formed in 1922 when the rural sections of York Township were separated from the southern urban communities, it consisted of 45,000 acres of farmland which remained more or less untouched until the end of World War II. Then Veterans' Land Act grants, which allowed a returning soldier to purchase a half-acre lot with a bungalow for $6,000, and the postwar baby boom changed all that. In 1946 the value of building permits issued by the Township barely reached $9 million; a decade later they were worth $129 million a year. The building boom began with houses, but in 1953 low-rise apartment buildings were introduced, and in the next year 245 were built. All this was needed to keep up with a population which nearly trebled from 45,000 to 130,000 between 1949 and 1954.

In 1949, though, when the Bells, the Bellmores and the Hartmans arrived in Dunview, it was like moving to the country. Local roads weren't paved and everything was deep in mud. Yonge Street was the only route into the city with more than two lanes, and it turned into a bottle neck; public transit was next to nothing and there were no public services beyond the basic police and fire detachments and a post office. The pressure of population was most immediately felt in the schools. McKee Public School and Earl Haig Collegiate were soon overwhelmed, so two new schools were hastily built. For some time there was little or no shopping in the area save for the Farmers' Market, which was still operating in the old car barn on Yonge Street at the city limits. The first shopping centre opened in 1953 at Lawrence and Bathurst streets, establishing the pattern for commercial development to follow lockstep with residential expansion. In 1953 planning began on a huge multi-purpose development, the first of its kind, at the forks of the Don River. Don Mills was a $200 million project spread over 2,000 acres of land, conceived as a

In 1949 the Hartmans moved out of Toronto to the new suburbs that began to spring up north of the city after the war.

complete community containing shops, houses and apartments as well as such facilities as a school, a church and a park. The development was completed in 1960, by which time the Township had lifted height restrictions, giving the world Flemingdon Park with its two twenty-eight-story towers. Four years later Yorkdale Plaza, a $40-million enclosed shopping mall with 120 shops and two department stores, opened amid declarations that the Township (soon to be Borough) of North York had come of age.

   None of this could have taken place without planning and investment on the part of a civic government to build the infrastructure to support the increases in population and traffic. The improvement of roads, water, sewage and transportation facilities, not to mention the expansion of police and health services, were necessary. The first major step was the merger of the thirteen municipalities in the Greater Toronto area in 1954 to create Metropolitan Toronto. The driving energy behind the "amalgamation" (actually it was more like a confederation), and Metro Council's first chairman, was Frederick

"Big Daddy" Gardiner, a lawyer from the affluent district of Forest Hill Village, who declared when he turned to politics at the age of fifty-eight, "I have always been more of a businessman than a lawyer. Now I am determined to be more of a businessman than a politician." True to his word, Gardiner's vision was the essence of business adventurism and, as such, fit right in with the prevailing view of development in North American cities at the time. It was an approach which drew little opposition until the seventies, and which saw growth – the bigger and the faster the better – as the key to prosperity. The alternative in Gardiner's view was "shrinkage and decay."

In the beginning the municipalities were not terribly willing partners in the merger, seeing it as a cosy scheme of the undeveloped townships to have the established areas of the city "share" some of the costs of expansion. But the municipalities shared Gardiner's attitude to development and eventually saw the advantages in co-operating. In 1954 Metro took over responsibility for issuing debentures, for assessing real estate, and for water, sewage, public transit, housing, welfare and the upkeep of main arterial roads. North York's reeve, Fred J. McMahon, first elected in 1953, became North York's first representative on Metro Council in 1954.

When Grace Hartman began working as a clerk-typist in the North York planning department, the boom was just gathering momentum. If managing the explosion which followed could be likened to a military campaign, she was working in the war room. She already had a good grasp of civic affairs in the Township, the outcome of the community work she began doing at Dunview and which she carried on through the fifties. At thirty-six she was a young woman with energy to burn; she liked the job and quickly worked her way to the top secretarial level. "It was a fascinating place to work. North York was mushrooming and everyone was learning about the planning and financing of new communities. There were the new subdivisions; the whole Don Mills project was considered quite utopian; the amassing of the land for York University which was supposed to have been a 'university city' with a real mix of people; Flemingdon Park and the Spadina Extension [which was eventually stopped by a movement of citizen opposition]. There were lots of debates and I heard all of them, for among other things I was responsible for the minutes of the planning board and listened to community groups who would come in to make presentations. It was a pretty frustrating business, though. I think the planners were visionaries, but I watched how they would design something for people and how it never turned out that way once the politicians got ahold of it. The ideas just didn't come through."

By the time Grace arrived at the Township offices, both the clerical, administrative and technical staff ("inside" workers as they were called), and the manual and maintenance employees ("outside" workers) had been organized for some time. Both unions (Local 373 and Local 94 respectively) were originally chartered by the Trades and Labour Congress (TLC) of Canada, and when the National Union of Public Employees (NUPE) was founded in 1955 as an affiliate of the TLC, became chartered by it.

In those days Section 78 of the Ontario Labour Relations Act gave municipalities the right to pass a by-law which exempted civic employers and employees from the provisions of the Act, such as the right to certification process and conciliation services. Coming up to the civic election in 1953, McMahon, who was running for the first time, had been approached by members of the building department (Local 373) over the issue. "North York had kept the inside workers out [under section 78] but not the outside workers," Grace remembered. "McMahon said if he was elected he would put us all back under the Act. So a lot of people went out and worked for him." McMahon has been credited with putting the affairs of North York Council onto a business-like basis; he also repealed the by-law invoking Section 78 and brought Local 373 back under the Labour Relations Act. When Grace Hartman joined a few months later, "the whole organization was floundering between acting like an association and a local union, and there was little militancy. What there was came from the building and plumbing departments where the men had been in construction unions. I began attending meetings; I'd have my say, and then, you know what happens – you talk and people give you a job to do."

Within a few months, Hartman was on the executive of Local 373 – something which required dispensation from NUPE president William Buss as the rules normally required membership in the union for at least a year before standing for office. "The president of the local was a young guy who also worked in the planning department. He was a nice man in a job no one else wanted. His father was a member of Joe's union so he came from a good union home and his instincts were right. But he was only eighteen and lacked the maturity to lead an organization, even in the fifties." Grace and several other women active in the local – Vera McGarry and Joan Flemming in particular – simply showed him what to do. Of course Grace had never belonged to a union before herself, never having worked in a place which had one. "Joe seemed to be constantly getting fired for union activities when we were first married, but I never felt I knew enough to try organizing any place I worked in," she said. Yet she had learned a few things about political organizing and she knew how to run a good meeting.

In 1954 NUPE was in the process of becoming a national organization, but the association of public employees in Ontario went back to the mid-forties when a loose federation of TLC locals in the civic, school and hospital sectors was created as the Ontario Federation of Public Employees (the precursor of the present day CUPE Ontario Division). Likewise, a grouping of Metro Toronto locals became active in the fifties under the name of the Metro Toronto District Council of Public Employees. Had the District Council not already existed, the creation of Metro Toronto, which virtually adopted the City of Toronto's collective agreement and pay scales whole cloth, would have demanded workers co-ordinate bargaining across the municipality. The inside workers were the greenhorns among unionized municipal workers though, and the role was not always comfortable. "There was lots of animosity," Grace remembers. "The blue collar workers in Local 94 hadn't much time for us and I think that happened a lot. It was usually the outside workers who organized first and, if they were lucky, the inside workers would get whatever increase they got but that never closed the gap. North York's staff was small and the majority were women. Local 373 was 65 percent female."

If clerical staff members were not taken seriously as workers in their own right, the fact was that the entire public sector was often dismissed within the labour movement. Trade unionism in Canada was built by large male-dominated craft and industrial unions, and the leadership of the movement (the representatives on the TLC, the CCL and, after it was formed by a merger of those two centrals in 1956, the Canadian Labour Congress) was almost always from the "heavy" unions such as Steel, the Autoworkers and the construction unions. Labour culture came by its *machismo* honestly. The arrival of public service unions was not therefore greeted with wild enthusiasm by other organized workers, who shared the prejudices of the population at large concerning city hall clerks, garbage collectors, school janitors and the like. Thought of as low status, low skilled occupations fit for the marginally employable, the popular sentiment was expressed by a sheet-metal worker who exclaimed at one CLC convention: "There's no way that a bunch of garbage collectors is going to tell us what to do."

Within a couple of years of her election to the Local 373 executive (first as secretary, then as vice-president and finally president), Grace Hartman was chairing the bargaining team and negotiating with the Township. There was not yet a personnel department, so workers bargained directly with the politicians. "I remember going in once when Vernon Singer was reeve. I had watched him at planning board and council meetings and he really was a brilliant man with a finely honed mind. I was dreading it and I remember Joe telling me that while Singer may know a lot about the politics of the municipality, that didn't make him a union negotiator. I thought Joe was right, and he was; the session didn't go badly at all."

It didn't take long for Hartman to find her bearings, and her tongue. "NUPE had no field staff to assist locals then. There was some advice from head office and some help in the crunch but with most things we were on our own, really flying by the seat of our pants. Once in a set of negotiations, when the municipality had settled – a fair settlement – with Local 94 and we were at the table with them the next day, I said that we would take the same increase (and with that our salaries would still not be on a par) and the reeve made the mistake of saying, 'Oh, but *they* are breadwinners and they *have* to have more.' I asked him if he knew how many women were sole-support mothers. He hadn't a clue. But I was always helping out women who needed a hand when they worked late and had to pick up their kids, and I knew."

With hindsight, it is easy to see the union and the Township were growing up together. Local 373 membership shot up from 60 to over 250 in the space of a few years. Soon after Grace Hartman joined the staff, the municipality brought in consultants to design a job evaluation program. The whole process dragged on for almost a year, and eventually a worker-management committee was set up to monitor the results. "In reality we didn't know what we were doing and neither did management. But whenever a new job was created we'd sit down and assess it. The fact is they could have snowed us then, but they didn't; the committee was left to do its job." By the late fifties, though, things began to change for locals like 373. "We would always have our demands checked by staff to make sure we weren't making mistakes. Then NUPE set up a research department and hired Gil Levine, who was able to arm us with information and data – a comparison of wages paid by municipalities across Metro, for instance. That sort of thing really made a difference." Bargaining was becoming increasingly complex and sophisticated as both sides strove to professionalize the process, the union often as not leading the way.

From the outset, Grace Hartman found herself dealing with injustices in the treatment of women which the union had not yet recognized and that went far beyond wages and salaries. In her own department, as she looked around and pondered the possibilities for promotion, she was tempted to go back to school and learn more about town planning. She was, in any case, taking on more and more responsibility. "I was not doing a secretary's job anymore, I was doing the work of a subdivision engineer and senior planner. I dealt with developers and builders where I'd be taking files to the works or parks committee meetings. Some politicians accepted me; others seemed not so sure I knew anything ... " She knew that all workers were slotted into male and female jobs, like caged gerbils, and yet she could see there were exceptions, a few women in the department in non-traditional jobs (there was one draughtswoman and one female planner). So when a new job was posted in her department calling for a man, she decided to apply anyway. "When I looked at the job description I realized I was already doing a good portion of it, and what I wasn't doing I could do. I was really angry that it was posted as a 'male job,' so I went to the department head and asked him. 'You know I can do the job, that I essentially am doing it now, and still you posted it male?' He told me it was between me and the personnel director, so I went to see Tom Murphy and asked for an application. Two of us applied. We had equal qualifications (although I had four years' seniority and he had a Monday and Friday drinking problem). Management stalled and stalled and finally announced they had decided not to fill the position after all. Some months later they posted it again, only this time they asked for a university degree – which disqualified both of us."

A fresh young university graduate was duly hired – and Grace got to train him in his job. But she gave the whole matter a lot of thought and discussed it with others, formulating her own convictions about what to do. "I saw the union as the only practical instrument for helping women overcome this barrier of discrimination – in pay as well as status" was her conclusion. The union was a natural choice for Grace Hartman, and for the time. There was, after all, no women's movement in the fifties. Although there were scads of women's organizations – Canadian Girls In Training, Women's Christian Temperance Union, the National Council of Women, the IODE, the YWCA, to name a few – none was organizing around women's rights, much less working women's rights. Looking around the North York planning department and counting her opportunities, she might very well have determined there was more going for her and more scope for her abilities in her union than on the job.

Whatever the case, Grace Hartman decided to bring her politics to the union as well. The fifties were an era of red baiting, fuelled by a good deal of political opportunism and the Cold War. It was a time when many people put their radicalism aside and turned to other more mainstream progressive causes. Grace Hartman had come of age politically in the late thirties. 1939 was the year World War II started, but it was also the year she got married, turned twenty-one and walked a picket line for the first time. The forties and the unusual circumstances of the war abruptly ended the Depression, creating a shortage of labour where for all those grim years there had been a shortage of jobs. Unions flourished. Union membership in Canada soared from 362,000 in 1940 to 832,000 by 1946, but so did the strife with employers. The war brought a host of wage controls and a string of regional War Labour Boards in which labour participated but seemed powerless to mitigate the anti-union and pro-employer decisions issued. This was when – and why – the famous Kirkland Lake miners' strike occurred. In the winter of 1941 and 1942, 3,000 men went out for union recognition and stayed out for twelve bitterly cold weeks. Despite a government conciliation board's unanimous recommendation that the strikers' position be accepted, the company owners refused. Backed by Premier Hepburn and his Hussars, the mine owners stonewalled. Prime Minister

Mackenzie King refused to intervene and the strikers eventually had to admit defeat. Those who weren't fired for their union efforts went back to work. Finally, in 1943, the King government was forced to act in the interest of social order, passing order-in-council PC 1003 which recognized the right to organize. This was the year one out of three union members in the country went out on strike, and more strikes were called than in any other year in Canadian history to that time. The unusual circumstances of the war had given unions the chance to recruit great numbers of workers; now they posed a serious enough threat to social stability to push the government into enacting legislation which would enforce collective bargaining and union recognition on reluctant employers, and gave unions the means to maintain their existence and status under the law.

1943 was a decisive year in another dimension, as the newly constituted Canadian Congress of Labour (CCL) passed a resolution at its annual convention endorsing the Co-operative Commonwealth Federation – the CCF party – as the political arm of labour. This signalled an important shift in trade union politics which came about with the advent of a social democratic party in Canada and the emergence of an ideology in competition with Communism on the left and within the union movement. The old division between the craft unions of the TLC and the CIO/industrial unions faded and was replaced by the fight for control of the movement between the Communists and the CCF. The late forties were dramatic years for trade unionists as organized labour reaped the rewards of a secure legal status. 1946 was another record year for strikes as unions pressed their advantage – with success. The ninety-nine day strike at the Ford Plant in Windsor produced an arbitration award creating a compulsory dues check-off (the Rand formula) and Canada's worst traffic jam as strikers blockaded downtown Windsor and surrounded the plant. Such conflicts, however, took a backseat to internal wrangling and the campaign to roust Communist leaders from the labour movement.

"Unlike many social democratic labour leaders, the Communists could claim with some legitimacy that they had entered the labour movement at the bottom and dedicated themselves to the painfully slow process of building their unions from the ground up. They could also claim to be heirs to the long struggles to create democratic all-inclusive unionism for Canadian workers." Historian Craig Heron is not alone in crediting Communist activists and organizers with many successes and most of the organizing work in the thirties and forties. But he also acknowledges the "debilitating deference to the Soviet relationship" which undermined the Party's credibility. From anti-fascism, the party line switched in 1939 to an anti-war position which switched again in 1941 when Hitler invaded the Soviet Union. "Bemused Canadian workers now heard Communist labour leaders discouraging strikes and attacking the CCF-dominated unions for fomenting them. The Party publicly threw its full support behind the King government and showed no such willingness to co-operate with the CCF." Between 1948 and 1951 the CCL expelled, among others, the International Union of Mine Mill and Smelter Workers, the United Electrical Workers and the International Fur and Leather Workers Union, and then orchestrated the ousting of the left leadership of the International Woodworkers of America, the largest union in British Columbia at the time. The fight was vicious and vitriolic, but the expulsions were accomplished without any official acknowledgement of the real reasons or the real issues. It was an era of anti-Communist paranoia, aided and abetted by the Gouzenko Soviet spy affair in Canada (the first salvo in the Cold War) and later by the McCarthy hearings in the United States. The TLC was somewhat slower to join the anti-Communist hysteria, but pulled off an astonishing feat in 1949 when it invited the gangster-ridden International Seafarers' Union, run by Hal Banks, into Canada to replace its largest Communist-run union, the Canada Seamen's Union – a feat accomplished with the collusion of the Canadian government and the shipowners.

Crusades mounted to stop ideas are usually ugly, and the anti-Communist purges in the Canadian trade union movement were no exception. They left behind them a nasty residue of suspicion and rumour which lasted into the sixties and seventies. Much genuinely worthy work and a good many careers were destroyed along the way, as expedience got in the way of truth and hypocrisy ruled the day. Drummond Wren, for example, was forced to resign from the Workers Educational Association in 1951 after a group of CCF and CCL labour leaders (including Charles Millard) began accusing the organization of having Communist associations. Despite the refutation of all the allegations, Wren eventually perceived what these men really wanted was control of the WEA or its dissolution in favour of union-run education departments. Although not illegal in Canada as it was in the United States, the Communist Party carried the same stigma here, with its connotations of hidden agendas and treasonous activities. Some accused were frank about their involvement, others felt compelled to deny it on principle, and many were falsely accused. When Wren was confronted and asked to sign a declaration denouncing the Communist Party, he offered to declare his non-partisanship with all political parties – to no avail of course.

The dilemma faced by many people who were or had been Communists or Communist supporters, was how to tread the fine line between outright denial and injudicious disclosure. Take Gilbert Levine. Levine had been working as a social worker in the Metro Toronto welfare department when the job of research director for NUPE came up in 1956. It was the time of the invasion of Hungary and a lot of people were leaving the Party. The NUPE job was precisely the kind of work Levine wanted to do, so he applied. "I came in to work one day and on my desk in the office was an envelope with my name on it. Inside was a red ribbon with the inscription 'Secret member LPP' [Labour Progressive Party]. I assumed that it was the response to my job application." It wasn't. Levine was offered the job and then he had to wrestle with the consequences and what might happen in terms of the current environment of the Cold War. "I didn't want to be confronted with my political background after having made the move with my wife and

two kids to Ottawa. So I decided to tell the interview committee."
Robert Rintoul, then the national director of NUPE, Bill Buss, the
president, and Pat Lenihan, a civic worker from Calgary and a
vice-president of the union, formed the committee. "I told them I
had been a member of the Party in my university days. They were so
surprised by my forthrightness – this was not what they thought a
Communist would do – that they listened and again offered me the
job. Bill Buss was an Englishman who believed in British fair play;
Lenihan had been a leading Party member in the thirties, and the
two of them convinced Rintoul." Levine wanted the job, the opportunity to make a living working for a cause he believed in, and the
chance to put his political knowledge to professional use.

Grace Hartman and Gil Levine knew about each other through
Communist and left-wing connections, but only met through NUPE
in the late fifties. When Grace joined Local 373 her past activities
hadn't been an issue, perhaps because no one there knew her from
the forties or the left. She landed in a small local in a minor-league
union which had barely passed the association stage. When she
became active and conspicuous, NUPE was on the fringe of the
labour movement – and not the radical fringe. It was, in fact, perfect
timing in the perfect place. There was space in the local for someone
like Grace Hartman, and as she made the inevitable moves onto
other committees and councils of NUPE, there were others to support her. In the first instance there was Vera McGarry. She and
Grace were a team for years on the Local 373 executive, and were
recognized as a couple of bright lights. Staffers like Levine and
Patrick O'Keeffe were drawn to them and supported their work.
O'Keeffe, who describes himself as a Fabian socialist, came to Canada in 1955, worked first for the City of Toronto and three years
later was hired by NUPE as the third of three reps in Ontario.
O'Keeffe serviced Local 373 and remembers how impressed he was
with Hartman and McGarry, particularly Vera McGarry who nonetheless never came forward. "Vera stayed on but could never be as
active because her husband did not encourage her. She was inhib-

ited, I think, by his family's attitude. With Grace, the opposite was true." She was also, as Pat O'Keeffe recalls, a good speaker with a lot of promise. "In a way we were developing people, urging them to run for executive office and so on. Eventually Local 373 became a predominantly female local and we encouraged that. I don't think there were any women on the executive of Local 79, the big [largely female] clerical and administrative employees' local of the city and Metro Toronto, believe it or not."

O'Keeffe was a CCFer, as was Vera McGarry, but he distanced himself from the anti-Communist crusades and from people he assessed as having no other agenda and no socialist vision. "I was with them a couple of years, hunting Communists, before I realized we were being used. I figured that out at a young age." The protocol among progressives in those days was simply not to ask. Pat O'Keeffe, like many people who might have known of Grace Hartman's work with the UE and SWOC in the forties, or of Joe Hartman's association with the Party, assumed Grace Hartman's association with the left without really knowing what it had been, and that is how the matter was left.

In the late fifties it may not have been Hartman's putative association with radicals that bothered people, but her gender. For starters, she became the first woman delegate to the NUPE District Council in an era when, according to O'Keeffe, "a woman at a convention was looked upon as a piece of ass." O'Keeffe was there when Grace attended her first Toronto District Council meetings, and observed the resentment. "I took my coat off to hit someone once because of the way he was treating Grace. She had followed on a speech I'd made and this guy – Bill Overcott of Local 43 – asked her what the hell she was doing interfering when she ought to be home with her family. Overcott was a rough, tough gravelly voice type who was very much opposed to women being involved in the movement. *That* was the kind of thing she had to fight."

Hartman's own story of that first meeting is indicative if less dramatic. "It was held in a courtroom at the [old] Toronto City Hall

Grace Hartman, Sybil Bellmore and Vera McGarry talking with Mayor Vera Jones of Hastings, England (left) at the North York Centennial Ball, October 1967.

and I remember as I walked in a couple of the guys growled, 'Oh boy, now we won't be able to adjourn to the pub tonight.' " It only takes one woman to interrupt the dominion of male culture. However, as things progressed and Hartman established herself as a leader, there were still those who found it uncomfortable, particularly as she brought more women along with her. After she was elected president of her local in 1959, both the executive and the negotiating committees ended up with a majority of women. "That was fairly representative of the membership of the local. However, up to that time the only positions routinely held by women had been secretary and social convener." It was too much for some people in the engineering department, who decided to run someone against Hartman once in the early sixties. "They decided on a man who was a very qualified draughtsman with a heavy drinking problem. I'd heard talk of this but didn't know that the women had gone through the building to get everyone out to the election meeting that night. I arrived early, as I always do, and found the place packed with women. When the men arrived, one of them griped, 'What's this? the women's auxiliary?' To which one of the women snapped, 'We aren't auxiliary to anybody.' I think the guy got two or three votes."

Management didn't accept her leadership without trials either. "In the thick of one set of negotiations that weren't going well, the committee decided to recommend a strike vote. I heard that the personnel director had gone around spreading the word that I'd never get the vote. To their surprise and, I have to add, mine too, we got 92 percent and we were back at the bargaining table at 8:30 the next morning." As public employee unions went in the fifties and sixties, Local 373 was reasonably stable. The relationship with the Township was basically sound: "We had a personnel director who believed it was best to have a union that worked, so he co-oper- ated." As a result, Local 373 acquitted itself well at the bargaining table, expanded the bargaining unit (to include swimming pool attendants, for example) and made gains outside the collective agree- ment on its own initiative. The women in the local organized a Sick Bay by having a small room connected to the women's washroom, and then they suggested the men follow suit. They took up the matter of lighting in the parking lot, and though she doesn't mention women specifically, the issue of their safety was obviously uppermost in Hartman's mind when she wrote in the *373 Reporter*: "It's a pretty dark place in the Winter at 5 o'clock, let alone an evening when you are late leaving the building."

There were bones of contention to be sure. On one occasion several activists in Local 373 decided to support a labour candidate when the Township set up a Board of Control in 1965. This, Hartman found, had a peculiar effect on some of the members, who felt the action overstepped the bounds of union business and who resisted taking on their employers on their own turf that way. Some members, too, were critical of the local's brief to the Township's Code of Ethics committee when it was holding preparatory hearings in 1965. The brief spoke to principle and policy, and noted: "Most matters of the Township are processed through regular channels. But sometimes one is processed with abnormal speed. Another concern ... is the use of political influence or position to pressure members of staff." The union expressed concern about the amount of expenses being claimed by elected officials, and suggested that they and staff ought to be prohibited from accepting gifts from anyone interested in municipal business. It was this warning about the possibility of political influence that almost generated a scandal. "North York Exposé Fizzles" read the Globe and Mail headline. "An expected exposé on political pressure in North York Township sputtered out in platitudes ... Grace Hartman, president of the North York Municipal Employees Union, told Council yesterday that certain parts of the brief had been blown up out of proportion. She said because the brief came from employees, 'everything we say takes a different colour. It was our intention to furnish suggestions and proposals; they were not intended to embarrass the administration.' " Apparently to some, mere mention of the possibility of influence amounted to an accusation, and to some of the more timid members of Local 373 it was too blunt for comfort.

All the same, Hartman's rapport with the members of 373 was easy and open. Though she shunned the stereotype of the female social convener, she did organize a lot of events anyway, since she saw the social side of union work as critical – the glue that would keep people together – especially with a group still establishing itself and its identity. There were children's Christmas parties and the Valentine's Day dances. Her mimeographed reports in the local's newsletter were colloquial and informative, frequently urging members to get active. "Let's each one of us really try to be the U in Union." She did not, for all her electoral success, take her leadership for granted, and she recognized she wasn't the only one on a learning curve (you could accurately say everyone in the Township offices was). And when the inevitable mistakes occurred, she faced them squarely – the time she signed off on an agreement before catching the fact that full retroactivity was not covered, for one example. "I went to the Board of Control to try to salvage the situation and was rebuffed. I guess they were hoping I'd go back to the membership and they'd throw me out." She did and they didn't; she was frank with the membership, lived down the ignominy and carried on.

It was the beginning of the sixties when Grace Hartman began her ascent through the ranks of her union towards a senior position in the Canadian labour movement. Who'd have thought a secretary would make the mark first for all women workers? As the cartoon on the front of one issue of *373 Reporter* mused: Chairman of the Board to his assembled directors, "To get an overall picture of our business, I suggest we call in the Switchboard Operator."

3

Sister Hartman
and Women's Liberation

N ot Impressed: She Looks After Job, Hubby Two Sons and 2 Labor Unions" blares the *Star* headline, announcing the official arrival of one "Mrs. Grace Hartman" on the labour scene in Toronto. It was 1960 and Hartman was president of Local 373, president of the Metro Toronto District Council of Public Employees and about to take up her duties as secretary of the Ontario Division of the National Union of Public Employees; busier than she could remember, working at full throttle in a field in which she was knowledgeable and fast gaining experience – but unimpressed? Perhaps this was a way to sidestep the Supermom image the paper was obviously after; maybe she was implying that her achievement oughtn't to be seen as something awesome. Even in this imperfect world what she was doing was not beyond any ordinary woman's capability.

For the media, Grace Hartman was a puzzle. Since she was a fledgling labour leader, they might have explored her politics as if they mattered, but it was her home life they were curious about. Even then they got it all wrong. Grace Hartman was the first woman to head the Metro Toronto District Council of Public Employees and she kept a clipping file, that much of the story was true. It was the part about looking after hubby and the boys that was fiction. (One wonders, did the reporter even ask?) The three other Hartmans were doing a fair job of looking after themselves and not only that; they were the backup system for Grace's union work. That was the real story, the one that eluded almost everyone at the time. Joe Hartman will tell you that when Ontario rep Bill Acton used to pick Grace up to go to Metro Council meetings, "I'd always be doing the dishes or cooking dinner and one day he told me I deserved a medal." Hartman's co-workers would sometimes needle him about "letting" his wife go to conventions. "Yes, I'd say, and she'd let me go to conventions too. They had a hard time figuring it." Like many who came into contact with the Hartmans, they couldn't help noticing the way the two worked as equals, how they shared the load whether it was political work or the laundry. It was not so much a case of Grace, housewife extraordinaire (speaking of stereotypes), as Joe, husband extraordinaire. The kids too came in for derision when they dared to cross roles in public. "Like any twelve year old I was not thrilled about doing chores," says Warren Hartman, shaking his head, "but one day when I was hanging out the washing a neighbour came by and snidely remarked as she passed that I was going to make some woman a good wife someday. I was livid and so was Grace when I told her." Not even the back yard was safe from that sort of prejudice.

However, it is quite possible that the only reason the Toronto *Star* paid any attention to Hartman's union activities at this stage was *because* of her gender, and the unlikelihood of her leadership because of it, a case of the notoriety with which sexism occasionally endows women. But even if it was coverage a man in her position might not have enjoyed, it was of the kind she could only thank you for spelling her name right. And perhaps for planting the notion that Grace Hartman was going places.

The evidence from history was not encouraging, for the labour movement is noticeably brief on herstory, having lost, mislaid or simply ignored it. Though you can certainly sense their presence, the most salient feature of our union foremothers is their namelessness. Sifting through documents and clippings from the early years, again and again the researcher finds references to "the ten girls who sparked the strike" or "the Italian lady who bravely stoked the courage of the men," but there are few names and no coherent narratives. We know strong women were there: in Toronto in 1907 when 400 Bell Telephone operators struck after management demanded a cut

NOT IMPRESSED

She Looks After Job, Hubby Two Sons and 2 Labor Unions

—Star Photo by Don Dutton

MRS. HARTMAN, ROBERT, HUSBAND JOSEPH
She Cuts Out Star Story of Her Election Victory

Working mothers, those housewives who have a job outside their home, often find they have little time to themselves.

Add the duties of the president of a union local and the president of the Metropolitan Toronto Council of Public Employees to those of a working mother and you have some idea of the task ahead of Mrs. Grace Hartman of North York.

But Mrs. Hartman isn't impressed by being first woman president of the Metro employees' council. She is surprised more women aren't in union work.

"There are a lot of women in our union local (North York Township Staff association, Inside Workers, Local 373) and their participation in union activities is increasing," she said. She is one of three women on the 36-member council.

Mrs. Hartman first became a union member when she started work as a secretary in the North York planning department six years ago.

She was secretary-treasurer of the local for a year, then vice-president, taking over the president's duties after the man elected to the job in 1957 resigned.

in pay in the midst of an "efficiency drive"; in Hamilton in 1929 when spinners at the Canadian Cotton Mills staged a spontaneous work stoppage after management tried to make them tend more machines than they could humanly handle. The strike committee of three women and three men showed skill and courage backed with the solidarity of 600 workers who stayed out for five weeks and engaged in mass picketing. There were anonymous union mothers in Montréal in 1937 when dressmakers organized by the International Ladies Garment Workers Union (ILGWU) struck for recognition and a first contract. Joined by the male cutters in the union who already had their contracts with the company, the strike lasted three weeks and that time the women won.

In 1937 Grace Hartman was working in the needle trades; not at a factory job but doing hand work in a warehouse with two or three other women. The fact that they were being paid close to minimum wage (which was not enforced in those days) indicates the employers regarded the work as indispensable even if they weren't paying male wages for it. As "women's work" it was safely undervalued. In the thirties, as historian Ruth Frager bluntly put it, it was rare for a woman worker to make enough money to be economically self-sufficient. "Like unskilled male workers, women frequently voted with their feet to protest the harsh working conditions and low pay ... For male workers, active participation in the labour movement required time, energy and dedication that was often extraordinary. For female workers, though, it was often impossible." She might have said "usually," for in addition to the circumstances of their working lives, women were more vulnerable to intimidation by employers and were hamstrung by the domestic mystique which discouraged married women from paid labour and found the idea of single women working "only slightly less socially unacceptable."

True, by the twenties there was a growing acceptance of single women working, but once they married they were expected to withdraw gracefully. Not that the majority of working-class families were able to live on the family wage of the breadwinning male. Until the forties it was the children who most commonly went out to work to secure a second income. Girls like Grace going to work at sixteen was not a new phenomenon. This stigma against women in the workplace meant that not only was it exceptionally difficult for women workers to organize – since they were often isolated in their work – but it was also hard for them to gain sympathy from the public, including their fellow workers, who figured they were only out for "pin money" and luxuries anyway. To Frager, the male culture of the labour movement was a significant impediment to women's participation. "If the 'real woman' belonged at home, the 'real man' belonged to the union." The labour movement was deeply ambivalent about working women, to put it mildly. In both world wars it supported the idea, but only as a last resort; that is, women could work if there were no men to be found anywhere first. Typically, approval was given amid florid expressions of concern for the need to protect women on the job "with a view to their responsibility toward the nation as the mothers of future generations." So too, labour's initial support for equal pay often seemed to have more to do with protecting men's jobs and job standards than improving wages for women. In fact, in some instances unionization worked to the immediate disadvantage of women, as employers, when forced to raise wages, refused to pay the higher rate to women and hired men instead.

During the thirties, women in the labour force continued to be mostly young and unmarried as well as unorganized and grossly underpaid. Females continued to function as a cheap and dispensable labour pool, hired as scabs in opposition to unionized men. As with all unskilled workers at the bottom of the pecking order, they were exploitable. Still, union organizers continued to lament the passivity of women in the face of appalling conditions. Even some women bought the cliché, as did Florence Custance, an early organizer and first head of the Communist Party's women's department, when she exclaimed in 1929, "Women do not take wage earning seriously. To them it is only a temporary necessity." Actually, the

Communist Party of Canada was one of the few places where women activists were tolerated. Custance herself was one of the first to rise to prominence. Yet her opinion was not peculiar. Only recently have writers and historians (including feminist writers and historians) stopped blaming the special difficulties of organizing women workers on their alleged socio/psychological make-up or on their "crippling femininity."

Wayne Roberts was one of the first to see through this prejudice and in his book *Honest Womanhood* he reconstructs the concrete reality of women's working lives before World War I, concluding the true miracle was that they organized at all. He catalogues the way in which technical innovation extended sexual discrimination into a new industrial setting: "By a whimsical throw of the loaded dice of sexual stereotypes, long recognized skills could be downgraded: the 'skilled' work of the male linotypist became the 'nimble' work of the female typist." Organizing was made more difficult because women were operating in an ideological vacuum, and those doing the organizing were small detachments without allies anywhere they could count on. "Not only were they politically and socially isolated, the fact that they also left the workforce upon marriage meant that they were deprived of a continuity of experience that might have allowed them to come to grips with the political economy of their experience ... Women entering the workforce [faced] a cruel irony. A whirlpool of industrially imposed sexism dragged them down to the least rewarding depths of the economy at the same time as it pinned them to the sidelines of action."

By the thirties women were no longer working in an ideological vacuum. With the advent of socialism they now had an analysis, an ideal and a place to do politics. Grace Hartman heard the names and knew the adventures of many – Annie Buller and Becky Buhay, for example. She knew of their radicalism, their leadership in workers' struggles, their jail sentences and tangles with the police (Buller was arrested with nine others at the Cotton Mills strike in Hamilton in 1929), and of their life-long commitment to the labour movement and the Communist Party. These women were Mary Hartman's generation, though, not Grace's, and it was a younger group of women activists that she came to know first hand, seeing them at meetings and political events around Toronto. That was how she encountered Pearl Wedro, a trade unionist who was drawn to the Party in the twenties through her organizing work and through the Jewish socialist movement. Wedro became a vocal and controversial leader of Local 40 of the International Fur and Leather Workers Union in Toronto, which was then engaged in an internal battle between Communists and social democrats. The conflict degenerated into physical violence, though no less violent invective was used as well "as Communists denounced the social democratic union president as a gangster and he responded by calling Pearl Wedro a Stalinist Fish Wife."

That account is to be found in *Dreams of Equality*, Joan Sangster's book about women on the Canadian left, which provides glimpses of disappointments these women had to surmount as they tried to mobilize workers. "Annie Buller, a Workers Unity League organizer for the needle trades, once lamented that she had seen 'a complete lack of organizing work among women' while Pearl Wedro was even more critical, claiming that women were simply prevented from taking a leadership role in union work. [Said Wedro] 'Usually in unions women took a back seat. They weren't elected and they were kind of looked at as people who paid their dues; they come, they go. Even in progressive-led unions, a woman's chances [were] less than a man's.' " *Dreams of Equality* gives substance to the work of women on the left, but also shows the tragic failure of both the CCF and the Communist Party to give priority and serious support to the Woman Question. Both movements were inhibited by the image of women as housewives which they adhered to, even during the employment crisis of the Depression, and paid only superficial attention to women's rights. "The transformation of family life, an end to women's unpaid labour in the home, challenges to the sexual division of labour, and women's reproductive freedom were either largely ignored by CCFers or assigned to the NeverNeverland of 'come the revolution' by the Communists." Indeed, despite women's important contribution to the making of Canadian social-ism and the place of women's equality on the left's agenda, writes Sangster, "one cannot escape the overwhelming fact of women's secondary status in both the CCF and the CPC ... In everything from policy discussion to graphics, cartoons and radical fiction, the man was given a lunch pail and the woman a broom."

It was well into the forties before Grace Hartman began to hear about women of her own age engaged in union work. Madeleine Parent was one of the first. Parent had begun working with Kent Rowley, organizing workers in the big Dominion Textile plants in Montréal and Valleyfield in 1943, just after Rowley was released from two and a half years' internment under the War Measures Act (no charges, no trial). Both were anxious to start an autonomous Canadian union but were constrained to work with the United Textile Workers of America in order to keep the TLC affiliation. "Kent was the first man to ask me to organize and when I said, 'Do you think I can do it?' even though it was the only thing on earth I wanted to do, he said, 'Of course you can, as well as anybody else. There's nothing you cannot do,' " Parent once told journalist Erna Paris.

In 1946, after they'd signed up workers in both plants and won certification, the company flatly refused to bargain. 6,000 workers struck. It was a nasty, violent, two-month strike, and the union had to take on the Union Nationale regime of Premier Maurice Duples-sis, and the Catholic Church, along with Dominion Textiles and its goon squad. At one stage in Valleyfield there was a pitched battle between the Provincial Police, who had ushered scabs into the plant, and 4,000 strikers and townspeople gathered at the gates. When the police hurled tear gas, the strikers responded with stones ripped up from the pavement and "in the end it was the police who put out a white flag – one of the rare times in history when the police were beaten," Parent recounted.

These were rough years in Québec for radicals, organizers and women; Madeleine Parent was vilified for being all three, but the most venomous slanders were reserved for her betrayal of "womanhood." She was called a witch and a lesbian and accused of perverting women and corrupting children. In Valleyfield she would walk by a schoolyard and see the nuns hurry the children off the playground so they wouldn't be contaminated by the sight of her. She also took to carrying her birth certificate with her at all times in order to disprove the tale that she was a Russian spy disembarked on the east coast by submarine.

What is remarkable – but not surprising – about leaders like Madeleine Parent and Pearl Wedro was the unorthodox approach they adopted in their private lives, which they saw as tangential to the political work that dwelt at the centre of their existence. Wedro and Buhay deliberately stayed single, although Buhay lived common-law with a co-worker for a time. Buller and Parent married union activists but did not lead anything remotely like conventional married lives, living for long stretches apart from their husbands. Just as they were unusual in the trade union movement, they were unusual in their disregard for traditional female roles at home, though the whole matter remained personal and was rarely mentioned.

Grace Hartman's induction into the Canadian labour movement was very different from Parent's. She didn't start out as an organizer fighting for the rights of disadvantaged workers, but as a rank-and-file worker herself within a pink collar ghetto. Her challenge was not to gain acceptance as an expert, but as an equal, and as a leader among the men around the table at NUPE council meetings. She accomplished this by dogged hard work, carried out with efficiency and panache. Reporting on elections in the 1962 Ontario Division convention newsletter, Bruce Martin (Local 101, London) solemnly records the acclamation of the two top male officers, Brother Fred Taylor and Brother Lee Johnson, and then turns to Hartman. "The old reliable (and this is said respectfully) Grace Hartman was acclaimed to her third term as Secretary. Grace is, in [my] opinion, one of the hardest working gals in the movement, and is a definite asset to our organization."

✳

As she rose through the ranks, Hartman grew with the union. In 1959 she was elected president of Local 373, a position she held until 1967. Between 1960 and 1963 she served as president of the union's Metro Toronto District Council and as secretary of its Ontario Division. In 1963 she became president of the "O. Div" and for a short while was president of three NUPE organizations. That was the year NUPE and its sister organization, the National Union of Public Service Employees (NUPSE), merged to form the Canadian Union of Public Employees (CUPE), and overnight became one of the largest unions in the country. Grace was elected a regional vice-president to the first national executive board (again the lone woman) and four years later, almost by fluke, wound up as secretary treasurer. The sixties was a decade of rapid expansion in the public sector and Hartman was in the thick of the action. By mid-decade she was deeply involved in issues that went beyond the nuts and bolts of business unionism to issues of justice and the basic rights of workers.

She didn't have to wait long for one festering situation to break in 1961, and of all things it involved the guards at Toronto's Don Jail. For some years, Metro Council and the province of Ontario had been buck passing, neither level of government accepting responsibility for establishing a proper wage structure, which left the guards earning less after four years on the job than an ordinary city labourer made in his first year. When the province took over the administration of jails in the late 1950s, all jail personnel become part of the Civil Service Association of Ontario (CSAO). (Originally they had been members of Local 79, City of Toronto inside workers.) In 1960 the president of CSAO, James Keatings, gingerly approached Pat O'Keeffe at NUPE for help. The following summer the province denied the jail employees the right to a grievance procedure, and their attempt to affiliate as a local of NUPE was refused certification by the Labour Relations Board. Shortly after that, the Don Jail's administration (which Keatings described as a petty dictatorship) was tempted to excess in its policy to prevent any organizing; it became known as the Dyed Hair Incident. A thirty-year-old guard, whose hair had turned white when he was injured in a gas explosion, decided for mental health reasons (to avoid embarrassment to his young family) to dye his hair back to its normal colour. The day after he did so he was suspended, along with the guard who advised him how to do the dye job. The department of Reform Institutions then set up an inquiry and the two guards, along with Keatings who was accused of leaking the story to the press against regulations, were called on the carpet and ordered to answer questions without counsel present. When Keatings refused, he was fired. Everyone was appalled; columnists called it "jungle justice by a kangaroo court" and the story made international headlines. It even hit the front page of *Pravda*.

In the midst of the brouhaha, Grace Hartman took the guards' case to Metro Toronto Council. It was her first public presentation of such a prominence, and Fred Gardiner, the original Metro chairman himself, was presiding. She was admittedly nervous, somewhat intimidated by the surroundings at the new City Hall and the spectacle of Gardiner glowering down at her from the chairman's throne like an immense bullfrog. However, he did want to hear and even asked her to slow down so that he could. The scene is worthy of theatre: diminutive Mrs. Hartman, North York secretary, dispensing advice to the big businessman. It was said at the time she received unusual attention from Gardiner, and you can imagine the impact of her words: "We respectfully submit that the morale of the Don Jail guards should be of vital importance to [you] ... The attitude of the guards has a profound effect on the rehabilitation of law breakers ... the first step in the direction of reform is taken in jail." She went on to describe a typical offender arriving angry, frightened and confused at the Don, emphasizing the obvious necessity for those frontline workers to be competent, properly paid professionals. Carefully dressed in a smart suit and hat, Hartman must have looked every

The first mass demonstration of public sector workers. Nearly 2,000 CUPE members gathered to protest provincial anti-labour laws in February 1966 at Queen's Park in Toronto.

inch the Willowdale matron, the last person Metro councillors might have expected to know what a jail guard does, never mind what he thinks about. The contradiction worked to her advantage. By spring 1962 NUPE Local 878 had been certified and Metro had agreed to bargain. The public outcry prompted a judicial inquiry. James Keatings addressed the Ontario Division convention in Niagara Falls in May, and shortly after a national defence fund was launched (Grace Hartman, chair) to raise money to help the guards and their families through the appeal.

At that 1962 convention, Local 373 brought in a resolution calling for the Ontario Division of NUPE to stage a demonstration at Queen's Park over Section 89 of the Ontario Labour Relations Act – which the papers noted had passed to a chorus of cheers. This was the old anti-union clause (formerly Section 78), which wouldn't go away, it seemed, no matter how much strife it caused. In 1958 a select committee of the Ontario Legislature had studied the provision and unanimously recommended that it be repealed. In its brief to the committee, NUPE had made the point that the provision not only was unusual among democratic nations, but it actually violated the International Labour Organization's 1948 Convention on Freedom of Association. Most significantly, the union stressed, it didn't prevent strikes. Since 1950 there had been nine strikes for union recognition by municipal workers in Ontario and 5,378 days of work lost as a consequence. Nevertheless, as the subsequent joint brief from the NUPE Ontario Division and NUPSE similarly decried in 1962, the government of John Robarts had left it intact in the 1960 amendment, changing only its place in the act from Section 78 to 89.

The Queen's Park demonstration took the form of a day-long legislative lobby which the Toronto *Star* called "one of the most intensive lobbying campaigns in recent history." Hartman and James Dowell of NUPSE presented the brief to the minister of Labour, Leslie Rowntree, and the minister of Municipal Affairs, Wilfred Spooner, while fifty other NUPE members fanned out through the building to buttonhole MPPs. Government ears were apparently still deaf; nothing budged while Ontario's reputation as an aggressively anti-labour jurisdiction, with a history of union-bashing going back to the infamous Hepburn's Hussars, remained unblemished. Now, however, the province seemed to be picking on public employees with a particular vengeance. Nowhere else in the country were they so hemmed in by restrictive legislation.

As if to emphasize the point, the Robarts government set up a three-man Royal Commission in 1963 to investigate legislation for compulsory arbitration in hospital labour disputes. Despite the evidence contained in its own report indicating that such measures almost never work to the benefit of workers or the bargaining process, plus a strongly worded minority opinion, the Commission gave the government the recommendation it wanted. Bill 41 was introduced and passed into law as the "Act to Provide for Settlement by Arbitration of Labour Disputes in Hospitals" in 1965.

With the clout of one of the country's largest unions behind them now, Hartman and her colleagues in the Ontario Division of CUPE finally decided they had had enough. Instead of issuing polite press releases they decided to hold a rowdy rally in Queen's Park where they would present the government with a *Bill of Wrongs*. It was slated for the first Saturday in February, chosen to cause as little disruption to municipal services as possible, the beef being with the politicians not the public. "As we drove down University Avenue to the Legislature I remember saying to Joe 'Who else but public employees would rally on a day like this?' It was so cold. We passed two buses from Sudbury and North Bay and I thought even if only they turn out we'll be okay." It was more than okay; it was a huge success. It was the first mass demonstration of public service workers, and close to 2,000 people turned out. The *Bill of Wrongs* was a newsworthy gambit and an early example of sixties-style pressure politics. The document listed ten pieces of legislation which explicitly discriminated against public employees, creating a second-class citizenship for some 35,000 workers in Ontario. "We have petitioned, talked, attended meetings where we have been abused and belittled ... We do not intend to sit back again and look with envy at our fellow workers. We came to Queen's Park today to demand relief – not beg."

To Grace Hartman it must have felt like the return of the thirties – only this time she was above the banners and behind the mike, addressing the crowd. Stan Little, national president of CUPE, also spoke, as did other labour and political leaders, but Hartman, as Ontario Division president, was in charge. "The government sent Allan Grossman, minister of Correctional Institutions. I read the *Bill of Wrongs* and handed it to him and asked him to respond. He wasn't happy having to do that and he fumbled through it. I remember him saying he considered the national president a labour statesman, and I took from that that he didn't figure me for one." Premier John Robarts did not attend and, on the pretext of a prior engagement, had tried upstaging the demonstration by asking CUPE offi-

Grace Hartman, president of CUPE's Ontario Division, reads the Bill of Wrongs on the steps of the Ontario Legislature in 1966.

cials for a meeting the day before. Hartman and Percy Huggett, a division vice-president from Local 79, had gone to see him, telling waiting reporters as they went in they expected to have twenty minutes with the premier; they were there two-and-a-half hours. The tide seemed to be turning.

Waiting for a dénouement, the perfect last straw materialized in Sudbury. Fourteen janitors and clerical workers at the Chelmsford Valley District Composite High School struck after attempting to organize and having the school board pass a by-law under Section 89 against them. Hartman fired off a wire to Labour Minister Rowntree, asking how many more strikes he wanted, and then turned all her energy, and the Division's, to the strike. Everyone -- police, politicians, workers and the media -- took it for the symbolic moment it was. The Sudbury and District Labour Council organized a public meeting to alert the community, the politicians and trade unionists to the strike and the larger issue involved. "On Saturday, March 13th, Brother Bill Acton [Ontario regional director for CUPE] and I attended the public meeting in Sudbury," wrote Hartman in a memo to Ontario affiliates. "We were well received and it was apparent that the people in the community were supporting the strikers. However, the local politicians were another matter; they seemed determined to keep the union out and three of the four municipalities supporting this high school passed by-laws invoking Section 89 although no organizing was going on in their particular municipality."

Sudbury's labour movement came out in full force and so did the police. There was a huge picket line, attended by students as well as workers, two car bombings and a mass demonstration organized by the labour council in which six Steelworkers were arrested. Howard Armstrong, a CUPE Ontario Division vice-president on the scene, wrote to Hartman in the midst of the strike: "We sure don't get lonesome for the law. Yesterday they had 9 cruisers, and 18 constables; Monday 11 cruisers, 22 cops and 2 police dogs. You would think we were a bunch of gangsters." In fact, the province had badly misread public opinion. The Chelmsford strike was settled without further ado and no reprisals; word came shortly after that the province was capitulating. In May the infamous section was repealed.

The *Bill of Wrongs* was a revelation to Hartman. She rediscovered the power of plain talk and forceful delivery, qualities she had witnessed in the old days when labour leaders were gifted orators. (She remembered George Harris of the UE as one of the greats, and was pleased to share a platform with him at a rally called by the building trades at Queen's Park around this time. "He was an old man struggling with throat cancer, and he'd lost none of the fire or appeal to the workers," she said.) Times were different, however; the sixties weren't about authority so much as experience, something Grace Hartman had in plenty. She also discovered that she could speak in public, hold an audience and play to the drama of the event. Her instincts on stage were excellent (though she quickly dumped the dark glasses) and it was at this point that she began to acquire a profile. Norman Simon was a rookie reporter for the Toronto *Telegram*, covering the labour beat in the mid-sixties. He remembers Local 373 as quite an activist local "at a time when white collar unionism wasn't mainstream. It got coverage the way kids organizing at McDonald's do today. It was cute, newsy, not real unionism. When journalists needed a quote about white collar issues or about women in unions, though, they would go to Grace. You would call her up at work, and she'd take time out from typing reports to talk to you." She was also getting invitations to speak; at Local 180's (the BC hospital workers) convention in Penticton in June, and to the Labour Day rally in Hamilton in September.

In British Columbia she gave the first of her "State of Women in the Union" speeches based on research done in the national office. She sketched in the outlines of women's changing participation in the workforce, growing three times as fast as the men's and accounting for close to one third of all workers, noting that where once a tiny minority of married women worked, now fully one quarter of them were employed so that the 45-54 age group had become the largest group of women workers. (Formerly it had been the 25-34 age group.) She warned about part-time work and its historical tendency to undermine union efforts. She also noted the attraction part-time work has for women, and concluded that trade unions oughtn't to be fighting these workers but should be making every effort to include them in collective agreements. Interestingly – or predictably – this was the section of the speech picked up by Canadian Press and carried in three-paragraph squibs in papers across the country, though CP neglected to mention Hartman's solution: to organize the part-time worker. Left out, too, was the bulk of the speech which was an exhortation to women unionists to get involved. She cited the fact that 15 percent of all union members were women and argued the need for daycare and maternity leave.

> *These are important rights for women and I could add many others ... However, Sisters, if we want these benefits which rightly belong to us we must take the initiative in the fight to obtain them.*
>
> *Too often we find that women are victims of their own propaganda. How often have you heard one of them say "I would like to try out for that position, but it has always been held by a man and they will likely give it to a man this time." This is negative thinking. If you feel you can do the job and have the qualifications called for then apply for it and if necessary fight for it through your grievance procedure ... Any decent conditions which we now have such as paid holidays, the 40 hour week, were fought for and won by workers who went before us. Anything we need, as women, to make our working lives more pleasant and profitable we will have to fight for and what better way to fight than through our trade unions?*
>
> *The reason that women's wages are so much lower than men's is not because we do not work as hard or are less capable, but it is to a considerable extent because women in the unions have not fought as hard for their rights ... In my opinion there are a great many women who still think the union is a man's organization and I think I can say without fear of contradiction there are many, many men who encourage this type of thinking. Let me assure you ladies,*

this is no longer true. It is our organization just as much as it is our
fellow male workers' and unless we begin to assume a more active
and responsible role in our union we are going to be a long time
achieving the things we want to improve our lot ... The men mem-
bers of our unions, and society as a whole must be made aware that
the women are in the workforce to stay. We are not going back to
the kitchen to spend our lives there. The sooner this is accepted the
sooner we are going to be able go forward together to win a better
standard of living for all. Because make no mistake about it,
Brothers, unless you too take up the fight you are soon going to find
your progress will be slower as the number of women in your
particular unit increases. This makes it your fight too.

The Hamilton speech was another fascinating address, made (as
the papers wouldn't let anyone forget) on the occasion of the first
woman ever being invited to the Labour Day platform in Hamilton.
This time Hartman spoke about her philosophy of trade unionism.
Some would call it social unionism, seeing the workers' cause as
connected to larger social and political causes. Hartman's approach
also owed something to feminism, though the word wasn't much in
use then.

At every turn of the road the Labour Movement is faced with
government and management intolerance. They regard us only as a
necessary evil and not as the vital responsible segment of society we
really are. We are constantly being criticized for our lack of partici-
pation in matters of social planning, social welfare, automation
and so on. But, how can we participate – as we want to – when every
time we offer our services we are rejected and told we are interfering
with management's rights? Not only are we ignored in the areas of
social reform, but even in dealing with our own trade union matters
– our voice is stifled by the preponderance of anti-union repre-
sentation. Instead of discussion as a wise preventative measure, the
Pearson government waits until great strikes are under way and

then comes down hard on the workers by imposing compulsory arbitration or some other unacceptable proposal ... And so the time has come when we must demand an equal voice in the economic running of this country, and not just consultation at the whim of government when things have gone from bad to worse.

We in the trade union movement are a very vital part of this great Canada of ours and we must insist on playing our true role. As responsible members of society we should look at ourselves and our own organizations and make sure we are not neglecting our role in society as a whole ...

As long as government and management alike continue to flaunt an irresponsible attitude in the face of the trade union movement, then they are deliberately inviting a like reaction and labour unrest will prevail. On this Labour Day 1966 our challenge to the government is "Adopt a new approach to labour and let us sit down together in honesty, without fear or favour, and try to resolve the problems that are plaguing this country's economy."

The mid-sixties were interesting times in Canadian politics – in the sense of the old Chinese curse. Not only was there a Quiet Revolution in Québec, but George Grant published *Lament for a Nation* at the end of the Diefenbaker era, inadvertently fuelling a renewed debate on the National Question among English-speaking Canadians that brought out the issue of Canadian autonomy in the labour movement. At the time, two thirds of Canada's unionized workers were members of the U.S. Internationals (the reverse of the situation today). Other communities were on the march as well: students demonstrating for an end to the war in Vietnam, First Nations' warriors occupying department of Indian Affairs offices, women demanding an end to their inferior status. It was the time of the Student Union for Peace Action, the American Indian Movement and the Committee for the Equality of Women in Canada

(CEWC). This last was the legendary coalition of women's organizations, led by Laura Sabia of St. Catharines, which badgered the Pearson government into appointing the Royal Commission on the Status of Women in 1967. The committee was in high gear by the spring of 1966. Sabia declared she had "donned the bloomers of an ardent feminist because up and down this country I have found prejudice," and with her steering committee she called for a meeting with the prime minister and cabinet.

Hartman and Sabia were bound to cross paths in these years, as the first steps towards organizing trade union women around women's issues were being taken and Hartman was front and centre in the endeavour. She once complimented Sabia on her ability at getting press coverage, but Grace Hartman wasn't bad at it herself; she could be heard doing commentaries on CBC radio about police harassment of youth in Yorkville, or the Goldenberg Commission report on a restructuring of Metro Toronto. At the Ontario Federation of Labour she chaired the first Women's Committee, set up in 1965, which sponsored a special conference on "Women at Work" in June 1966 at the Westbury Hotel in Toronto. Attended by 140 delegates, not all of them women or union officers as men and ladies auxiliary members were welcome, the conference featured sessions on women in offices, women workers in the plant, and women in service industries. Sabia saw Hartman would be an asset to the committee.

Hartman joined the CEWC steering committee in July to replace Christine Bennett of the Steelworkers, and did so as the chair of the OFL Women's Committee. By the time the delegation went to Ottawa in November to see the prime minister, she officially represented the Canadian Labour Congress (CLC) as well as CUPE. She immediately took up the task of manoeuvering the labour movement into backing CEWC, starting with the CLC endorsement, which was no mean feat. CUPE was not in good standing with the CLC establishment at the time. As Canada's second largest union it had been insisting on representation at the executive council, and the old boys were not amused when CUPE president Stan Little ran for office at the spring convention against their slate. Little lost, but was not forgotten. And now along came Hartman, agitating about women and a Royal Commission. A silly volley of letters ensued as Donald MacDonald, CLC secretary treasurer, demanded official requests from Sabia for representation and so forth, his missives to Hartman so formal as to crack with brittleness, in striking contrast to his pleasant letters to "Dear Mrs. Sabia." Hartman's attempts to get the CLC and CUPE offices in Ottawa to send representatives to the November meeting were not successful, but she didn't let up, writing to chastize MacDonald for leaving her to be labour's only rep in the room. "However, we were all introduced and the government people at least knew we had someone there."

The prime minister was a disappointment too. He sent word twenty minutes before the presentation was due to begin that he could not come after all. Hartman's letter to him was even harsher than her letter to MacDonald because Pearson's replacement, Lucien Cardin, had the gall (or stupidity) to try sweet-talking the delegation: "I think anyone will agree that there is discrimination against women, but men do not want to discriminate, they love women!" Said Grace D. Hartman to Lester B. Pearson, "I do feel, though, when you have a group of determined women dedicated to a just cause you should not send someone who attempts to dispose of sincere questions with flattery. We did not travel to Ottawa to be flattered. We travelled to Ottawa to earnestly request that the government establish a Royal Commission to enquire in some depth into the problem of the tremendous waste of brainpower in this country."

A new year, no word and no Commission; behind the scenes, Hartman was working the New Democratic Party, corresponding with Grace MacInnis, then a member of Parliament, and the federal leader, Tommy Douglas. MacInnis, along with many NDP women, was not terribly keen on Sabia's committee which she felt was made up of business and professional women with a middle-class outlook on life. She also took exception to the brief, which paid no heed to the concerns of working women. Fair enough, responded Grace Hartman. But "I think it would be wrong to sit back and let the other women carry the ball and lay down the ground rules for a public inquiry." She suggested another strategy: "Once this Commission is established then our various organizations will make representations to it and thus be able to bring out these matters in a manner WE think best and not in the manner that other organizations think." In other words, she knew at what stage to take on the demographics of the CEWC.

Early in January 1967, catching the mood of growing impatience of the committee, an insistent reporter pushed Laura Sabia into speculating about what she could see happening if nothing were done. This produced a headline promising a million women on Parliament Hill. In a panic, Sabia dashed off a memo to her committee, explaining the circumstances of her remark and backpedalling furiously for fear of alienating her staid membership. The same day Hartman wrote her a personal letter:

> *Dear Laura,*
>
> *Don't apologise too much for the* Globe and Mail *article. I know that won't be the thinking of some of the other women, but I don't think it does a darn bit of harm. From personal experience I know that in order to get a few changes in provincial legislation affecting public employees I had to lead about 1800 to the Parliament Buildings one very cold February day and present a "Bill of Wrongs" to the Robarts Government. We did then get some of the changes we had been requesting for years.*
>
> *I had a long chat with (M.P.) Jim Walker who has been quite close to the P.M. for some time and he feels we will get the Royal Commission if that is what we really want. However, he did mention that while the presentation to Mr. Cardin undoubtedly was complete in its research and arguments, no one but those present at the meeting knows what those arguments are. He claims the majority of M.P.s are not really aware of the discriminatory legislation*

etc. This may be, or it may be just an excuse but maybe we should make sure they have no excuses. He also suggested that we might not receive much support from the French members because "status of women" is not very important in Québec. However, I know that when I ran in my own union as a general vice-president, the French delegation – all of them men – guaranteed me almost complete support.

I also noticed in this morning's Globe that [Secretary of State] Judy LaMarsh suggests we quit harping on a Royal Commission and not suggest a march on Ottawa. The fact that she went to the trouble of mentioning it indicated that your comments were very effective.

When she joined the CEWC, Hartman understood she wasn't joining a working women's group. She was the only trade unionist present and, along with Kay Macpherson of the Voice of Women for Peace, the only one with a political perspective to the left of the Liberal Party. She nevertheless recognized the significance and potential of the action in terms of the work she was herself doing around women's issues in the trade union movement. It fit in with her philosophy of taking trade unionism to the lives of the people – the whole person approach – and it fit in with a political agenda which saw organizing as a feminist issue and feminism as a working-class proposition. "[The committee] started out as a committee of middle-class, professional women from groups like the IODE, the B'nai B'rith and the Canadian Federation of University Women, people who didn't know what a worker was and who were not necessarily sympathetic to my cause as a unionist, but who accepted me because we agreed on women's issues." To them, Hartman must have seemed out of place at first, for she was coming from the mainstream of a labour movement which was a very long way from equality or feminism – to say nothing of the left. Her cachet and position as a trade unionist was important to them nevertheless. It could also be fairly said that the CEWC women had their middle age in common; they were mid-career women, as was Hartman, and they shared the experience of having achieved some prestige and a modicum of power in the world. However, she and they were about to be confronted by a generation of women (myself included) just coming of age in the sixties, who had a completely different view of feminism as well as power.

In February 1967 Laura Sabia's committee succeeded in getting its Royal Commission appointed. Hartman then made sure to organize briefs from the labour movement so that working women and trade union issues were well represented and had an impact. By the autumn of 1968, when CUPE presented its own brief, she had become the union's national secretary treasurer and was working out of the national office in Ottawa. Shirley Carr, a CUPE member from Niagara Falls who had followed Hartman onto the board of the Ontario Division, worked on it with her; research director Gil Levine drafted the paper. Even by today's standards it is a striking document, thorough and thoughtful and self-critical. Beginning with a list of "mid-Victorian myths" about women workers, particularly married ones, it goes on to comment on the status of women in the labour movement and their general absence from the councils of labour, including CUPE's own. "We differ from other labour organizations which state that the labour movement is in the forefront of all organizations striving for the equality of women. CUPE does not feel that the labour movement does enough to fight discrimination against working women ... The majority of female workers who fight for true equality do so without the wholehearted support of their fellow trade unionists, male and female." Taking equality in employment to be the key to achieving equality for women in other spheres, it made a series of recommendations relating to equal pay, daycare, labour standards, maternity leave, unemployment insurance and abortion (which it advised "be granted on the request of the person involved").

CUPE's document was also striking for its contrast to the CLC's brief which made no recommendations and shied away from mentioning abortion (despite the fact that a motion in support of unrestricted abortion had been passed at the 1968 CLC convention). The

SEX
DISCRIMINATION

IS IT OUR OWN FAULT?
ASKS A FEMALE UNIONIST

By WENDIE KERR

MRS. GRACE HARTMAN 'Employers learn they can't count on women.'

Trade unionist Grace Hartman has some very definite ideas about the status of women in commerce and industry.

"Either we're being discriminated against or our own problems are our own damn fault," she says.

President of local 373, North York branch of the Canadian union of public employees, Mrs. Hartman, 7 Kenton, recently went to Ottawa with a delegation to ask the government to appoint a royal commission on the status of women.

This Willowdale resident is optimistic about the eventual results of government action.

However, she admits some women are the authors of their own misfortune in the business world.

"Many really do not have any sense of responsibility to their employers; when the going gets tough, they feel they can always sink into the security of their family. Employers learn they can't count on women."

WASTE TRAINING

Others, she feels, especially those with technical or professional training, are not using their resources.

"University graduates seem content to sit at home — wasting their training."

"They may plan to return to their field after their children grow up, but if you don't use your skills for 20 years, you've

feminine propaganda for so long, that now they "are victims of it themselves."

But, said Mrs. Hartman, for the woman who does wish to persevere in industry or the professions, many obstacles lie in her path.

"You can't always legislate these things, but maybe sometimes you have to," she says.

Advertisements specifying "no women need apply" and "men only" are among the obvious signs of sexual discrimination.

NOT FEMINIST

"In industry, unless men open barriers to women, they are not going to be able to fulfill their optimum standards. Usually about half the employees in a business are women, and if they don't participate actively, they'll pull down the men."

Mrs. Hartman doesn't consider herself a feminist, although she admits her recent involvement in women's affairs may have made her sound like one.

Representing her union plus the Ontario federation of labor's women's committee and the Canadian labor congress in Ottawa last fall, Mrs. Hartman was accompanied by 79 women from across the country.

The group requested a study into anti-female discrimination in hiring practices, incentives, promotions, legislation concerning marriage, divorce and domicile, state

WHAT DO OTHER WOMEN THINK?

MRS. J.J. WATT, 32 Felicity, president of the Scarboro University womens club: "The schools of medicine, architecture, engineering, and denistry have quota systems to restrict the number of women enrolled. We need education and interest on everyone's part to combat this social ill. Fortunately, teaching is one of the more equal areas of employment because candidates are given equal salaries and hired on qualification."

CECELIA WALLACE, 475 Rosewell, North York, a secretary at the faculty of theology at Toronto university and an organizer for the St. Joan's International Alliance, a suffragette movement active in the early 1900's in Europe: "Women are still regarded by many theologians as having a functional role only . . . to bear children. Times have changed. Laws in Canada and canon laws of the church do not give women the status that they deserve. There should be tax concessions for mothers and wives who work, adequate day nurseries, equal pay, equality for women in legal cases."

MRS. THELMA POWELL-BROWN, director of a school for emotionally disturbed youngsters in North York: "Women working in the nursing field are not paid in accordance with their abilities. The great relationship a nurse has with human life should be recognised and her status and reward should be increased in our society. As far as women marching on Ottawa to demand certain rights, I personally feel that this type of bombastic approach is not a workable technique for this time. A collected, careful approach is far more successful."

Does sex discrimination really exist or do women imagine it? This article was published in the North York Mirror a few days before the federal government established a Royal Commission on the Status of Women. Hartman did not consider herself a radical feminist, but she did call herself a feminist. In February 1967 it was already a loaded word.

Congress was in the position of having to make a presentation, but one gets the distinct impression – as did Grace Hartman and Shirley Carr – that the CLC brass was holding its nose as it did so. Recalls Carr, "The criticism was that it was watered down so badly that you wouldn't know that it had anything to do with the status of women.

It was all generalities; it was yes, girls are girls and boys are boys. Grace and I were there along with Huguette Plamondon when the brief was presented [by Donald MacDonald] to Florence Bird, the Commission chairwoman. Afterwards, during the questions, Huguette, who was then a CLC vice-president and who is so bubbly and so strong coming out of Montréal and the United Food and Commercial Workers Union, made it very clear that so far as she and Grace and I were concerned, freedom of choice was a fundamental women's right. That was not in the script, they would not allow us to have it in the brief, so we made the point verbally. Well, god, I thought Donald MacDonald would have a fit."

Grace Hartman was in her heyday as president of the CUPE Ontario Division and Shirley Carr was a steward in Local 133, Niagara Falls, when the two women met. "Grace came down to one of our weekend seminars. I had known about her for years; our guys would talk about her all the time as this very strong feminist. So she delivered a major address to this little group of ours. One thing about Grace, she never turned anything down because of the numbers; she went regardless of whether there were two or ten or two hundred people. I went to tell her afterwards how much I appreciated the fact that she had come down to see us and for what she had to say. And from there we started to get to know each other." And to work together; it wasn't long, either, before there were cute remarks about kewpie dolls – which is why Carr always pronounces the CUPE acronym as a single syllable – and rumours began circulating about the rivalry between the two "girls." With no other women contending for leadership positions the assumption was these two were in natural competition. "It was tough, tough politics in the trade union movement because you had the political factions as well as the man-woman thing, and the men were very nervous about these two strong women coming on trying to 'take over' – which we weren't. We were always being challenged by our male colleagues to run against each other, and little did they know. Early on Grace and I had had a discussion about that and I told Grace that she should never be afraid of me, that I would never run against her. We made a pact as two women that we would not run against each other, and we never did. We never spoke publicly about it either."

At various times colleagues tried to persuade one or the other to compete, to no avail. When Shirley Carr made the decision to run for the CLC executive in 1974, thus removing herself from contention for CUPE's top jobs, a group did try to persuade her to stay. But she and Hartman had thoroughly discussed the options and decided it made more sense to go for two top jobs in two separate organizations rather than slug it out over one in CUPE. To this day, some of the men who were at that meeting characterize Hartman's refusal to discourage Shirley Carr from leaving CUPE as cowardice on her part, fear of the younger competition, fear of sharing the stage with another women. As Carr says, little did they know.

When Grace Hartman arrived in the job of secretary treasurer at national office, she brought the women's dossier with her and simply carried on the work she was already doing. Stan Little was cagey enough to realize that, with CUPE's female membership growing the way it was, resistance might be more trouble than it was worth. He concluded it "couldn't do any harm." From Hartman's point of view, it was not easy talking about the status of women. "I was considered some kind of oddball when I raised women's issues, especially around unions which judged you for your strikes. It was the CLC convention, in 1968 I guess, I happened to be walking past a table of men when one called out, 'Hey, I understand you're the new secretary treasurer of CUPE. Imagine that, a woman looking after the money.' 'Yeah,' I said, 'Who looks after yours?' ... I was becoming known as a leading trade unionist and a spokesman for women and I heard many jibes when I spoke to labour groups in those years, telling them that women were going to come into their unions and into leadership positions. I recall presenting a brief to the government of Saskatchewan on behalf of my own union whereupon the president of the Federation of Labour told me, 'That was a pretty good brief and a good presentation, for a woman.' Well, by then I figured I had earned my spurs and I didn't need anyone's approval. I didn't care that he was the Federation president, he couldn't make remarks like that. According to my colleagues I went up one side of him and down the other – pretty good for a woman. The labour movement was much more patronizing than the men's clubs who were beginning to invite women like me to speak to them then. I was something different. I remember going to one [such luncheon] and the president looking at me and exclaiming, 'You don't look like a trade unionist.' So I asked him what I was supposed to look like, 'work boots and a flannel shirt?' That caught him off guard; but actually those men had respect for my position in CUPE."

Following the tabling of the report of the Royal Commission on the Status of Women in 1970, Hartman moved to introduce a comprehensive policy on women's equality within the union. She and Gil Levine took all the report's recommendations relating to working women and all those within CUPE's purview, and shaped a statement around them. (So, for example, the CUPE brief to the Commission had called for equal pay between untrained male orderlies and trained female registered nursing assistants. This became a recommendation of the Royal Commission which was now put forward for official endorsement by the delegates at the 1971 CUPE convention.) *The Status of Women in CUPE*, as it was called, was a simple, effective statement. It addressed wage and job discrimination, pensions, maternity leave, part-time work, rug-ranking, day-care, and the participation of women in the union, calling on locals and regional bodies to set up women's rights or "Implementation Committees."

By 1971 Shirley Carr was a general vice-president on CUPE's national executive board, and the two women approached the convention with tactical zeal. Grace wanted to be the first speaker on the resolution endorsing the statement. "I said to Stan Little that I didn't want the five-minute red light [time limit] put on me either. He said he couldn't get away with that forever; I said that it wouldn't be forever. I'd learned by that time how key the first and last speakers are, and how the first can set the whole tone of the discussion. I was determined to do that. So I carefully made notes and I was first up at a floor mike (I always preferred that). After it was over, some male colleagues told me they wouldn't have dared vote against the resolution. 'Why not?' I asked. 'Just they way you put it, we knew we'd better not.' 'What could I do if you had voted against it?' I pressed. 'We weren't sure,' they laughed." What Hartman had said when she called for adoption of the motion in the crowded convention hall, was that women needed the support of men, that it was not special treatment any more than particular policies for hospital workers were special treatment, adding, "You know, women have been held back and put down for so many years, don't do it again. Don't do it to us this time."

A few people did speak against it – including one woman – but the resolution passed with little opposition, and a red letter day it was for trade union women. No other major trade union was working on anything so extensive as CUPE's policy on the rights of women workers. But it implied a great deal of work. As Hartman wrote in a memo announcing the policy to all CUPE affiliates after the convention, "The whole process of obtaining equality between the sexes, within our organization or anywhere else, is going to require an intensive educational program at every level as well as discussion, explanation and some truly sincere efforts to encourage the many capable female members we have to take their rightful places in the life of their local union ... So let's really start working."

We called it Women's Liberation and we thought of it as a movement, a radical movement based on an analysis of sexual politics and class oppression, consciousness-raising sessions, self-help projects and political action – the non-violent direct action pioneered by civil rights and peace groups. Demonstrations, sit-ins, marches. We were an uppity bunch of young women who tended to regard the women of the Committee for Equality as reactionary, which of course was to disregard what they had accomplished and how they had had to do it. It was, as well to discount where some of them had come from politically. Radicalism was not something we believed had ever existed in Canada – or so we were taught in school. (1837 and 1885 were called rebellions not revolutions.) So far as we knew, women had organized to get the vote at the turn of the century and had done very little since. A handful had managed to get elected to the House of Commons over the intervening forty years, and just two had ever had a seat in cabinet. (As Judy LaMarsh told friends, she had to trudge along miles of corridors to get to the women's washroom closest to the cabinet meeting rooms, and there was zero interest in making any change as the necessity was assumed to be temporary.)

Our minds were not on partisan politics anyway, but on things like access to abortion and contraceptives, affordable daycare, sexism on the job and in the law. Just as my mother had been shocked to learn that she was not a person for the first nineteen years of her life, so I was shocked by the "dum casta" clauses in the divorce laws which granted women rights so long as they remained chaste. In Toronto there were many WLM groups – the New Feminists, the Radical Feminists, Toronto Women's Liberation – working on projects and actions like the annual International Women's Day march, the Women's Place on Dupont Street, and a WLM newspaper called *The Other Woman*. I was part of a loose coalition of collectives in Toronto Women's Liberation and a member of a legal committee which ran a community referral service. When word came in the spring of 1972 that there was to be a major conference of women in Toronto, Maryka Omatsu and I, for reasons I don't recall now (perhaps our membership in the legal collective), were delegated to attend. I was twenty-seven years old and had been in the movement for two years.

It was called "Strategy for Change" and it was organized by the ad hoc National Action Committee on the Status of Women, a much expanded version of the Sabia committee which had pressed for the Royal Commission. The agenda was to take stock of the response to the Commission's 167 recommendations and to strategize around their implementation. We were skeptical, but looking down the list of groups represented on the conference steering committee, we couldn't quibble with the likes of the New Feminists or the Ontario Women's Abortion Law Repeal Coalition or Women's Liberation. We arrived at the King Edward Hotel and quickly noticed that the podium was filled with Liberal party women (save the conference chair, Laura Sabia), and the halls lined with government bureaucrats. We knew the federal government had funded the conference, so we figured the fix was in. What we couldn't figure out was *where*. After a day of workshops on political action, mass media, daycare, economics, direct action techniques and community organizing, a radical caucus of women was announced and about sixty of us came together to put out a critique of the event. It took us most of the night and the debate was gruelling. But we managed to produce a two-page statement calling for a more radical assessment of women's problems. We were definitely the jeans and bandana set. A few older women joined us nonetheless, notably Kay Macpherson (then the president of the Voice of Women) and Madeleine Parent (secretary treasurer of the Canadian Textile and Chemical Union), though it was Parent who stayed the course and made the contribution which changed the outcome of the conference. She had spoken on a panel at the opening plenary on Friday, and I had admired her clarity and the way she addressed the audience as "Sisters." I'd never heard anyone speak of working-class women with such respect and admiration. Now we were hearing her explain how the conference was being asked to manufacture endorsement for a government-appointed advisory council on the status of women – recommendation #166 of the Royal Commission's report. It sounded benign enough, but as Madeleine talked we realized it was no substitute for an independent women's movement, and might well preclude grassroots organizing. That was easy enough to understand: we called it being co-opted.

At the next morning's plenary session a huge debate roiled around the proposed federal advisory council. If the objective of the Liberal women was to get approval for such a council, they were out-manoeuvered. The discussion that morning – and I can still see the details right down to the chandeliers in the ballroom at the King Eddie – was a revelation. I heard women of my mother's generation espouse politics closer to mine (despite the girdles and bouffant hairdos) than the thirty-year-old right-to-lifers' at the mikes. I was astonished by the statements of women like Grace Hartman and Ursula Franklin, who got up to plead the case of the younger women, and Madeleine Parent's eloquent, "What we need is not an advisory council responsible to Parliament but a Parliament which is responsible to the women of Canada ... "

Madeleine Parent remembers: "Laura Sabia told me that she had asked Grace Hartman to be one of the panel speakers. Rather, the way she put it was that she had asked Grace's advice about a speaker from the trade union movement and Grace had suggested two names, one a more traditional type 'or else there's Madeleine Parent and she's livelier anyway.' Grace didn't tell me, Laura did, and I suspect that Grace didn't feel she wanted to speak as a trade unionist, for as a trade union officer she would have found herself having to speak in her official role. With me there was no question of my having to be in such a role.

"Well, it had become obvious to me what was going on. There were government women everywhere and when we got out of the workshops on Saturday, after asking questions of a few friends, I discovered that all the workshops except the one I was in had come out with a recommendation in support of asking the government to set up an advisory council – rather than setting up an independent coalition of women. I had help from Yvette Rousseau who was leading the Québec delegation, and because of that was favoured with an invitation to attend the [closed] cocktail party. She told me a government leader amongst the women there had said we must fight for the government to set up an advisory council. It was in the sense of an either/or proposition, she said. Don't bother to organize was the message. They'd set up a council, there would be funds and we could suggest nominations. But of course the government would decide. On that basis Yvette and I concluded this was the occasion for women to set up a coalition. We had never had such an opportunity before, backed up as it was by the Royal Commission. So Laurell Ritchie and I talked to Kay Macpherson about setting up an organization and right after supper the three of us went to talk to Laura Sabia. Laura was very interested ... While we were talking we spied Yvette down the hall with her delegation and made a bee-line for them. We opened up the issue to them and they, it seemed, were split but at least there was another group who thought as we did. Laura kept calling for a real debate. She was a Tory, you know, and no servant of the Trudeau regime. She had this whole thing at heart, too, and wanted to see it come to something. She didn't want to see the effort fall flat or into the hands of the government. So, Susan, that's how I landed in your caucus."

Looking back on the conference now, and reading the statement of the Radical Women's Caucus, I realize how much our commentary was directed to the conference organizers and not the government, the public or other women. The points were valid but there was no location in the real time and space of a *realpolitik*. Without Parent we would have twisted in the wind, accomplishing little tangible. Almost in spite of ourselves we did some useful coalition politics that weekend, and everyone came out of it with NAC and an independent movement. The *Strategy for Change* document published in the wake of the conference tersely noted on the inside cover page: "The first item of business of the Sunday morning session was a discussion of the desirability of a federal Status of Women Council. The convention rejected the concept of a federally appointed, federally constituted Status of Women Council."

Twenty-three years later NAC carries on, but the Advisory Council on the Status of Women has come and gone, axed by another Liberal government in the shortness of time.

4

The Secretary
Takes National Office

Montréal in November can be bleak as a park bench in a late afternoon drizzle or glamourous beyond description in the lacy first snows of winter. It's hard to predict, so you wouldn't elect to have a convention there at that time – except everyone chose Montréal in 1967 because of Expo, or because it was Canada's centennial year, or, if you were Stanley Little and the incumbent president of CUPE, because you had a large and reliable base of support among the francophone members of *le syndicat Canadien de la Fonction publique*. The Sheraton Mount Royal Hotel accommodated the 600 delegates to the third biennial convention of CUPE in the third week in November. By then most of the public celebration was done, although the euphoria lingered like incense in the air. Montréal had staged a party and invited the world, the world had shown up and, as the columnists crooned, "put Canada on the map." All of Canada had joined in and people were still absorbing the extravagant success of it. Yet things were not rosy or quiet, and you didn't need to speak French to detect the malaise beneath the city's cosmopolitan surface. The president of France had touched it when he leaned from a parapet at City Hall and intoned to the crowd "Vive le Québec libre!" In that moment, everyone could see the nerves laid bare.

1967 was an auspicious moment for the Canadian Union of Public Employees as well. Though only four years old, CUPE was straining at the seams, torn between its founding factions just as the country was. It had come into being in 1963 when the National Union of Public Employees (NUPE) and the National Union of Public Service Employees (NUPSE) joined forces to create one organization. The two had been operating in similar fields: NUPSE concentrated on electrical utility workers, some hospital and municipal workers; NUPE mainly represented municipal workers, school employees, and hospital workers. The overlap was no secret, reps from both unions passed each other on the road and stayed in the same hotels. By the same token, there was talk in labour circles as to the advantages of reducing the number of unions in Canada generally. CUPE was simply the largest merger attempted. The newly minted Canadian Labour Congress made it clear that one public employees union was preferred, so the writing on the wall warned merge or risk being pushed from the field. This was the situation that gave some NUPSE loyalists, Stan Little included, reason to believe that NUPE was a "paper organization," deliberately set up in anticipation of the CLC merger to counterbalance NUPSE.

In 1963 neither NUPE nor NUPSE had been around long, although both had locals with roots going back to the early years of the century. (NUPE Local 43, the City of Toronto outside workers, had been established in 1917, for example.) NUPE was chartered by the TLC in 1955, although it originally applied in 1951 at which time the Congress deemed a national association inappropriate. NUPSE was recognized by the CCL in 1947. Both unions grew quickly, though NUPE was considerably larger by the time amalgamation talks commenced in 1957 – it had 200 locals in ten provinces to NUPSE's 60 locals in four provinces. And there the similarities ended. NUPSE and NUPE belonged to the same labour movement, but their culture and associations were entirely different. Some claimed the difference was due to NUPE's having been affiliated to the TLC which had a history of conservative craft unionism, while NUPSE had been affiliated to the CCL with its tradition of activist industrial unionism. Certainly NUPSE was a centralized organization with a large staff in the national office supported by a high per capita tax ($1.40 per member per month) paid by the locals. NUPE had a diffuse structure in which local unions had more autonomy and the national office less responsibility (and a 60 cent per capita tax) for servicing the membership. NUPE locals had developed a significant degree of self-reliance since there was only a tiny staff to service locals. NUPSE, with its high staff to membership ratio, had tended to encourage greater dependence on the central office for guidance and assistance.

Aside from financial savings there were political reasons for the amalgamation. NUPE had managed to organize very successfully right across the country but had no base in Québec. NUPSE, on the other hand, had in its assistant director, Francis Eady, someone who was fluent in French, at ease in Québec, and able to establish a rapport with Québec public sector unions which helped bring them into NUPSE. It was plain to both executives that, combined, they would add up to something substantially greater than the sum of their two organizations, forging a credible national force and acquiring unassailable status as the new power block in Canadian labour.

The original proposal submitted by the CLC (under whose aegis the merger talks were carrying on) called for the president, the secretary treasurer and three vice-presidents to come from NUPE and two vice-presidents from NUPSE. The formula was a fairly good indication of who originally approached who, or who needed who the most, although it is unclear which was ultimately the more reluctant partner. Between 1957 and 1961 both organizations were otherwise preoccupied and months went by between merger meetings. Neither party pushed it; neither withdrew. Finally, in the spring of 1961, Stan Little, formerly NUPSE's director of organization who had become its full-time paid president in 1962, seized the initiative.

The line-up at CUPE's national office in Ottawa, 1966. Left to right: Francis Eady, Ben Coffey, Bob Rintoul, Roy Laberge, Stan Little, Charles Bauer, James Dowell, Gil Levine, Mario Hikl.

In a letter to the CLC's executive committee he complained that NUPE's structure and low per capita tax were serious impediments to the merger. He charged that NUPE's national office was "starved" for funds, and the structural "lack of control can mean inadequate supervision over local union funds." Little could not see how NUPE would be able to foster identification with a national organization among its large membership without a strong central administration. NUPSE still favoured the merger, he assured the executive members, but only if NUPE faced its problems.

The tactic did not endear Little to the NUPE people, who responded with their own document rebutting his claims, but it did have the effect of stoking up the merger debate. Talks resumed and that September, at NUPE's seventh annual convention, President Bill Buss, National Director Robert Rintoul and the incoming executive were given their marching orders. The delegates instructed them to negotiate "all the terms and conditions" and to "act as they see fit" so that a merger could be consummated as soon as possible. Between that motion and the founding convention of CUPE in Winnipeg two years later lay yards of politicking and square miles of diplomacy. But Stan Little's advisement to the CLC that NUPE and NUPSE's differences concerned "trade union outlook, philosophical and political viewpoints in their broadest sense" turned out to be truer than he realized. Aside from the per capita tax question, prickly because it touched on the political ethos of the organization as well as its manner of administration, there were other matters dividing them.

The main difference involved structure. NUPE had evolved into the more activist organization. Its members had developed a network of district councils and provincial divisions over the years which undertook collective action on their behalf; it was a bit like having three unions for the price of one. NUPE had a presence and a lobbying capability at all three levels of government, achieved largely because its members and elected officers were willing to put in the free time. Yes, NUPE aficionados like Grace Hartman would agree, "loose structure and local autonomy can weaken a union as a national force, but it also strengthens the members' commitment to the organization if they can belong and have a say." To someone used to NUPSE's simple two-tiered structure of locals and a national executive board, however, NUPE must have seemed a bewildering phenomenon. And NUPSE's bureaucratic operation must have alarmed many NUPE people, who tended to regard NUPSE as the weaker union anyway.

The final deal turned on a simple exchange: NUPSE needed numbers and a nation-wide base, and NUPE wanted Québec and guaranteed status. Yet it almost derailed over the question of leadership. Normally, the larger of the merging groups takes the top job, but that is not what happened in CUPE's case. Stan Little was known to want the position and had prepared the way for himself by the creation of a full-time elected president position in NUPSE. Bill Buss was also known to want it. It was only when Buss yielded the position to Stan Little for the sake of the merger that everything fell into place. Possibly Buss realized he wouldn't have solid support in his own union as long as Bob Rintoul, NUPE's national director, who possessed the necessary full-time experience, was available. NUPE's structure, with its part-time elected president and full-time national director employed by the executive board, meant it had no clear candidate. In the event, the merger agreement named Little president and Rintoul secretary treasurer, and provided for the NUPE convention to elect three general and six regional vice-presidents, and for NUPSE's to elect two general and three regional vice-presidents to the new executive board.

The merger took place in September 1963 when the two unions each held a final annual meeting and then combined to ratify a constitution forming the Canadian Union of Public Employees. Within NUPE, each provincial division caucused ahead of the convention to decide who its candidates for the national executive board would be. "Eight of us ran in the Ontario region. I was the only female and I topped the poll," Grace Hartman recalled in a long interview with Wayne Roberts in 1989. "The convention was very well attended. Even small locals sent delegates. My own local in North York, which had about 275 members, sent three delegates because we felt the importance of what was happening to us. Of course there was a fear of the merger, a fear of losing your identity. If you believe in a union you develop certain feelings for it. We had strong feelings in my own union about the new president coming from the smaller union. There was no great harmony in that last convention. The decision to merge had to go to a roll-call vote which was most unusual, but there was no question about the final decision. It was the art of compromise." And of trade-offs, for if NUPSE got the presidency, NUPE got to keep its structure by bequeathing it to CUPE.

After the wedding, the hard part begins. Melding two large and unwieldy organizations isn't an overnight job. It takes many meetings and many conventions for new relationships and loyalties to cement. CUPE's founders knew the real merger would take time and, in the interest of "stability and confidence," appointed Little and Rintoul to four-year terms so that neither would be up for election until 1967. They had hopes that four years would give the two men enough time to consolidate the union; pious hopes given the two characters involved for, in the four years, Little and Rintoul were never able to work out a *modus operandi*. They were at odds the whole time. The concept behind the accommodation had been one of parity. Although it was not articulated in the merger agreement, the idea was for each organization to provide one top officer. Furthermore, the constitution described these positions in equal terms and provided for each national officer to report to the national executive board (NEB). Both were paid the same salary. "I never considered myself second in command as national secretary treasurer and I made that quite clearly and concisely understood. Little and I were going in as equals so far as status and authority were concerned," Rintoul always maintained. But Little showed scant appetite for consultation or discussion with anyone other than his executive assistant, Francis Eady, who was also reporting to him on organizing in Québec. To his way of thinking, the president was the CEO of the corporation and the secretary treasurer simply an administrative officer. He tended to act on his own and Rintoul would learn of meetings when the bills came in. This did not sit well with Rintoul, who was a proud man and used to being in charge of things at NUPE. He knew what NUPE had accomplished during the eight years of his leadership and he found it difficult to take second place in the merged union. It wasn't long before the two men fell to accusing each other openly of being obstructionist and difficult, even paranoid, each blaming the other man's staff at every turn.

According to the terms of the merger agreement, the staff of both organizations were to be offered employment by CUPE. So along with Little and Rintoul came their respective executive assistants,

Francis Eady and Ben Coffey. NUPSE's Mario Hikl as director of legislation and James Dowell as director of education, and NUPE's Bill Buss as director of organization and Gil Levine as director of research, all came to work at the new national office. On paper it looked like the perfect solution, but in reality it was like putting a dozen praying mantises in a jar. People describe the place as so divided a Maginot Line might have been dug down the middle. The metaphor was apt, for Little had unleashed a demon when he accused Gil Levine of being a Communist. "What irritates me to this very day is the lengths they went to," Rintoul said in an interview in 1977. Hikl had confronted Rintoul with the information and Rintoul had been unimpressed. Then "S. A. Little came to me and said he could prove it if I would come with him to a meeting at RCMP headquarters in Ottawa. This I agreed to do. After going through five or six security doors, we met with a member of the RCMP who started telling me all the things Gil Levine was doing that they had proof of, and that I was pretty naive to think he was no longer associated. I asked if he was prepared to stand up in court and say so and he said they couldn't do that. In that case, I said, the matter is closed so far as I'm concerned. And I went back to the office."

The matter, of course, was not closed; it hung in the air, turning a foul atmosphere toxic since even one incident involving Mounties leads to questions about who else is under surveillance and whether the information is being passed in one direction or two. Answered or not, the questions set a tone. Whatever one thinks of Communists or the Eastern Bloc, the red baiting played havoc with staff morale. The disaffection between Little and Rintoul went beyond their office doors. Coffey and Eady fell to sniping at each other in lengthy letters, written to their respective bosses and then copied to the other national officer, in which they denounced each other's alleged infractions in increasingly prolix language. Eady at one point accurately described the attitude (his own could be included) as "niggling and picayune."

In such an atmosphere, people's worst invective becomes the

Bob Rintoul, CUPE national secretary treasurer, and Grace Hartman, Ontario Division president, at the opening session of an education seminar in 1967 at Niagara Falls.

norm. Eady and Little were more and more contemptuous of Rintoul's operation ("This union has struggled under an incompetent, inefficient and bureaucratic administrative setup under the leadership of the National Secretary Treasurer and his assistant [which] has done untold harm to the Union," shot Eady), while Rintoul and Coffey became more and more outraged by Little's breaches of procedure.

Meantime, the young organization was maturing at a remarkable rate. A thousand workers were joining up each month, making CUPE the fastest growing union in Canada. At merger the combined membership was approximately 80,000; only the Steelworkers, which had been Canada's largest union for decades, had more members. By 1967 CUPE had grown to 115,000 and was the largest national union in the country. Of course this was partly a reflection of the tremendous expansion in the public service and in public enterprise generally. But it was also a function of CUPE's growing strength and influence. If head office was split (with former NUPSE staff siding with Stan Little, and former NUPE people siding with Rintoul against him), the merger was quietly happening in the field, and in the public arena CUPE was beginning to wield its increasing weight. The proof of the pudding was in victories like the repeal of Section 89 of the Ontario Labour Relations Act in 1966, and the successful campaign to prevent the new Canada Pension Plan from bring integrated with existing municipal pensions.

As 1967 dawned, Little was facing the big disadvantage to his having come from the smaller union. Heading into the convention election he had a base of support of less than a third of the membership of CUPE to count on. Should the NUPE forces run someone against him, it would be an uphill struggle to the end. At one point he approached Bob Rintoul about running as a team, a logical move which Rintoul rebuffed, leaving Little to assume (correctly) that NUPE was planning its own slate. In January, Grace Hartman was writing vice-president Bill Black in Vancouver: "Bob and I had a long talk the other day and we both feel that whatever happens, it should be a team effort for the top two posts. One possibility is you for the top and Bob stays where he is. That would create the least disturbance, I think, and give us a good chance to go to town. However, another combination being bandied about is Bob for the top and me for his spot." Black was well known in labour circles in British Columbia, a former president of the BC Federation of Labour and long time business manager of Local 180, the provincial hospital workers. He was a flamboyant, wiry, hard-talking man and not particularly left wing, a rather conservative-type democrat.

By now relations between Little and Rintoul had reached a nadir. Something had to give, and that turned out to be Bob Rintoul's health, forcing him to resign in late February. The NEB meeting in March agonized, then decided to sidestep his decision by granting him accumulated vacation and a leave of absence until the convention in November. Rintoul had threatened to resign many times since 1963, but that didn't make his leaving easier to digest. (And worse, though he might be gone from the office, no one expected for a minute that he would be uninvolved in the race.) That weekend in March, as the men looked around the room desperately for a replacement, for the first time in Canadian history they fastened on a woman. Grace Hartman was NUPE, she was a vice-president from Ontario with the numbers and the pull, and even though Bill Black had pulled a higher vote as a general vice-president, Hartman was in a position to pick up and move to Ottawa. At a breakfast meeting at the Hotel Vancouver, Kealey Cummings, a NUPSE vice-president from Local 1000 (Ontario Hydro), nominated Grace Hartman for national secretary treasurer. National office issued a press release, Hartman took a leave of absence from the Borough of North York, and on May Day she took over full time as CUPE's acting secretary treasurer.

When Sister Hartman walked into Brother Rintoul's office, she wasn't in the least prepared for total chaos. Apart from everything else, she found the three individuals on whose support her job as secretary treasurer depended – her secretary, the bookkeeper and her executive assistant – were under a cloud, their jobs in jeopardy. So she reported to the CUPE national executive board at its meeting in June. "The last meeting of the national executive board was held in an atmosphere of crisis and bitterness," she began,

> *The regional vice-presidents especially felt that they were not being given the true and full facts of the problems that existed within the national office ... [When I arrived] my executive assistant was newly reinstated after an eleven-day suspension, the head bookkeeper had submitted her resignation because of interference in her department, and my secretary was accused of advocating an illegal strike – a charge, made by Brother Eady which was neither supported nor withdrawn.*

> Lest any of you feel outraged by this situation, I think I should
> mention that in the minds of many of our members, the national
> executive board members are themselves held responsible for the
> situation that has been created. As one delegate to a Division
> convention put it, "fourteen people should be able to control two
> officers." I can assure you that it was not my intention to allow this
> type of situation to continue or to assume any responsibility for the
> mess that existed. Consequently, I went through the records and
> examined the operations as time permitted, to determine, if possible,
> the cause and source of the problems. However, I want to make it
> very clear here that I do not intend to point a finger at either of the
> officers but merely to lay facts before the board. It is to be sincerely
> hoped that once these matters are aired and decisions reached for
> their solution, that there can be beginnings of some real harmony
> at national headquarters.

The crisis Hartman refers to was the uproar caused by the resignation of Rintoul. It was going to be difficult to explain for, even
though health *was* the reason, or at least the immediate one, people
would suspect otherwise. Trench warfare at the national office had
become a subject of much speculation, as the editorial in the Ontario
Division newsletter illustrated: "The resignation of Brother Rintoul
cannot be brushed off or forgotten by the membership of our union
... The national officers will undoubtedly be required to fully explain
the truth or falsehood to the rumours that all is not well at 176
Gloucester Street ... For our part, it is now clear this union cannot
continue to operate on the 'two head' concept that was born of the
merger ... [We] must make the decision for a sane and logical line
of command."

The minutes of NEB meetings in March and July indicate that
board members also felt the resignation was symptomatic of "conflict and lack of trust" between Little and Rintoul, and the climate of
"gossip and character assassination" at national office. At one point
late in the meeting, Bill Black suggested the executive board draw up

lines of authority and insist that the general vice-presidents exercise theirs more vigorously: "Between now and convention the house has to be put in order ... We have to show the rank and file that we are capable of doing our work." The minutes of the July meeting, a special two-day session called to deal with ramifications of the Rintoul crisis, are three pages long. After a day and a half spent in a committee of the whole, the board voted to destroy the minutes and all documents pertaining to the discussion. These were duly "torn up and placed in paper containers for destruction." (The script presumably calls for a bonfire at this point.)

The suspension of Hartman's executive assistant, Ben Coffey, like the resignation of the bookkeeper and the accusation against the secretary mentioned in Hartman's report to the NEB, were symptoms of an office in trauma. Coffey had been suspended by Stan Little in March when Rintoul was out of the office and Grace Hartman had not yet arrived. In reviewing his notes and preparing the minutes of the Vancouver NEB meeting, Coffey had spotted an apparent discrepancy in the tally of the vote to hire the new director of public relations, and had taken it upon himself to contact board members to confirm their votes. It wasn't an insignificant error he was attempting to correct, however, for the vote had been close. Little had, in fact, called it a tie and then cast the deciding vote for his own choice; Coffey's investigation was in effect a challenge to chair.

Obviously the big question in 1967 was, if Rintoul and Little couldn't merge the national office, could Hartman and Little? In her first few months as secretary treasurer, Hartman decided to approach the situation directly and start off where she wanted to end up. She was not going to participate in a power struggle as Rintoul and Little had, she would focus instead on clarity and procedure. With her June memo, Hartman came clean with the board about the troubles in the office. Her strategy would be to keep things in the open and to share responsibility with her colleagues on the executive board. She took the precaution (since she was responsible for planning NEB meetings) of circulating her report beforehand, so that when

Stan Little objected and insisted that the NEB executive committee deal with it first (a special session had to be scheduled overnight to do so), the cat was out of the bag. The report could hardly be "unread" by the board members, and the executive committee could not ignore her recommendations. These included confirmation of her duties as national secretary treasurer, a directive to the two national officers to bring matters of policy to the NEB for resolution when they failed to reach agreement between themselves, and an instruction to officers and (staff) directors not to involve the clerical staff in their disputes. Hartman's report can be read as an attempt to pull the organization back on the tracks, indicating how far she figured the two men had let the office careen out of control.

For all her tough words, Hartman was in a delicate situation. She had a job just getting a grip on the secretary treasurer's portfolio and preparing the budget and programs for the November convention. To be suddenly responsible for a $1.2 million budget, and for administering the finances and staffing of a national operation with 103 full-time staff and 577 locals, was overwhelming at first. But now that she was in the job, it was obvious she ought to run for the position and that Black should run for president. Black held off announcing his candidacy until the very last moment, however, leaving Little to the rumours and a sinking feeling. What Hartman did not know was how dirty Little was prepared to play it.

On the third day of the convention, nominations for president were called and Grace Hartman rose to present Stan Little's challenger, Bill Black. Delegates arriving at the convention had received Little's flyers listing several CUPE vice-presidents as supporters, with an invitation in a small note at the bottom to Grace Hartman: "This candidate has not indicated her desire to associate herself with this team of officers, however, her name is included to encourage teamwork and unity." Right up to the convention, people took Hartman's silence for neutrality, but she and other NUPE people had been working behind the scenes for months preparing a campaign, as they saw it, to reclaim their union. It was now or never.

Hartman kept things close to her chest until the convention, trying to separate her tenure as acting secretary treasurer from her campaign for the job. Little and Co. found out about Black's candidacy by accident, when Norm Simon (CUPE's new PR director and a Little supporter) came across Bill Black material being printed by Pat O'Keeffe (who was with Black's campaign) at Thistle Printers, a well-known union printing shop in Toronto. Stan Little remembers going through the motions of the convention feeling "the thing was doomed," and all the while fighting for his political life. All through the corridors, the elevators, lobbies and cafeterias of the hotel, the campaigns raged and stories circulated with increasing quantities of muck and acid. The Québec delegation floated a rumour that they would bolt *en masse* if Little was defeated, and they voted for him *en bloc*. The hospitality suites were working overtime with promises, liquor was said to flow freely, and one story had a couple of "all paid for" prostitutes "building delegate support" in one of the suites. With the scent of blood, the newshounds were also out in full force, and when the ballots were counted Little had 285 and Black 275. Grace Hartman won by acclamation, Stan Little by a hiccup.

CUPE's new national secretary treasurer was hardly through the door of her Ottawa apartment before the press was calling up to get her reaction to allegations that there had been election irregularities. The weekend after the convention ended, Ben Coffey issued a statement claiming that as many as twenty-three delegates had been seated illegally. Coffey had supervised the elections. Because he attended NEB meetings, he was also aware of the motions which had been passed the previous October effectively waiving a section of the CUPE constitution which barred delegates from being seated if their local was more than three months in arrears in per capita tax payments to national office. Under this rule, a large delegation of

The 1967 CUPE convention in Montréal: Stan Little wins re-election as president, Grace Hartman is acclaimed secretary treasurer.

Little supporters from the recently organized Québec Hydro local would have been excluded. Little had convinced the NEB to waive the constitutional requirements in this case, and also to blink at the rules by permitting large locals additional delegates. Coffey may never have said so, but others certainly did: the changes shifted the balance in Stan Little's favour, just as holding the convention in Montréal had favoured him, probably enough to give him the election. Coffey was perplexed as to why questions weren't asked and why the Credentials Committee never reported the NEB actions to the convention. He felt that the membership ought to know and that he had an obligation to tell them. For the second time in six months the national executive board met in special session to deal with the fallout. What emerged was a three-page resolution, rendered in several capitalized sequences, insisting that what happened at the convention was quite legal, being the convention's will and the convention being the supreme body of the union, period.

Hartman had gone to Montréal hoping the convention would heal the rifts; she came away feeling CUPE was more divided than ever. She called in Coffey and asked him to draft a report of all his findings. He did, and also secured a legal opinion on the NEB motions. An ad hoc Committee on Elections formed in Toronto meanwhile, involving Locals 43, 767, 79, 503, with 373's Vera McGarry acting as recording secretary, calling for an investigation. They secured a second legal opinion which also concluded the proceedings had not been according to the CUPE constitution but gave no advice about what to do in the circumstances. The group asked for an audience at the emergency NEB meeting, and a four-man delegation was received. The board listened, thanked them, and later issued its decision.

And what the sixteen members of the NEB seem to have decided was to jump clear if possible. How indeed do you rectify a procedural blunder of this magnitude? How is democracy best served? There was an argument that nothing could undo what happened in Montréal or correct it even if it were illegal. Furthermore, no one could foresee what a re-election would yield. It was reasonable to assume that neither Black or Little would emerge with a clear mandate – another election would not change the fact of a close vote. Another election would, however, aggravate the strife and soak up time and money. For all that, the decision to ride it out was a deal with the devil. The CUPE leadership was on the brink of collapse. Perhaps, then, the NEB's decision, though not on the side of the legal angels, was on the side of wisdom and expedience.

By 1967 Grace Hartman had been active in the trade union movement for nearly ten years. Her passage through the ranks had been a steady forward march at a bracing clip, and from a distance the performance appeared effortless. But the turn of events which put her into the secretary treasurer's chair was no fluke. Hartman was in line for the job and she had even been considering it. Agreeing, on the spur of a weekend, to take the post temporarily meant she was putting herself in the running for it permanently. The decision she had to make, then, was whether to carry on or to step aside so someone else could run. "I remember we had a meeting here one Sunday morning breakfast – my two sons and my husband and I. Their attitude was 'go for it,' even though they knew the disruption it was going to make in the family. When you have that sort of support, you figure, well, you should." Bob was about seventeen at the time and still at home. Warren had returned to his roots in downtown Toronto and was working in the theatre. He went home regularly for Sunday breakfast, which was a family ritual and the place where decisions, especially momentous ones like this one, got talked out.

True to form, the Hartman family handled the logistics of Grace's move to Ottawa in an unconventional and thoroughly sensible way. Two-city relationships – never mind commuter marriages – were far from popular in the late sixties, they were unheard of. Yet here was a couple choosing to live apart after twenty-eight years of marriage, *and* it was The Wife who was leaving town to take the high-powered job in the nation's capital. The idea was for Grace to live in Ottawa during the week and return home on weekends – as many as she could manage. This way the entire family did not have to be split up, the base of operation could remain where it was. Despite the amount of travel implied, there was a lot to be said for simply leaving things as they were. Grace would have a minimum of organizing and moving to do. So for the next several years she lived out of a suitcase among unpacked cardboard boxes in a small apartment in Ottawa, and every two or three weekends she'd drive back to Toronto. Occasionally Joe drove up to Ottawa, and sometimes old Dunview friends Ray and Sybil Bellmore would join him and the four would "do the town" a bit. Sometimes Grace and Joe met halfway for a weekend at the Silver Lake campground. But mostly Grace did the driving. For one thing, Joe was never as comfortable as she was driving at night, which their schedules pretty well dictated, and Grace preferred leaving in the evening as morning was her worst time of day. She liked cars and liked driving – something she shared with Bob who will admit they both drove fast. (Her record, door to door, for the 425 kilometers was three hours and forty-five minutes.) The quiet and space gave her time to think and meditate, out of reach, incommunicado and in control as she floated through the Southern Ontario countryside. Everything could be in disarray at work, but she could count on calm at the wheel of her Chrysler. In Toronto, Joe could tell she was about to arrive when the phone started ringing. When she didn't turn up on time there was the worry, trying not to think of things like Vera McGarry's tragic death in 1972 when her car skidded into a ditch one winter night as she headed home from a union meeting.

Hartman came to see the 1967 convention as a blood-letting, and the Coffey affair as part of it. She was sympathetic to the man and recognized that he was motivated by principle, but she felt his loyalties were misguided and, as the person for whom he was supposedly working, was unnerved by his penchant for maverick acts. She also didn't think it wise to leave the legal interpretations to everyone else's lawyers, so she called up Richard Rohmer, a prominent lawyer she met when he was elected to North York Council in 1957/8, and asked him for a private opinion. "In conclusion, it looks as though you have a mess on your hands," he told her, confirming that the seating of delegates from Québec Hydro and the extra credentials given the six large locals were in violation of the CUPE constitution and that the NEB motions permitting them were invalid. There were those who viewed these events as nefarious, the NEB members complicit, and Coffey shabbily treated in that both times he stepped out of line it was to shed light on improprieties that ought to have been addressed. It seemed that Little's tactic was to focus on the messenger instead of the message.

For her part, Hartman did not lead a move to annul the election, and she did not go to the wall to save Coffey. So far as she was concerned, Ben Coffey had acted on his own and had taken more authority on himself than he had a right to as a member of staff. The constitution of CUPE tried to be explicit about that. "We decided we didn't want a staff-run organization, that the politicians would run it even if they ran it badly. We didn't think staff should be involved. Not that they don't get involved – they do. And in the '67 convention they were up to their eyeballs in politics." Ralph Maillet, the education rep in the Atlantic region in 1967, was posted in a little corner of the hall with the educational display during the convention where he observed the goings-on. "The staff wasn't supposed to get involved but I honestly don't know of anyone who wasn't. I could see people from the other camp who were also education reps freely politicking, and being that I was living for NUPE at the time, twenty-four hours a day, it didn't take me too long to cut loose. I did my little share of politicking."

Once the dust settled, Hartman reassessed her situation. She had been roundly criticized by some members for playing politics in office and for her conduct in support of Bill Black at the convention. Nevertheless, she realized she had an opportunity she hadn't counted on. Whereas Little had become a divisive force in the leadership, she was the national officer no one had voted against; this gave her a kind of diplomatic immunity and the chance to heal the merger. Hartman once described her sentiments to writer Gloria Montero: "The staff had taken sides, no question. It had been a bitter battle and I remember saying to someone at the time, 'If only he'd remember the story of the English king who upon coming to the throne and being handed a list of the barons who'd opposed him, threw it in the fire.' " Stan Little didn't do that, and it was quite some time before Hartman felt an accommodation between them was possible.

The two couldn't have been more different. Stan Little was "volatile and bombastic" in contrast to Hartman's soft-voiced and even-keeled demeanour. She would sit out the explosions. "He would rant and rave and shout and then look at me and ask why I wasn't saying anything. 'No sense in us both yelling,' I'd say. 'I'll say something when you finish.' " Hartman didn't appreciate his tendency to resort to high-handed action, such as the way he assumed authority over her executive assistant and disciplined him out of turn, but she was very aware of the power Little wielded on the executive board and the advantage he had because the work, for him, was a full-time occupation whereas for the rest of the board (save herself now), who had full-time jobs elsewhere, it was volunteer work five or six weekends a year. Nevertheless, she felt Little had a real feel for the organization. "He'd been in it a long time, had come up through the ranks, and he was very possessive about 'his' union." He could be very persuasive as a leader, too, though many people didn't like his roughshod ways. Some were put off by his enigmatic executive assistant, Francis Eady, who was alternately described as Machiavellian and the "brains" behind Little. Bob Rintoul once characterized the relationship as Eady preparing the bullets and Little firing the shots, which at least credits Little with the up-front political savvy. Whatever the balance of talents between the two men, they were a formidable combination.

Eady was Stan Little's greatest asset and his worst liability. He was an Englishman who could "speak volubly of trade union trends and policies throughout the world," Dominique Clift said of him in the Toronto *Star*'s coverage of the 1966 CLC convention. Eady attended the convention with Little, who made an unsuccessful run at a vice-presidency, but it was Eady who did most of the talking and was the man the CLC establishment feared most, according to Clift. "As he goes on in the intellectual and high-strung fashion which is said to be his trademark, his complaint is that the present structure of the CLC prevents it from ever being able to act decisively, so that it remains little more than a lobby at the federal level." It is striking how the executive assistant overshadowed the president at that convention, and how Eady took on a high-profile role. Subsequently he seems to have withdrawn, but people on the NUPE side of the staff divide continued to find him too devious by half. Hartman appreciated his ideas (the *Bill of Wrongs* was one of them), yet she always felt he was working against her and never trusted him. She put Mario Hikl in the same category, having clashed with him early on when CUPE Ontario Division was preparing a brief for the Ontario gov-

ernment which he challenged in a manner she considered deroga-
tory and untoward. Like others, she heard stories about the "shit
files" he kept on people.

Hikl and Eady are no longer alive to tell their side of the story, but
like Little they seem to have believed the NUPE staff were following
"outside orders." Norman Simon, the young PR director hired in
1967 and ostensibly one of Stan's men, didn't share the prevailing
view. "Hikl, to his dying day, could have passed a lie detector test
that Grace Hartman was a Commie menace placed there by the
Kremlin." Eady's departure in 1970 to take a job with the Manitoba
NDP was a blow to Little who was losing his chief strategist, back-
room organizer and the man he had worked closely with since before
the merger. The replacement he chose was a disaster from just about
everyone's point of view, including that of the man he hired, Allan
Millard. Millard, who had just resigned from External Affairs, was
the son of Charles Millard, the Canadian director of the Steelworkers Union in the forties and fifties. Little, it seems, made the fatal
error of mistaking the son for the father, and eventually discovered
that instead of hiring a politico in the Eady tradition, he had, in fact,
hired a technocrat. Millard chafed under the false expectations.
"Stan Little made it clear he wanted me to be his eyes and ears, to
be his spy, if you will. I told him I wasn't going to be another Francis
Eady." Little was worried about a Hartman faction building at national office, and he indicated to Millard that he was in touch with
the RCMP. "I don't remember the exact incident, but one day he
called me into his office and told me he had lunch that day at the
Talisman Hotel. I asked why that should be of interest to me and he
said [making the motions of someone riding a horse], 'The Horse-
men, the Mounties!' " Millard maintains that Little shared information "he had via the RCMP" about Grace Hartman's movements –
mundane information about trips she had made, who had met her
at the airport and so on. "He was convinced that Gil Levine was
pulling the strings and Grace was just dancing." Little denies the
story; Grace herself was guarded, acknowledging only that she
"heard things" but had no proof.

Now in his eighties and retired, Little is still critical of Hartman's abilities as a financial officer and skeptical about her union background, a skepticism often translated by people around national office as contempt. Hartman's supporters, and even some of Little's, felt he treated her like a glorified bookkeeper and regularly encroached on her authority. They were uncomfortable with his propensity (when talking among the boys) for disparaging references to her as "that fat ass over there" or "that Commie." Such epithets sound as dreadful now as they did then to the men who never forgot them but who recognized them, nevertheless, as the dirty style of union politics not yet out of fashion. One can also recognize Little's discomfort at having to share the political limelight with a woman – in his view, the proverbial secretary who got promoted beyond her station.

Whatever history they may have inherited, Hartman and Little were adversaries in their own right. There might have been some hope initially that Hartman could be, if not won over to the NUPSE side, at least mollified, which the gesture of Kealey Cummings's nominating her to replace Bob Rintoul hinted at. But whatever thoughts anyone had about a *rapprochement* during that first year evaporated when Hartman nominated Black at the convention. "She wasn't as hip as she might have been as to what the hell the whole story was," chides Little. "She was fed their line of stuff to the point she was absolutely convinced it was the thing to do." NUPSE hadn't run anyone for secretary treasurer because they had wanted to avoid the "our side/their side split that had been killing the organization. I was prepared to work with whoever came along as long as I was at the top of the heap." Following Montréal, and once Grace Hartman had been acclaimed by the membership, she was in a position to make some demands. The two of them sparred first over the hiring of an executive assistant to replace Ben Coffey. Although the decision should, by rights, be the secretary treasurer's, Little insisted it be decided by the whole executive board. Hartman acceded. "Stan had someone from Québec Hydro all lined up but my choice was bilingual and his couldn't speak English. I had to fight almost to the point of being prepared to pack it in, but I had my way," Hartman recalled. Both candidates were actually interviewed by the full executive board, but Hartman got her man – Ralph Maillet – and avoided Stan's rather blatant bid to extend his control into her office.

Grace had caucused with Gil Levine and John "Lofty" MacMillan, CUPE's new director of organization, about the candidate and the strategy, accurately ascertaining that she could win it at the executive board. MacMillan, who replaced Bill Buss after his death in 1966, had been CUPE Atlantic regional director, having started out as a staff rep for NUPE in 1957. Tall and imposing as the nickname implies, he was a well-known union activist from New Brunswick who had brought his local union (Local 61 of the Saint John Policemen's Protective Association) into NUPE in 1955. He had been in the union movement since the thirties, was an excellent organizer and a dynamic politician in his own right, having served as president of the New Brunswick Federation of Labour and been elected to the Saint John Common Council. Director of organization was the first national director's position to come vacant since the merger, so it was bound to be politically contentious. If the unwritten rules were to be followed, the post ought to go to a NUPE person, which MacMillan certainly was, but it had taken a year for the appointment to be made. One can understand Little's reluctance to bring such a high-powered NUPE partisan into national office.

In early 1968 Little moved to consolidate his presidency. The 1967 election had left him in a vulnerable position. Stories were circulating – deadly serious as well as funny ones – about ballot stuffing and other mysterious irregularities. Instead of symbolizing unity, Little had become controversial. It was a situation that had to give him pause, and it meant that he needed Hartman in a way he hadn't needed Rintoul. Both of them played their hands at the first regular NEB meeting in 1968.

First, Stan Little produced a special report requesting endorsement of his executive authority as CUPE's president. He was not going to carry on without assurance that he would not be repaid with "the kind of cut-throat action that took place at the last convention." He referred to "an underground campaign of innuendo and half truth" and "the silly games" which had preceded Montréal, but at the same time called for an end to hostilities. He enjoined members to be prepared to bring their differences to the board, and requested their backing to put an end to the rebellious conduct of the staff. Most significant, he wanted to make "decisions which have financial aspects," implying by his criticism of Rintoul (as being unwilling to make unpopular decisions) and Hartman (for not being stringent enough with the budget in the last six months of 1967) that *he* had nothing to do with the current financial squeeze, but that he *did* know what to do about it. It was an odd report – vague and score-settling all at once – and what it asked for was a blank cheque to "rectify the problems besetting this union." In the ensuing discussion, Little backed away from his rebuke of Hartman, saying he had been making a general statement.

In contrast, Hartman made a financial report to the same meeting which was the real stuff of problem solving. She and Little had projected a deficit of $300,000 for the year and she had to come up with an austerity program that was wide ranging and detailed to save the debt from accumulating; hiring was frozen, one or two offices closed, officer and staff expenditures curtailed, and prompt payment of per capita taxes was vigorously pursued with checks to eliminate cheating. Hartman realized this had to work. She had to exert fiscal control on a day-to-day basis and this left her and Little at a standoff. Little refused to allow Hartman full control of the financial agenda, but she in turn refused him full control of the political agenda. As Little says, they operated at arm's length for some time.

In these circumstances, it was probably a blessing Hartman had to start out with a new executive assistant for it gave her a chance at least to break the cycle of inter-office warfare. So far as national office was concerned there was no getting around the fact that she represented the NUPE/left axis. "Even though I was elected without opposition, life wasn't easy. I was always considered a left winger and Stan was anything but. I never did trust Mario Hikl, and Stan was distrusting of Gil Levine. Even the clerical staff was split in national office. The sides were very harshly drawn." Levine had been a close associate for a long time, she knew MacMillan well too, and frankly respected the skill and dedication of both men. But she didn't always take their advice. "Sometimes I'd go along with it and find it didn't work. I didn't necessarily disagree but I was going to do it my way, and it was not my way to go into executive board and roar and shout. Lofty always wanted me to do it that way." Ralph Maillet was also frustrated by her apparent passiveness. "Most of my arguments with Grace were about exactly that. That she didn't stand up for what obviously were her rights. I was present at meetings where I was fit to be tied because she would clam up when in my view she should have exploded. She would be challenged on issues that were 110 percent her right, and she would back off. Behind closed doors I'd ask her why she didn't call for a vote when she could have won it. 'Yes, I know, but we'll get back to it,' she'd say. So not only did she have to take it [the haranguing] from Stan she also had to take it from me!"

In time, though, Maillet began to see how these things *weren't* being dropped, and how they would find their way back onto the agenda. "In her own way she was a very smart person; what she couldn't accomplish today she would get passed tomorrow. Eventually the issue would become active again." For him the merger was one of those matters. It may have taken her a long time to effect, but he came to believe if any one person was responsible for finally making it gel, it was Grace Hartman. Hers was a long-term strategy, and one thing Hartman was sure of was that time was on her side. With each passing year and each new CUPE member the NUPE/NUPSE divisions receded; slowly, very slowly, the trench down the middle of national office began to fill in.

From the beginning, the understanding between Grace Hartman and Stan Little may well have been unspoken. Some speculate that it was a sort of MAD standoff, a mutually assured destruction pact in which each had something to hold over the other. Had there not been dirty tricks at the 1967 election? Didn't Grace Hartman have a radical past? As things evolved, though, their styles seemed to mesh into a sort of live-and-let-live M.O. It was still a long while before they buried the hatchet, if they ever did, but one day Grace decided it was time to try. "I sat down with Stan and told him, 'You know, it's no use you and I being enemies. You're never going to like me or the things I do and say any better, but we have to work together; we have to build this union,' and he agreed."

This was the period when CUPE was coming into its own as a force in the trade union movement, even while the shakeout from the merger was still going on. Local 43, City and Metro Toronto manual workers, which left CUPE over the issue of per capita rebate, returned in 1967; Local 180, BC's hospital workers, stayed with the new organization for six years and then disaffiliated. There were disputes with Local 1000 (Ontario Hydro) and other large locals about the status of self-servicing unions which had their own staff. With such an expansive membership it was almost inevitable that CUPE's finances continued to be chaotic. The secretary treasurer's constant challenge was to ensure that per capita taxes were properly paid in the first place, and to calibrate revenues to the needs of organizing and servicing new members. The gaps at times were frightening, which is why Hartman applied the brakes in early 1968. At the 1967 convention CUPE had set up a Defence Fund (on an assessment of $1 per member and 10 cents a month with an overall objective of $1 million) for supporting strikes as well as work actions by unions forbidden by law to strike. It was a concrete illustration of CUPE's growing militance. Likely as not, CUPE strikes in those years concerned issues of principle and the basic rights of public sector employees. Late in 1967 the Don Jail guards

were back in the news when the Robarts government, after transferring the administration of justice to the province, passed an order-
in-council declaring the guards would henceforth be civil servants.
This meant they had to join the Civil Service Association of Ontario
– an association Robarts fondly referred to as "our union" and which
CUPE considered a creature of management. There had been no
consultation with the workers or the union, CUPE Local 878. The
guards walked out on December 30; by the time the strike was settled
two weeks later, there had been a large demonstration at Queen's
Park with the threat of a one-day work stoppage by 40,000 public
employees across the province. The government, portrayed as rail-
roading workers into a union they hadn't chosen and didn't want,
backed down for a time. CUPE was allowed to continue representing
the guards and was invited to make representations to the (Judge)
Little Commission, then studying collective bargaining in the Ontario government service.

Early the following year, Grace Hartman's own Local 373 became
embroiled in what the North York *Mirror* dubbed "an unprecedented twist in labour-management relations" when the Borough
council decided, out of the blue, that the public interest would
somehow best be served if labour negotiations were conducted in
open forum. Bizarre as the idea was in terms of industrial relations,
it garnered support because it sounded so reasonable. From the
workers' point of view, however, it amounted to intimidation and
the local was prepared to charge the council with refusing to negotiate in good faith. Each time the negotiating committee turned up for
a meeting, they would find the press present and leave. After two
months, Hartman wrote Mayor James Service from Ottawa, entreat-
ing him to meet with the department of Labour's conciliator and to
consider the fact that the union would be in a legal strike position if
he didn't. "Your unwillingness to conduct these negotiations in the
tried and tested way has stood in the way of talks. Not even the most
basic issues have been discussed because of the roadblocks you have
put up." She made the point that politicians may be used to conduct-

ing *their* business in the goldfish bowl, but ordinary workers were not. The presence of the press turned negotiations into public events where comments had the weight of published statements. Obviously it skewed the process and, in due course, North York quietly abandoned the idea.

It seemed as if the province's coercive attitude to public employees was contagious and the disease incurable. In 1969 CUPE Ontario Division decided to stage another mass demonstration at Queen's Park on a Wednesday in early June. This time the *Bill of Wrongs* was two feet long and accompanied by two coffins representing the dead bodies of collective bargaining. 3,500 workers turned up with a forest of placards enumerating public employees' grievances against a government which continued to treat them as second-class citizens. Grace Hartman spoke that day, as did Percy Huggett, her successor as president of the Ontario Division, and Stan Little. Hartman emphasized the economic plight of hospital workers and the huge disparity between the wages the province was prepared to pay some workers and not others. Electricians were making $248 for thirty-seven hours of work a week, more than some health care workers were paid in a month. The same week in Edmonton, 1,500 hospital workers turned up on the steps of their Provincial Legislature to demand that the province intervene with the Alberta Hospital Commission to guarantee the $1.75 per hour minimum that had been set for hospital workers.

Public sector workers led by CUPE were clearly on the move. They were asserting their dignity as well as their rights as workers, and no strike epitomized that better than the 1971 Ottawa Garbage Strike. Although brief, it happened in the high heat of August when the ninety-two members of Local 1338 struck Ottawa Disposal Systems Ltd. after eight fruitless months of negotiation. The company had won an $8 million contract with the city in 1970, and since CUPE's policy when faced with such contracting-out situations was to follow the workers, Local 1338 carried on trying to secure an agreement. The company simply refused. When the workers went out, the

CUPE president Stan Little on the picket line with his members during the 1971 Ottawa garbage strike.

company hired strikebreakers – students and hippies, mostly – to man the trucks, and security guards, to whom they issued baseball bats, to "ride shotgun" with them along their routes. From the first day there was violence, massive police presence and arrests on the picket line. Twice over the ten days, the Ottawa police sent in its riot squad – fifty men fully outfitted in combat gear – and at one point the company had to declare a moratorium on collection. Several times CUPE appealed to city council and the Board of Control to take responsibility and intervene. As CUPE rep Normand Bourque pointed out repeatedly, the company may have been privately owned but garbage collection was still a public service. At the heart of the matter was the phenomenon of "privatization." Bourque had warned city council when it decided to take this route that the profits from garbage collection would be at the expense of the workers, and of taxpayers whose service would deteriorate. (Indeed, complaints had more than doubled with the new service, and the strike, of course, spoke for itself.) The strikers were also making a point about their dignity as workers. "We're garbage men, not garbage," proclaimed the signs. And there were many who walked the picket line in solidarity, feeling the emotion of that struggle. The end came early on a Monday. The front page of *Le Droit* carried a photo of the workers parading back into the yard, a Scottish piper leading the way, Bourque on their shoulders and Grace Hartman marching along beside them in victory.

Not unexpectedly, finances dominated the 1969 CUPE convention in Toronto. The highlight of the proceedings was Grace Hartman's report and the discussion of *Action 69-71*, a two-year strategic plan for the expansion of the research, service and organizing facilities of the union, which she presented along with a proposal for a $1.60 hike (to $2.90 a month) in the per capita tax. The funds, she argued, were necessary "to develop an organization capable of meeting the advance of automation and technological change. We must face this challenge armed with information, determination and militancy." The proposal and its pricetag (which would bring in $4 million a year) consumed three days of debate at the convention, during which the executive board presented two substitute motions as they tried to ease the delegates' objections and still wrest an increase from them. The objections didn't only have to do with money; they were also about confidence in the leadership and about CUPE's future. Some people said the plan was a blueprint for turning CUPE into a "centralized union like Steel"; others suggested the burden of the increase could be more equitably shifted by having a sliding scale. Many just couldn't get past the deficit. "CUPE was perpetually strapped for cash but I always felt there was nothing wrong with that. We were turning money back to the membership, expanding some departments and adding a whole new job evaluation department," Grace later remarked. Once it had become clear that the $1.60 would never fly, a revised recommendation with a lower per capita was put before the delegates. After some debate, the question was called and Little declared it carried. He was challenged, and when it was discovered there were more voters than official delegates in the hall, another vote had to be taken. This one fell three votes short of the needed two-thirds majority. Finally a third proposal – for a 90 cent per capita increase over two years, plus a $3 assessment for the Defence Fund – was put to a roll call vote and carried. Of course the newspaper reports played up the irony of the CUPE leadership's uphill slog. "CUPE has found that it is as difficult to negotiate with its members for a dues increase as it is to bargain with employers for a raise," chortled the *Globe and Mail*'s Wilfred List.

Throughout the debate there were hints of the old rivalries and unfinished business of the 1967 convention. Don Roach of Local 767 (Toronto Housing), a leader of the Committee on Elections (renamed the Committee for Constitutional Responsibility) which had remained active into 1968, ran for the presidency against Stan Little on a platform of non-confidence. Wallace Higgins, president of Local 79 (Toronto municipal inside workers), also challenged Little on the state of the union's treasury, charging that 75 percent of the deficit was attributable to mismanagement. When the count came in, Little won by 459 votes to Higgins's 148 and Roach's 21. Hartman was also in a race, though less seriously contested, and she won by 501 to 108. Hugh Lennon from Local 134 (Toronto Board of Education) humbly confessed, after the applause and "vivas" had died down, that he had only run against Hartman because he felt the top posts in a union should always be contested. This was the convention where the merger really took place. Little and Hartman were elected handily, as if they were a team. And there was no question that the convention succeeded in formulating an ambitious plan for the future – something unimaginable two years before.

The convention two years later, in 1971, was almost placid by comparison. Stan Little, in his president's address, speculated it would prove to be CUPE's coming-of-age convention. Membership was nearly 130,000 and a new organization was taking shape. For the first time, neither Little nor Hartman were challenged for their positions. In addition to a string of constitutional amendments, the 695 delegates discussed matters which ranged far beyond the usual bargaining table issues to larger social questions of the day. They decided CUPE should oppose the War Measures Act and strengthen bonds between organized labour in Québec and other parts of Canada, endorse the National Farmers' Union boycott of Kraft, protest the nuclear blast off Amchitka Island and all nuclear testing by the world's superpowers, and actively work to eliminate any form of discrimination against women inside the union and on the job site.

This last declaration was easily the most revolutionary statement of the convention. Furthermore, *The Status of Women in CUPE* was a departure for CUPE since policy wasn't normally developed by two members of the executive board without the involvement of the president's office. But Hartman and Shirley Carr had the credibility

Grace Hartman at the 1971 convention, which passed CUPE's first policy on the Status of Women. Stan Little is on the right.

and weight of the Royal Commission on the Status of Women to lean on, and the work of women unionists contained in that document supporting them. Thus the premise and analysis could be presented as motherhood statements, and the recommendations as positions of principle. As a result, the discussion on the floor was subdued. Several men spoke in favour (including Kealey Cummings) realizing, as the women did, that with its passage the motion would make trade union history. While it made sense for a senior union with 40 percent of its membership female to tackle the rights of women workers, it was still a proud achievement and a legitimate first.

If the delegates were in a fighting mood about anything in 1971, it was over governments' intransigence about compulsory arbitration and the right of public servants to strike, or about the Canadian Labour Congress. There were several items on the CLC list, to which Hartman added the shoddy job it was doing representing women. She noted during her lead-off speech on the Status of Women motion that the CLC had given as much space to the problems of the Basques in Spain as to women in Canada in its annual brief to the cabinet, and she criticized the Congress's leadership for refusing to set up a women's committee or give the matter serious study.

The CUPE membership was equally determined to take on the CLC over the matter of Canadian autonomy in the trade union movement. As with the issue of women's rights, independence in the labour movement was far from being a closeted, sectorial concern. By the late sixties, nationalism was a political force in Canada, accompanied as it was by a radical analysis of Canada's colonial situation in world economics. The cause was gaining strength among liberals as well as the left, and the public debate touched on every aspect of Canadian life – economics, defence policy, research and development, science and culture. Within the labour movement, Kent Rowley and Madeleine Parent had already set up the nationalist Confederation of Canadian Unions (CCU), and the struggle to Canadianize unions in Canada was in the open. CUPE had taken up the issue early, and at convention after convention had returned to the matter, broadening and intensifying the demand. The CLC was then dominated by private sector, U.S.-based unions that hadn't welcomed the arrival of large public sector unions in the first place, and were especially loath to make common cause with unions like CUPE which insisted on the principle of national control. The argument was that the international unions' major contribution had been to take money from Canada and orders from Washington. In the context of the Cold War, the debate took on ominous political overtones, signalling to many that it would be best to keep their nationalist objections private. Stan Little and Grace Hartman weren't so constrained and both found themselves speaking out on the issue, and not only to trade union audiences.

In 1970 Hartman was invited to participate in the Teach-in on the Americanization of Canada, sponsored by the University of Toronto NDP Club and the Waffle Movement (an NDP minority faction on the left mainly concerned with the Canadianization issue) at Convocation Hall on the U of T campus. She presented a paper on "Organized Labour and Canadian Independence," sharing the session with Kent Rowley, secretary treasurer of the CCU, and Michel Chartrand, president of the Montréal Council of the Confederation of National Trade Unions (CNTU). Her presentation had been meticulously prepared by Gil Levine, using new government statistics to show that of the $35 million in union dues sent south of the border annually, only $18 million returned. "The disclosure that the international unions are operating at a profit of about $17 million a year on their Canadian operations should effectively demolish the argument that Canadian labour cannot be financially self-supporting," she said. And she reiterated CUPE's long-standing demand that the CLC adopt standards of autonomy and urge its affiliates to work to attain them. The newspapers leapt on the speech, noting the unusual candour about a taboo topic. "Criticism of mainstream Canadian labour represented by the U.S. based unions is rare from union leaders," said the Toronto *Telegram*. And indeed, the international unions were as skittish as sacred cows about the issue. Complaints were made to the CLC that Hartman had attacked international unions – in this speech and others – and had been agitating for full autonomy for their Canadian sections. "Every time I spoke about autonomy or women I was jumped on," she would say.

It was mainly the spectre of nationalism that made the CLC establishment of U.S.-based unions truly apprehensive. CUPE had tread softly around the issue through the sixties; its brief to the Congress's Commission on Restructuring in 1967, written by Francis Eady, was extremely cautious although it did refer to the issue. Recognition of the contribution made by U.S.-based unions had to be tempered by recognition of the rights of workers to associate freely and to decide on the structure and scope of their own unions. However, the press release announcing CUPE's 1967 submission did not mention the proposal that an international committee under the chairmanship of the International Confederation of Free Trade Unions be set up to investigate and provide guidance. A leitmotif in the brief was the matter of jurisdiction and the "need for the unification of small and unco-ordinated groups with larger organizations with which they have a direct community of interest." Since 1963, CUPE had been the designated organization for provincial and municipal employees (with the exception of British Columbia public employees who were already affiliated with the CLC). But as CUPE went out to organize these provincial workers, it found its efforts constantly being undermined by the CLC leadership who were encouraging direct affiliation to the Congress. By 1971 Stan Little was claiming the CLC actions constituted a deliberate campaign. "CUPE started making inroads which was the only reason the provincial associations suddenly became interested in the CLC." In spite of its policy of promoting mergers, the CLC seemed bent on preventing CUPE, its largest national affiliate, from getting any larger.

In 1973 both sides took off their gloves. First CUPE presented a brief to a special session of the CLC executive council, stating its case. It rebuked the CLC for its history of interference and double dealing, and denounced the provincial associations for not being representative or effective or even bona fide trade unions under the law. Then in September the Congress voted to grant affiliation to three provincial civil service groups in Alberta, Newfoundland and Prince Edward Island. CUPE arrived at its 1973 convention in a white rage that erupted as delegates debated a motion to pull out of the Congress. Many observers felt a majority would have voted for an open break, a position taken by Shirley Carr among others. The opposite view was expressed by Louis Laberge of the Québec Federation of Labour who advised: "Stay in – don't get out. We never won a fight by running away." Little and Hartman took the middle road and, in the end, a resolution was adopted calling for CUPE to stay in the CLC until the 1974 Congress convention; remaining after that time only if the convention adopted a reform program – rather vaguely defined as "revitalizing and changing the CLC leadership to prevent further breaches of faith and moral responsibility on the part of the CLC." Otherwise, the executive board was empowered to pull CUPE out.

Much has been written about the famous 1974 CLC convention and the reform movement that wasn't. Following its convention the previous fall, CUPE met with five other public sector unions – the BC Government Employees' Union, the Canadian Brotherhood of Railway, Transport and General Workers, the Canadian Union of Postal Workers, the Letter Carriers' Union of Canada, and the Public Service Alliance of Canada – and over the next few months spearheaded a move to contest the CLC slate for its four full-time executive positions. (For a while, Hartman considered running herself.) The group produced a document identifying five areas requiring critical attention: Canadian autonomy, industrial democracy,

social unionism, effective servicing, and the rationalization of jurisdictional structure. CUPE undertook a major assault on the Congress, pulling out all stops to encourage members to attend. In 1972
there were 414 delegates at convention; in 1974 in Vancouver there
were 1,057, 569 of them from CUPE. The CUPE *Journal* proclaimed "the CLC will never be the same again," but to many people
the promise of the reform program was not fulfilled. In the end, only
three reform candidates were nominated: Shirley Carr for executive
vice-president; André Major from the Canadian Paperworkers Union, which had recently voted to separate from the international
union, for executive vice-president; and Don Montgomery of the
United Steelworkers, and president of the Toronto Labour Council,
for secretary treasurer. Montgomery was nominated from the floor.
All of them won, although only two of them actually ran as renegade
candidates. Carr was drafted onto the official slate, probably because
she was thought to be unbeatable and possibly because she was a
woman. She joined Huguette Plamondon, who had been a CLC
vice-president for almost twenty years and was the only woman on
the thirty-member board despite the fact that union women had been
calling for better representation the whole time.

For those anxious to see a changing of the old guard, Vancouver
was an anti-climax; the expected confrontation over the National
Question didn't happen. According to Robert Laxer in his account
of CUPE's challenge in *Canada's Unions*: "The main problem was
a crisis of the leadership among the reform group. Various deals and
trade-offs made in the months preceding the convention seriously
damaged the impact of the fifty percent of the local union delegates
who came from Canadian organizations." One major deal bruited
about was over jurisdiction. Incoming CLC president Joe Morris
was understood to have promised support for CUPE's effort to solve
the jurisdiction dispute by allowing a separate national union of
provincial employees as a compromise. In return, Stan Little and
Claude Edwards of the Public Service Alliance of Canada (PSAC)
were believed to have agreed not to run anyone against Morris.

Whatever the exact nature of the accommodation, when the time came for CUPE to apply its numbers to advantage on the autonomy resolutions, Little seemed to collapse. He actually spoke in favour of the executive's recommendations, which fell a long way short of his own union's position. To nationalists, the resolution on autonomy called for only slightly more than the minimum standards for Canadian sections of international unions passed in 1970 – standards that had never been enforced. The only significant addition was a clause authorizing the executive council to discipline member unions for not meeting the standards. What the convention did do, in defiance of executive recommendation, was pass the Québec region's autonomy program which included the right to conduct its own educational campaigns and to retain a larger share of dues to finance these activities. In some delegates' view, Laberge and the Québec delegation stole the show and demonstrated what passionate oratory and good organizing can accomplish.

The CUPE leadership's cold feet may have had something to do with the feeble support from its allies. "From the outset it was clear that the expectations of the leadership of the other unions were not as high as we would have hoped," said the executive board in a statement to affiliates. There was also fear that if they were pushed too hard, the international unions might make good on their threat to withdraw. "It must be pointed out here that in all our plans we were walking on a precarious line. We needed to bring new faces and new ideas to the CLC, yet we could not push the CLC to the point of destruction." In the months preceding the Congress convention there had been a great deal of pressure applied. Stan Little was also on the CLC executive council by then, having been elected because "they couldn't ignore us any longer. I guess I particularly got in their way because I was sitting on the inner core and they couldn't do a damn thing without me knowing about it. But those six or eight months were bloody hell! I'd walk into a room and they couldn't throw me out but they'd do everything else but. Those international unions had an absolute free hand over there. They'd have me up all night trying to 'straighten me out' as they called it." The deal was presumably the result of the straightening-out program. Some considered Little's abilities as a dealmaker one of his strengths, but there were also those in Vancouver who felt deceived, and Little's own executive assistant was one. In a chance conversation, CLC vice-president Lynn Williams convinced Allan Millard that everything had already been decided: Shirley Carr would be an executive vice-president and all the rest was sound and fury. "Here the members had spent thousands of dollars sending delegates to Vancouver when there was nothing for them to do." At the CUPE caucus session on the Monday night, Millard asked Little point blank if a deal had been made. "Stan ignored me for the rest of the convention, and when I got back to work the phone call came in. He wouldn't speak to me, I got the message from the secretary. You're fired. Clear out."

Hartman seems to have sat this one out on the sidelines, leaving Little to make his various deals; she did not try to lead where he wouldn't. She really tried to chart the middle ground when it came to splits. "Stan was up on the platform most of the time and I was down with the membership, and oh! were they [the international unions] giving CUPE a hard time. Bob White got up and spoke about all the things he had done for CUPE and how he wanted us to see reason, and I remember asking Stan who that guy was as I'd never seen him before. Steel was saying the same thing. They were really uptight and annoyed at our resolutions and positions. Lofty came to me at one point and said, 'Let's take 'em out of here.' 'Well,' I said, 'if we walk out we have to leave the door open a crack so we can get back in. We can't be stupid about this; we need the Congress.' "

It was Grace Hartman who wrote CUPE affiliates in September, reporting on the NEB decision to stay with the CLC and passing along the board's resolution and accompanying statement. On the question of jurisdiction it read: "Our key resolution was debated, our points were made, the mood of the convention clearly favoured the

CUPE position, and most important we got an 'on-the-record' commitment from the newly elected president. Brother Morris told delegates he favoured a national organization for the provincial government groups and that further entry of these associations should not be allowed until the national organization exits."

It could be argued that the 1974 reform convention was a watershed for the National Question and the Canadian labour movement, and that it had a greater impact than nationalists and leftists like Laxer gave it credit for – although that would have required clairvoyance. Attitudes on union autonomy were changing and the balance was already beginning to shift in 1973 and 1974. Certainly it was a boon to CUPE to have its jurisdictional differences with the CLC settled, and wily Joe Morris immediately put Shirley Carr in charge of the dossier supporting the creation of the new provincial government workers union (the National Union of Provincial Government Employees, NUPGE, established in 1974). Despite the disappointment with the outcome of the 1974 CLC convention, CUPE had come to symbolize the new emphasis on national unions in Canada, and Stan Little had made a reputation for himself, summed up by Wilfred List as "annoying other union leaders by championing the right of the public employees unions to a greater role in the CLC, elbowing for wider jurisdiction for CUPE, and raising his voice on behalf of greater autonomy for Canadian sections of international unions." Part of the role CUPE took on in these years was supporting the struggles of other Canadian unions, such as the Canadian Textile and Chemical Union (CTCU), a CCU affiliate, in its three-and-a-half month strike against Artistic Woodwork in Toronto for a first contract in 1973. It was a really nasty strike involving immigrant workers and reactionary owners, and it aroused a great deal of sympathy and support from artists and students as well as other workers who were all branded dangerous outside agitators by management and the police. The picket line grew larger and larger as the strike continued, and Metro cops were sent to initiate most of the violence. There were many arrests, and videotaping from unmarked cars. Several CUPE members marched on the picket line daily and, at Grace Hartman's instigation, CUPE National sent a telegram to Premier Davis expressing support for the strikers and condemning the violence.

CUPE took its leadership role on women's issues equally seriously and publicly. This, of course, was due to Grace Hartman's presence and the fact that she had the union's support (or lack of interference) when she needed it. She was willing to work with middle-class women and when she did she brought the authority of thousands of workers with her. She was willing to work with an all-male executive but when she did she had the strength of several hundred thousand women behind her. The politician in her was able to weigh the advantages in each situation.

Sometime in the middle of 1975 CUPE overtook the Steelworkers to become the largest union in Canada. 1975, as it happened, was International Women's Year and the same year Grace Hartman became president of CUPE. For the first few months she also found herself president of the National Action Committee on the Status of Women, a position she took on after Laura Sabia retired. The choice was deliberate and reflected NAC's multi-partisan nature, for Sabia was a middle-class professional and a Conservative woman while Hartman was a left-wing (NDP by this time) working woman. She had also been NAC's treasurer for three years, and part of the backbone working committee of women who got NAC on its feet and the coalition running. The generational differences evident at the "Strategy for Change" conference in 1972 were augmented by other splits, between liberal women and radical feminists, between traditional middle-class women's organizations and activist groups which were then emerging from grassroots movements, the "jeans and the suits." The working women there (Madeleine Parent and Laurell Ritchie from the CCU, and Grace Hartman) were able to bridge some of those differences. Hartman, for instance, could be said to represent both mainstream labour and radical working-class feminist perspectives and constituencies, and she brought both to her presidency. "I think it was good that we had a person of her standing there at that time for want of a more active person," says Parent. Her tenure, though, was brief. Heading into election year at CUPE she didn't have the time to be much more than a caretaker president of NAC, and after the first year of her term she had to withdraw. Bev Stager and Kay Macpherson, as vice-chairpersons, saw to the day-to-day office administration, assisted by Ruth Chud, "our office person." In her report to the 1975 NAC annual general meeting in Winnipeg, the first outside of Toronto, Hartman spoke of the period of adjustment which necessarily followed Laura Sabia's retirement. It was a year of stabilization which included the appearance of NAC *News* edited by Moira Armour, a grant from the Secretary of State to help pay for travel to meet women across Canada, and some reorganization. In parting, she urged NAC to political action. "As a trade unionist I know that is the only way legislation gets changed."

Over the previous six or eight years, Grace had passed up few invitations herself to speak at educational institutes, conventions and rallies, and she encouraged women trade unionists to do the same thing. "The men won't take up cudgels for their female counterparts. Even in CUPE, when we were preparing our brief we knew the men weren't really enthusiastic. Few will go out on strike to support equal pay for women," she told a reporter in 1968. In 1970 she was at the microphone at the CLC convention in Edmonton, pressing for establishment of a women's commission. "We are going to be heard, and you'd better start listening," she told the men on the platform. At the Brantford District Labour Council she spoke of the history of women's struggle for recognition and their rights over the century, and commented, "It is men who are deciding how much money will be spent on defence as compared to housing, whether women have the right to abortion or to exercise control over their

own bodies, what to do about unemployment and high prices ... "
And she warned that women are certain to rebel: "The rebirth of the
women's rights movement is inevitable." To the CUPE New Brunswick Division convention in Moncton: "Genuine equality for women
workers will come only when unions refuse to sign agreements that
give advantages to men over women workers in any way ... Women
are tired of being taught to package and sell themselves as sexual
commodities to the male populace with the emphasis on fashion,
figures and uplift brassieres." To the CUPE Manitoba Division at
Dauphin in 1971: "The majority of working women will continue
to turn their backs on unions until union leaders begin to treat them
as persons with equal status." At the Canadian Hospital Association
convention in Vancouver she talked about the caste system in hospitals, "I know of no other industry which so blatantly attaches male
and female to job titles and so consistently pays women less for doing
virtually the same job as men." At other times she spoke with
admiration of the Women's Liberation Movement, and in support
of the focus it was giving to daycare and abortion, critical issues for
working women.

Hartman's message was direct and unvarnished and unaffected.
She used words like "oppressed" and "exploitation," and she let no
one off the hook, directing her attention to both sexes, reserving
criticism for both. She didn't spare the men in the union who sided
with management in discriminating against women, or the women
who colluded with discriminatory practices and were "all too willing
to let the men do it" – or anyone, in fact, who accepted the status
quo without a fight. Throughout these years she lent her own and
CUPE's support to other women's struggles: orchestrating a CUPE
hospital workers' boycott of Texpack products during the strike by
the CTCU in 1971, or joining a demonstration in front of Ottawa's
tony Rideau Club in 1972 when two government lawyers were
barred from attending a luncheon to which they'd been officially
invited, because they were women and the club was segregated.
Grace MacInnis, the only woman MP at the time, Pauline Jewett,

then head of Canadian Studies at Carleton University, and about fifty other women milled about on Wellington Street, sipping iced tea and eating sandwiches set out on a little table by the organizers, the Ottawa Women's Resource Group. Later in the day, during Question Period, Treasury Board chairman C.M. Drury was greeted with shouts of "male chauvinist" when he told the House he had consulted with "the gentler sex" about the policies of a private club which was often used for government functions. Hartman was quoted in the Ottawa *Journal* expressing the opinion of many Ottawa residents (she figured) that the Rideau Club was so far removed from everyday life neither she nor her secretary had a clue where it was. Successful women didn't usually take to the streets in protest. Even Grace MacInnis was careful to tell the press she was there as an individual, on personal business, but this group was learning something about the efficacy of public action from workers, peace activists and radicals. Grace Hartman was there to cheer them on.

While Grace remained connected to the organized women's movement (she remained on NAC's Survival Committee after 1975) she was still critical of feminism as she saw it evolving. She always asked where working women were. "So women can't be firemen in Scarborough," she remarked in 1974, in the wake of a story of women being refused employment as firefighters. "That brings us to the basic dilemma about what is more important to women in the long run: making a symbolic infiltration of the fire department or having enough money to put bread on the table?" She despaired of academic discussions, such as the one over the use of "Ms," which "working-class women regard as remote and meaningless. It is exactly the kind of discussion which has turned the majority of working-class women away from the women's movement and the reason why the movement has failed to catch on with anybody but middle-class and upper middle-class women." When women's liberation talked about housewife-slavery in the home, she thought of women working nine hours a day for poverty level wages, standing on the cold cement floors of a fish packing plant, ankle deep in slime, and knew beyond the shadow of a doubt that "she would feel much more fulfilled staying at home with her children than slaving all day in the stench of the fish plant." Hartman was aware of the class contradictions in feminism just as she was aware of weakness in labour's commitment to women's rights. Her approach, by now well established, was to play devil's advocate to both camps – to inject a working-class consciousness into the women's movement, and feminist consciousness into the trade union movement. It was a bit like freelancing at the revolution; her political stance and style were not especially radical, but to rebels like Madeleine Parent, Hartman was a beacon. "I couldn't tell you how a person like Grace, who was part of mainstream labour with its very right-wing leadership, was limited in what she could do, but within the women's movement my experience of her was that she was on our side. She was not always the most hard-hitting spokesperson but she would support the most hard-hitting spokesperson. She would add her reputation and credibility to positions we were taking and that was very important."

5

Leading Canada's
Largest Union

Thanksgiving Monday, 1975. A black, rainy, rotten night greeted Grace Hartman as she drove back to Ottawa from the long weekend in Toronto with her family. The CUPE convention was a week away so there had been no question of her staying longer. The car purred reassuringly as she slipped along Highway Seven, listening to the iridescent notes of Oscar Peterson's piano tumble from the radio. Her mind drifted back to that trip to New York in the mid-fifties with Edna, when they did the jazz clubs 'til dawn, calling home intermittently to see if Rae's baby had arrived yet. She thought of the piano, and her father. Here it was International Women's Year, and she was about to become the first woman in North America to scale the senior ranks of labour. Reporters would ask about that, but it wasn't affirmative action that had brought her here. (Unless you count Joe as affirmative action which, come to think of it, she was inclined to.) Nor was it tokenism, she firmly believed; it had more to do with synchronicity. There was a very good chance now she was going to be in a position to actually make change. With Stan Little, it had been the vision of one big union for public employees. His twelve years at the helm hadn't realized that exactly, but CUPE was one big union nonetheless and its status had been established. Her vision was of broadening the influence of CUPE in the social and political affairs of the nation. Whatever happened, she expected it would be interesting.

Then suddenly she was aware that the music had stopped and the news had come on. Prime Minister Pierre Trudeau was announcing the imposition of wage and price controls and the establishment of an Anti-Inflation Board. "I remember it as if it were yesterday," she said in 1989. "The Conservatives under Robert Stanfield had run in the 1974 general election on a platform of wage controls as a means of combating soaring inflation. Trudeau had been elected on a platform opposing them, saying they simply would not work, yet we kept hearing threats. People like Gil Levine had good contacts in the department of Labour and elsewhere. And here they were, the prime minister's gift to us for Thanksgiving. I drove the rest of the way into Ottawa thinking, 'What a way to start out!' "

That announcement changed the tone of the seventh biennial convention which took place in Toronto. A thousand delegates converged on the Royal York Hotel, a larger than usual contingent, a larger proportion (35 percent) of them women, and their collective mood angry. Organized labour hadn't been alerted, let alone con- sulted about the government's change of mind, even though con- trols were undeniably going to affect workers first. By chance, CUPE's was the first union convention after the declaration and all eyes, especially those of the media, were upon it. John Munro, the federal minister of Labour, wanted to address the convention. "We weren't going to let him and then we thought if we don't it will seem to the public that we won't even listen. So we gave him twenty minutes. He took thirty-five and spoke very fast because he had a long speech. All through it the French-speaking delegates were com- plaining because there was no translation (we found out later the cables had been cut). I'd asked the delegates beforehand to let the minister speak, but to respond with absolute silence, no applause." There were jeers and groans and obscenities shouted as Munro tried to sell the audience the notion that the anti-inflation measures were not anti-labour in intent. They were not, he said, "a crude attempt to zap labour, or to make labour the scapegoat for inflation." He asked delegates to reconsider their opposition, while threatening that the government would not budge from its commitment even if there was to be solid opposition from labour. When he finished he looked out over the crowd. A few signs held aloft silently screamed "*Non au 10%*" (the ceiling on wage increases); people coughed, muttered to their neighbours and waited; no one applauded. Munro seemed unnerved by the reception. Pale and sweating profusely, he left the platform, saying to his aide, "Let's get out of here, I'm only making things worse."

Coincidently, Pierre Trudeau turned up at the Royal York later the same week to speak at a service club luncheon. He arrived with Margaret and infant Sasha in tow, and was mobbed in the lobby by delegates and demonstrators. One woman walked straight up to him and demanded to know if he realized what he was doing to the poor and the elderly, and didn't he care? "You wanted leadership and you got it," shrugged the prime minister, "and you are going to be stuck with controls for a while."

There had never been much doubt about CUPE's response. Stan Little led off the convention with an attack on controls for "making public employees cannon fodder in what will surely be a phony war on inflation," and on the government for "trying to trick the Canadian people into believing that it is actually going to try to control prices. In fact, all the government is going to do is treat the bosses to a wage freeze." The members cheered when he exhorted them to resist. "We will go about our business as if they didn't exist." The executive board presented Emergency Resolution 201 which denounced the program as "unfair, unworkable and undemocratic" and "contrary to the basic interests of all Canadian workers and the right of free collective bargaining." It called for a vigorous campaign to oppose wage controls. The resolution was ardently debated and sent back to the Resolutions Committee twice for redrafting, with instructions each time to make the English more precise and the action more explicit. The final version urged all CUPE locals to defy the legislation by continuing to negotiate for improvements they deserved and their members had decided democratically to seek, and called for CUPE to meet with affiliates immediately to plan a campaign in collaboration with other labour bodies and community groups. This was passed with sober intent; the membership wanted action and for CUPE to take the lead.

Such assertiveness was becoming a tradition at CUPE conventions. Delegates insisted on making decisions their own, and often refashioned executive board motions to alternative, more radical versions. This was the beauty of CUPE's structure, which permitted a level of local control and membership participation that few other mainstream unions would. This was NUPE's great contribution to the merger. The curse of it, though, was the unpredictability, the energy and creative patience which democracy demands. CUPE's opposition to the government's anti-inflation program was adamant, and its refusal to appear voluntarily before the Anti-Inflation Board controversial. "We came in for a lot of criticism for that from other unions," Hartman recalled. "Sure I wondered if our quick decision was the correct one, if we should have been going [to the AIB]. But we were trying desperately to bring up a lot of our low wage groups." The position was reviewed, but only in the final year of the three-year wage-controls program, when the power of the controls over the long haul had became painfully evident, did CUPE try working within the system.

The 1975 convention was a tumultuous one, complete with a bomb scare, Margaret Trudeau being jostled by CUPE protesters, and the membership calling for a general strike. Grace Hartman's election message addressed that militancy. "The new program of wage controls demonstrated to all of us the urgent need for CUPE to get involved in political action." It wasn't sufficient to support the NDP in elections or pass motions at CLC conventions, she said, not for a union like CUPE whose members were feeling the attacks of the government so sharply. She sailed through the election which was contested at the last minute, winning 668 to 208. Grace Hart-man had learned a thing or two about union politics and how to get elected by then. She had support among staff across the country and was also well known to the CUPE membership. She was fortunate, too, to have good news to take to the convention: a small surplus in place of the usual deficit, and a Defence Fund back in operation after a moratorium of almost two years.

In 1975 CUPE had a membership of 210,000 and a budget of $7 million – austere compared to the Steelworkers' plush $13 million for a membership of 187,000. Hartman had acquitted herself well in the position of secretary treasurer, she was a good manager, and although there are various opinions as to how much credit her designs and decisions deserved vis-à-vis Stan Little's, the fact is she was more conscious than most managers of the degree to which her own effectiveness depended on others, especially her support staff. In the beginning she could probably have used better – that is, more sophisticated – financial and administrative assistance than young Ralph Maillet could offer, but the two of them worked and evolved together. With her adeptness at staff relations, her warmth and openness, Hartman had an easy affect which invites confidence and confidences from others; she could never have navigated the Byzan-tine politics of the early years without it. Finally, she made a point of keeping part of herself reserved from the fray, cultivating an outsider's perspective which her gender provided in any case. In the long run she even came to appreciate Stan Little, and eventually revised her judgment about who really was the better choice for president in 1967. Bill Black was very much a one-man band and might have been quite authoritarian in the position. When Little announced his retirement in January 1975, Hartman approached him to endorse her candidacy, calling in the last card. He agreed and even cleared the way for her to take on some of the presidential duties during the last few months of 1975. For her part, Hartman accepted Kealey Cummings as secretary treasurer from the Little/NUPSE faction.

For Grace Hartman, the convention must have been exhilarating but at the same time the sort of experience you need only once in a lifetime. It was both a personal triumph and a moment of terror as she was dropped over a precipice into the middle of the action. "I remember the election was on the Wednesday and on Thursday Stan Little, who was still on the CLC executive, left to go back to Ottawa for an emergency CLC meeting on wage controls. It wasn't normal; newly elected officers usually assume their duties at the close of the convention, but I took over as president on the spot." She had, of course, dropped into chaos before, but this was of a different level and import, and in front of television cameras. Still, she came out of the convention and into office with a mandate to take decisive action. "We will turn the heat on; we will melt the wage freeze," she promised.

One of the first things Sister Hartman did as president was demand thirty-five minutes to address the Liberal national convention taking place in Ottawa in early November. "They had never heard of that before, but we had given John Munro thirty-five minutes and I told them if we didn't get equal time the world would know. By then I was riding a crest of publicity. I could hardly cope with the number of interviews, and they knew CUPE could pick up press." They gave her fifteen minutes on a panel with Donald Macdonald (the finance minister) and John Munro. Her speech was timed to the minute. She didn't expect applause and she wanted no surprises. "Our staff had made sure there was a step for me to stand on; being so short I'm buried by the microphones otherwise. I was sitting beside Donald Macdonald, who said I could speak from the table if I preferred, but I'd seen Pierre Trudeau come in and sit down right dead centre. It was him I wanted to speak to, not those guys." The news reported scattered applause when Grace Hartman spoke, and it was clear from the questions that people sympathized with the situation of the nursing home employee earning $2.75 an hour whose annual wage would be frozen below the poverty line and who asked "Why Me? Why Now?" It was not that Hartman felt she could win over the Liberal faithful; her assertion that controls would hit low-income earners hardest was not what they wanted to hear. (As it happened, the conference didn't take a clear stand on the anti-inflation program.) It was rather a matter of exacting attention – and respect. They would have to listen to the truth, a truth that included the articles in the financial press advising professionals and executives how to beat the controls, games that wage-earners would not be able to play. "I don't want to leave the impression that we are not concerned about inflation," she told them. "The low-paid woman who works at that nursing home has been hit harder by inflation than middle and upper middle income earners. She spends a much larger portion of her income on food and housing – items which have been rising faster than all other components of a family budget. Now you tell her to tighten her belt. You tell her to get on the front lines. And when in disbelief she turns to me, what am I supposed to tell her?"

The next months were a-frenzy with meetings, speeches, interviews, rallies and strategy sessions. A key note in the debate was the matter of legality, with Joe Morris of the CLC sounding the "We're law-abiding citizens" line and stalling for time in contrast to Grace Hartman's "Reject the legislation" position. Hartman accused the prime minister of deceiving voters, suggesting that his timing was deliberate. "For this new program to occur in International Women's Year has the distinct ring of male chauvinism," she told the First Unitarian congregation in Ottawa in December. The Ottawa *Journal* ran a news item on her lecture, heading it "Restraints tinged with sexism: Hartman." She was talking about the changing role of women in society, and about what was happening to the vast majority of working women at the low end of the wage-scale, caught in the pincers of inflation and the government's nasty anti-inflation cure. "The government says it is trying to stop inflation. The real intent of this program is to bring an end to free collective bargaining. They have rolled back wage settlements but they haven't done anything about rolling back prices," she told the Calgary Labour Council in January. When asked about the penalties for defying the law,

October 14, 1976. A year after wage controls were introduced, Grace Hartman addresses demonstrators on the national Day of Protest at Memorial Park in Winnipeg.

she faced down *Globe and Mail* reporter Virginia Galt with "There aren't enough jails in the country to hold us all." Hartman could smell a vindictive edge in the government's action, and felt the old resentment at being treated like a servant. She had the facts, the militant backing of her members, and very quickly she became a household name in Canada, a sweet voice of reason offering scathing comment about the anti-inflation program on radio and television. She took to calling it the Wage Measures Act.

Late in March 1976, 30,000 workers gathered on Parliament Hill in sub-zero weather to protest government wage controls, the largest demonstration on the Hill since the dairy farmers' protest in 1967. People carried balloons and sang songs with irreverent lyrics, while overhead two biplanes pulled a message to Trudeau from CUPE

Local 767: *The Universe isn't morally unfolding as It Should*. A carnivalesque atmosphere, but the messages on the placards were grim: "Whatever happened to price controls?" "Fuddle Duddle to Trudeau and the wage freeze." The crowd was a good deal larger than the Canadian Labour Congress, which had called it, had expected. It was ample evidence of gut level opposition to federal controls, if evidence was needed. From the day controls were announced there had been activists clamouring for a national strike, but no one in the senior ranks of Canadian labour seemed willing to lead it. The CLC had undertaken a PR campaign with posters, newspaper and radio ads exclaiming, "Why Me?" – that is, "Why should Canadian workers and consumers be the ones to pay the price of a war against inflation?" To many people it sounded a bit like the Liberal government's insipid slogan for International Women's Year, "Why Not?" with about as much political edge to it. Within CUPE, senior staff spread out from national office across the country to meet with division staff to lay out the program and answer questions at meetings about implementing the convention's planned tactic to "bargain as usual." Lofty MacMillan reported to Grace Hartman that there was real support out there for a general strike.

It was not immediately clear why Trudeau had invoked controls when he did, but the changes in the share of profits and wages in the national income explained a lot. Corporate profits had more than doubled between 1970 and 1974, rising from 17 percent to 22 percent of the national income while wages fell from 72 percent to 67 percent. Then, as organized labour started to negotiate back some of the ground lost to inflation, the trend abruptly reversed, producing a profits squeeze (or the hint of one) as some $4 billion in corporate profits was "redistributed" to wages and salaries in the first half of 1975. Wages and salaries, on average, were rising faster than prices as businesses, stuck in a major recession, found they could not pass the cost of wage increases on to consumers. The financial community convinced the government that inflation was carrying the country straight into chaos and with a million and a half workers due to sign new contracts in late 1975 and 1976, the time was right to act. They might have said the same for unemployment, which reached its highest level in fourteen years (7.3 percent) that November, but obviously it was the disappearance of profits, not jobs, that panicked the businessmen.

For the second time in his career as prime minister, Pierre Trudeau resorted to extraordinary legislation to curtail the civil rights of citizens in response to an apprehended catastrophe. The first time, during the October Crisis of 1970, he had rounded up dissidents and held them in jail without charge. This time, workers were told to accept a 10 percent ceiling on their wage increases with no guarantee in return, only the fond hope that prices would stabilize too. The AIB balance sheet: after the first year, inflation was down to 6.2 percent (from 10.6 percent the previous year) and the average wage settlement to 10.2 percent (from 14.4 percent); after the second year, inflation had risen back to 9.5 percent and wage settlements were further depressed to 7.7 percent. That year, 1977, food prices shot up almost 18 percent, all of which gave the lie to the government's line that wage settlements were the cause of inflation. Wage controls tightened as time went on, and public sector workers, as predicted, saw their wage increases rolled back a full percentage point further than those of private sector unions.

From the moment controls were introduced, it was obvious who was going to get hurt the most. Because they were living at the bottom of the wage scale, with no margins, the freeze on wages cut deepest into women's standard of living. Hartman spoke about this incessantly, but it was Madeleine Parent, according to Grace, who carried the ball politically on the issue of wage controls and women – at NAC especially.

CUPE was certainly in the front lines of the equal pay struggle, having first addressed the issue of "equal remuneration for work of equal worth" in its brief to the Royal Commission in 1968, and it was some advantage to the cause that Hartman's election to the top position in CUPE coincided with International Women's Year. CUPE had also been promoting the participation of women in the union, and encouraged all members to become active and knowledgeable about the discrimination women face at work and in the community. An "Anti-Discrimination Check-List" was produced, special bargaining workshops were organized, and an update of the 1971 plan of action prepared. Until wage controls hijacked the agenda, the 1975 convention's major focus was *The NEW Status of Women in CUPE* which reported, on the plus side, more active participation by women in CUPE, the elimination of wage discrimination between male orderlies and female nursing assistants, and the inclusion of maternity leave in most collective agreements. On the negative side, women remained badly under-represented on staff and in elected positions, wage discrimination was still widespread and daycare generally did not exist. The 1971 directive to set up Implementation Committees had been ignored. Informal status of women committees had been set up in Victoria and Toronto locals that year, but there was no concerted organizing happening. Undaunted, the convention reaffirmed the original sixteen-point policy and passed resolutions calling for the decriminalization of abortion and the release of Dr. Henry Morgentaler from prison, for CUPE to press all governments to institute equal pay for work of equal value practices, and most significantly, for CUPE to institute its own internal affirmative action plan. This was a milestone, moving the union from theory to the practice of combating sexism in its own ranks. Hartman pitched in and encouraged women to run for union office, urging them to apply for senior positions in the union whenever and wherever she could. There was much she did privately to advance women and the debate on social justice within CUPE. And when she went out as CUPE's president onto the national stage to debate economic policy, she was prepared to talk about it as a women's issue.

Oddly enough, it wasn't so easy for the National Action Committee on the Status of Women to make the breakthrough. There were conflicts about whether it was appropriate to take on wage controls at all, and arguments were made by some executive members like Lorna Marsden, NAC president between 1975 and 1977 and a prominent Liberal, that NAC should not get sidetracked and should only take on women's issues which were not being tackled by anyone else. Others, Madeleine Parent, Laurell Ritchie and economist Marjorie Cohen included, felt the anti-inflation program was *the* women's issue *par excellence*, of extreme importance to their constituents. The crux of it was the catch-up exemption in AIB regulations, intended to allow adjustments which would otherwise have been illegal in order to eliminate sex discrimination in pay. Predictably few applications had come in under that exemption – by early 1977 twenty applications had been received – because the onus was on the employers to apply for it, the same employers who profited from paying women cheap wages. The subject came up at the NAC annual meeting in March 1977, which Grace Hartman attended. "The Liberal women were out in full force, I remember. Madeleine Parent and I talked about how we were going to get a resolution condemning wage controls through. It didn't look easy. Both of us spoke with a fair amount of knowledge about what was actually happening and we did get the resolution." It was a solid one which condemned the discriminatory treatment of all workers but especially women, reasoning that because controls limit low-income workers to smaller increases, they widen the wage gap between low- and high-income workers and prejudice the position of women workers further. The catch-up exemption was less than useless window-dressing. Later that spring the evidence emerged when one employer, who had been forced to admit malfeasance, was given a rollback on an increase negotiated to eliminate discriminatory pay scales. CUPE Local 1500 had laid an unequal pay complaint with the Manitoba Human Rights Commission in 1973 against the Health Sciences Centre in Winnipeg, and a key issue in the subsequent dispute between the union and the hospital had been the implementation of a job evaluation program. One was recommended by the Industrial Inquiry Commission though, and catch-up increases were included in the collective agreement signed in June 1974. According to its terms, 936 of the 950 female staff were to receive pay increases to put them on a level with male staff. These were not high incomes and not large increases – the base wage rate rose from $3.39/hour to $3.69/hour. But the AIB rolled it back anyway, reducing the increase from 16 percent to 12 percent. The AIB, CUPE discovered, was hewing to a feebly narrow definition of equal pay, claiming the exemption didn't stretch to include work of equal value. The union responded with the charge that the definition was not in keeping with the government's own Human Rights Act, Bill C-25 passed in 1972. This meant, as Laurell Ritchie pointed out, the government had been caught in the act of putting its seal of approval on discriminatory practices.

The wording of NAC's resolution had been strong, but the follow-up was anything but. The presentation made to parliamentarians after the annual meeting pointedly raised the effects of anti-inflation regulations on women. But beyond that the NAC executive waffled. When Grace Hartman invited NAC to be part of a meeting she was arranging with Finance Minister Donald Macdonald to press for a clearer definition of the sex discrimination clause, the NAC executive argued itself into a compromise and sent one of their number, Kay Macpherson – unofficially. There was further political paralysis on NAC's part, and a withdrawal into "further study" and consultation with the membership. "We argued very strongly that fighting the AIB was a women's issue, but we lost the day on that one," says Marjorie Cohen. If NAC's contribution was muted, at least when it spoke it was on the right side of the debate. The government-appointed Advisory Council on the Status of Women couldn't even muster a mild public rebuke of the government's attack on working women. The appointees were mostly Liberal party members and adamantly "unwilling to criticize their own," as Hartman found out. She had been appointed to the council to replace Laura Sabia when Sabia was retiring from NAC in 1973, and despite reservations she stayed for two terms, hoping her presence would have symbolic effect if nothing else. There was never any question in her mind, though, of getting anything progressive past the Advisory Council. There were twenty-nine other women on it, and Hartman was by herself. Among that group of "very bright, intelligent women who were all active in their own areas and who *knew* how controls were affecting women," she carried no weight on wage controls. She watched them tune her out, though she talked on anyway. In mid-1977, after the Health Sciences Centre rollback, she decided to force the issue. "My position has always been that the government was not sincere, that the exemption was a token one, and that June's [Menzies] appointment was a sham. Now I have proof," she told her assembled colleagues. She challenged them to take a stand. "We should support NAC's position. We should call for June Menzies's resignation."

June Menzies had been a member of the Advisory Council until 1976, when she was appointed vice-chairperson of the AIB, replacing Beryl Plumptree. Hartman had written to her at the time, warning her of the stakes she was playing for. "I do not have to tell you that most of the low-paid workers in this country are women and the decisions of the AIB are creating greater and greater differences between low- and high-paid workers. If the program continues for the projected three years, equal pay for women workers will be set back so far you and I will not likely live long enough to see equality reached." Within six months Hartman was calling on Menzies to resign. She didn't limit herself to one call, either, but continued attacking for months, deliberately using Menzies and her token position as a metaphor for all that was wrong about liberal feminism, and unfair about the government's policy. Hartman knew she risked seeing her comments reduced to a cat fight in the women's pages, but that didn't stop her from using an International Women's Day speech in Vancouver to taunt Menzies for promoting "50 percent equality" along with her 50 percent rollbacks. Menzies occasionally reacted, saying the feminist criticism was misdirected, that the AIB was not responsible for the fundamental problems of women workers and was not being unfair to them. Like June Menzies, the Advisory Council denied the problem and sidelined Hartman's plea.

This left CUPE out in front, leading the Great Women's Battle of the day, a trade union willing to travel further down the feminist road than the official advisory council of feminists. Grace Hartman didn't let up, of course, which was the whole point. Her commentary kept its focus. At an ACSW conference in January 1978, she spoke of how the times were particularly hard on women workers and warned, "The women's movement might be becoming a bit removed from the realities of women working in hospitals, factories and typing pools. We may have to reassess some of our attitudes and positions." Immigrant women and women of colour would have agreed with her, and Grace may have been thinking of the native woman who had been on an earlier council with her. "One native woman, one trade unionist. You know, the tokens. I sat down beside her one day and we began talking. She was very angry – not at me, at the council. 'You're talking about things that don't mean anything. What my people want is running water and inside toilets.' I asked why she didn't tell [the other women] what she thought. Well, the next day she did. She attacked us for being white do-gooders, which we were. But she didn't say what she had said to me which was the crux of the whole thing. She walked out and never came back."

"WHEN GRACE HARTMAN SPEAKS – PEOPLE LISTEN." So said the campaign slogan. "As president of the largest union in the country you'd expect she'd be called on to voice opinions on behalf of workers. But the clarity of her statements, the power of her personality and the conviction with which she speaks has captured the attention of the media and the public beyond normal expectations." Hartman's 1976 bid for vice-president of the Canadian Labour Congress was aggressive in a somewhat offbeat way. Though she was replacing Stan Little on the official slate, she was determined to win on her own merits. Her campaign flyer speaks unapologetically of her stature and influence, suggesting that the CLC would be lucky to have someone with Hartman's reputation. That she had a constituency beyond her own union made for good leverage. Hartman had been sitting on the CLC executive council for six months by this time, having taken over from Stan Little mid-term when he stepped down as CUPE president, and knew what she was up against. What she hadn't known until very shortly before the convention, even as a member of the council, was that a "Labour Manifesto for Canada," proposing a form of tripartite co-operation with government and business in the development of national economic policy, would be the main thrust of the CLC's proposed action plan against wage controls. There was an assumption being made in some quarters that after controls came off, the federal government would continue with some form of economic monitoring, and the CLC leadership wanted in on it. The term used was Social Corporatism, which stuck in many craws and drew immediate denunciations from the convention floor. The Program of Action accompanying the Manifesto rang no clarion calls for national resistance either, though work stoppages would be considered "if and when necessary." The CLC was hardly spoiling for a general strike; it was only willing to invoke the threat of one in lobbying its tripart partners.

Once again Grace Hartman found herself betwixt and between. Here she was, a new member of the executive council, running for office for the first time, out of sync with the council's stand on the main issue facing labour but believing strongly in the principle of keeping things within the Congress and fighting differences out on the floor rather than in the press. "If you appear to be going in a different direction than the Congress the news hawks are fast to pick it up – and ask." Like Stan Little, she was prepared to do business with colleagues on the CLC executive council. She was critical of them on a number of scores, but she was not prepared to take the high road, as C.S. Jackson did in the 1940s, and become the Congress's in-house antagonist. Nor was she about to become one of the boys, an option Little had. In the first instance she might have taken them on over a general strike. Lofty MacMillan and other advisors were in favour of pushing the CLC on it, and one has to wonder what would have happened if CUPE had struck out on its own. Grace Hartman was not about to speculate or fantasize about the leadership heroics involved in such independent action. Instead she pulled MacMillan off the road. "I'd been planting resolutions all over the place, and locals had been voting unanimously for a general strike and sending them in to the CLC," he recounts. The CLC was not amused. And it had other plans.

Despite the unorthodox procedure of springing the Manifesto on delegates the first day of the convention, it passed. A legion of delegates spoke out against it, including several CUPE delegates such as Larry Katz (from the research department in national office), Lofty MacMillan and Judy Darcy (the Toronto Library Local 1582). Shirley Carr, as an executive vice-president, spoke glowingly in favour; Grace Hartman reserved comment, choosing her battles.

The battle Hartman was prepared to fight at the Québec City convention was over the changes in delegate selection which the CLC executive proposed in hopes of reducing the size of conventions (an unruly 1,500 to 2,000 delegates by then). However, the changes would have altered the character of the Congress. In most labour centrals in the world, delegates are chosen by their national affiliates and are usually the national officers of the union – full-time paid trade unionists. In Canada, in addition to two full-time officers of national or international unions, each local of every affiliated union is allowed representation by rank-and-file members, which is why CLC conventions wind up being so much larger than their American or European counterparts, and why they have a significant number of working union members as delegates. The new rules would have eliminated local delegate selection; instead, selection would be done in head office and according to membership size. Hartman contemplated going along with the proposal since the formula would still favour large unions. "I laid out the resolution, which would be going to the floor, to the CUPE caucus [the opening night of the convention] and suggested we could live with it. Well, they told me in no uncertain terms that they could *not* live with it and I wasn't going to live with it either. That proposal stirred up a nest of hornets in our union as well as many others. I told the CLC Executive then that CUPE wasn't buying it and that I would make our position known on the floor." Making CUPE's position known included accusing the resolution planners of transferring local authority to national officers so they could play God with the members. "Lynn Williams from Steel was chairman of the committee and he was extremely angry when I said that I was not going to support it. The ethic of the Boys Club and cabinet solidarity and so on. But when I spoke at that convention (and I can tell you I was a long time at the mike before I was recognized) I got such a round of applause I had to ask people to stop to allow me to finish in time." The support was overwhelming, and the resolution was overwhelmed, two to one.

If Hartman was willing to break ranks (along with Louis Laberge) over CLC voting structure, she was not willing to fight the executive over the Manifesto in public, not before she really knew what to make of it herself. She was quite happy, nevertheless, to see the criticisms registered. Similarly, she wasn't prepared to endorse Lofty MacMillan's challenge to Joe Morris for the presidency at the convention, although she indulged his effort. "In fact the CUPE executive asked him not to run, but he went ahead. Lofty's Lofty. And he did quite well, you know. He's the kind of guy workers like and he's colourful." And he was articulate. "This document is here to deceive workers," he charged, waving the Manifesto in the air, "rather than doing something for the millions of workers who are out there waiting and hoping that at this convention in Québec City some-

Shirley Carr and Grace Hartman at the first CLC Women's Conference in 1971.

thing will be done to protect their incomes and the collective bargaining under which they are negotiating their contracts." MacMillan pulled a quarter of the vote and went back to work as CUPE's director of organization the following Monday as usual.

Over the next few months, CUPE took a long look at the Manifesto, produced a critical analysis in late 1976, and at the 1977 convention recanted its original lukewarm support. "CUPE was a hold-out. Our membership was up in arms about getting involved in such a thing," Hartman said in 1989. "We thought, and I still think, it added up to a two to one situation; management and government would side together against the workers. In CUPE it touched a chord; and it seemed for years after, tripartism would come up at conventions and be condemned again."

The one big change in Hartman's political life after assuming the presidency of CUPE was taking her seat at the CLC executive table. Hartman was third woman in, after Huguette Plamondon and Shirley Carr. "[Shirley and I were] two pretty high-powered women from the same union. I got the feeling that CUPE was not at all popular there, that we were considered Jennie-come-latelies in the movement, though some of our locals went back further than many of theirs. The industrial unions seemed to see our growth as a threat too; when CUPE became the largest union, well, that was a bitter pill for the Steelworkers to swallow." The rivalry rumbled through the 1976 convention but didn't openly erupt. Buried there too, and not very deep, was the attitude that public employees weren't real workers and had pantywaist unions, lame enough to elect a woman president, left-wing enough to reject structural changes on the grounds that democracy and the rank and file would be constrained. "Here our union was taking militant positions and at the same time becoming the largest union in the Congress. I was always being told CUPE was full of crazies. So there were a lot of things against me, but I knew they'd be there. I decided I was going to do the best job I could anyway."

There were times to marvel and times to grit your teeth – the meeting with Trudeau and his cabinet, for example. "It was supposedly very democratic; we met round a huge square table and were served a buffet lunch. Joe Morris was pressing Trudeau to get out of controls. Shirley and I were sitting one on each side of Marc Lalonde as he was the minister 'responsible' for the Status of Women, and we wanted to talk to him about the Advisory Council. After Morris's pitch Trudeau said 'Well, how do I get out of them? Do I take his people out first?' pointing to Mahoney [of the Steelworkers] 'or your people,' pointing to McDermott [of the Autoworkers], 'or,' waving his hand down the table in our direction, 'shall I take her people out?' That really annoyed me. 'That "her" is our union, Shirley,' I said, which I guessed he didn't like though he didn't say anything. I remember asking Lalonde if he was telling us they put on the controls without having any idea how they would get out of them. He replied that they thought they had three years to do it. This was mind boggling to me – because I have to say I had great respect for Trudeau's intellect – yet here he was a year and a half into controls and still they hadn't figured out a way to lift them."

The admission was startling. Grace Hartman had always been wary of close huddles with management, suspecting collusion was inevitable in such situations. The sharing of insider information alone renders them privileged, and potentially corrupting. She answered Lalonde with: "People out there should know what you're saying." In meetings like this, much, obviously, depends on the balance of power. During these years the government had every reason to fear unrest among Canadian workers, and felt the need to develop some kind of ongoing relationship with labour leadership. The ministers were listening. But most of the time, for instance when the CLC presented its annual brief to the federal cabinet, Hartman was sure they weren't. She detested "going cap in hand to give a brief to a bunch of guys who don't care and aren't listening." No one was more delighted when the CLC broke off relations with all government agencies, and labour reps resigned from boards, in the wake of wage controls. Yet Hartman was also the CUPE president who resisted her members' periodic attempts to pass motions boycotting certain officials or ministers, explaining that she didn't want her hands tied. "I'd meet with the devil himself if I could get a better deal for CUPE workers," she'd say.

*

A dance with the devil is one way of describing life as political leader, where every step is critical and the choreography so complex as to defy straightforward motion, where people's real lives can depend on your performance; you have to be nimble, you have to have abnormal reserves of energy and a thick hide, and you have to love dancing. Sometime between 1963 and 1967, Grace Hartman made the transition from union activist to labour politician. She had risen to leadership through volunteer activism, now she turned "pro," running for election to a full-time paid position. Of course this implies a different relationship with the membership, if only because the stakes are higher on both sides. In CUPE, moreover, there are only two such positions, both of which are vested with immense political status, if not the executive power of other unions where the chief officer negotiates contracts and has the authority to call strikes. By 1975, when Hartman emerged in the public eye as a national leader, she had the confidence and enthusiasm of someone ready for the job. She was ready, but hardly prepared for the unrelenting workload which the political crisis created. Even more unexpected given her history, Hartman discovered she had a cast-iron constitution. She was rarely ill, had the stamina to work for long hours at a stretch, the ability to operate on small doses of sleep and to sleep anywhere – "on a clothesline in a windstorm" as Kealey Cummings would say. She was a nighthawk and a speed reader, and her domestic arrangement meant she could concentrate on her work and compartmentalize her life.

For many of her sixteen years in Ottawa, Grace shared a house with her son Bob who moved to the area shortly after she did, and who became a single father with a toddler named Danny to raise in the early seventies. Grace did not bring CUPE home with her to the house in Dunrobin, but she did bring her briefcase and work late at night on her own, after Danny was bathed, fed and in bed. And she would take her needlework with her to work. It was a therapeutic occupation on the road, and she was constantly travelling after 1975, speaking against controls, mobilizing forces in support of the October 1976 Day of Protest (the CLC-sponsored national work stoppage called to mark the first anniversary of wage controls). Needlework was better than worry beads, the perfect way to spend dead time in airports and still have something to show for it. Naturally it made for amusing encounters with members of the patronizing class, who occasionally mistook her for someone's kindly auntie and initiated conversation, only to find themselves stuck beside one of the country's more controversial union leaders. There was the Newfoundland MP who asked Hartman if she was someone important because of the treatment she was getting from the Air Canada crew, and the young executive who stared at her nonplused when she answered his "Visiting relatives?" inquiry with "Well, no. I'm going to speak to the convention of the BC Provincial Division of CUPE in Vancouver," followed by her credentials. Hers and CUPE's. "I like to give it to them in full: name, rank and serial number. President of the Canadian Union of Public Employees, with a membership of about 250,000, the largest union in the country." That time the conversation continued pleasantly. They shared a bottle of wine and the fledgling businessman learned a few facts of life about the steno pool in his company.

A woman turning up in Grace Hartman's position was still noteworthy, yet between 1967 and 1975 there had been changes in the public attitude. In 1967 it was "Mrs. Grace Hartman Mother-of-Two" who became CUPE's national secretary treasurer. In 1975 it was "Woman, 56," who became national president. That or "Friendly Feminist atop tough union" as, eight years into the women's movement, the press corps had come to see the feminist factor as more of a story than the woman factor. What sort of feminist runs a union? the reporters wanted to know. Not the kind who backs you into a corner with arguments, not one of the strident ones. In 1967 the *Globe and Mail's* Wilfred List wrote, "Mrs. Hartman, a soft-spoken mother of two ... had no intention of becoming a union executive when she went to work for North York Township ... Today her name is a byword within CUPE for active, intelligent union leadership." In 1975 it was "Grace Hartman may soon have to exchange her gentle tones and soft smile for a table-thumping performance as North America's first woman to hold top office in a major national union ... It will be an extraordinary transformation for this apparently gentle grandmother." List (who practically never wrote about Grace Hartman without using the word "soft") couldn't resist comparing Hartman's style to Stan Little's, noting how she steered away from mingling and glad-handing at functions – Little's forté – in favour of quiet talks about the problems of individuals or locals. "The qualities of a union leader as she sees them include a basic understanding of the problems of the members. And coming from the rank and file she feels she has acquired those insights." Another of her tenets of leadership was the absolute necessity of staying in touch with that membership. This she assuredly did, in a different way than Stan Little, and taking full advantage of the gifts of circumstance. She had to travel all over the country tending to CUPE business – logging 200,000 miles in 1978 – giving speeches, attending conferences and rallies, walking on picket lines. She joined striking Edmonton hospital workers (Local 1158), and maintenance workers (Local 1392) at Dalhousie University in 1978; she demonstrated with nursing home employees (Local 2103) at Grove Park Lodge in Renfrew, Ontario, who were protesting a two-year dispute with the new owner who refused to recognize an arbitration award and fired three workers for union activities. "We are being harassed but we have a moral right to belong to a union and we'll take legal action to ensure the agreement is implemented," Hartman told the demonstrators, adding that government ought to be operating nursing homes, not private enterprise. "No one has a right to make a profit off the old and the sick," she said. "Instead their money should go towards good care and decent wages."

Although Hartman always made the point that she was elected by women and by men and paid to work for both, she carried a particular brief for women which she never denied. She identified herself publicly as a working-class feminist and put herself on the line to make affirmative action work. This meant recruiting women to political action within the union, as well as into senior staff positions, wherever she could. The scarcity of women reps was a sore point, and she was determined to change those statistics if nothing else. The barriers were real and badly damaging to some. What she heard from other women was horrific, reflecting the relative good fortune of her own experience. She had been mocked and taunted and disregarded, but never sexually assaulted or harassed. She had never had her confidence shaken by a colleague propositioning her, as happened to one of the first women reps in the Atlantic region. Nothing seems to stop those ancient assumptions, she thought to herself, not even signs on the walls, or rational intelligence. Men coming into the CUPE office would routinely dismiss her and speak to the nearest male – usually her assistant, Ed McAllister – as the person in charge. Be they janitors or lawyers, some men can not bring themselves to speak to a woman in power or as a superior. Grace Hartman listened to stories of relationships ending over union commitments, lovers unable to accept the absences, husbands jealous of time taken away from the kitchen, families opposed to the politics and skeptical of the usefulness of unions to begin with. She talked to women and encouraged them to be activists; she told them to stay in touch. She herself stayed in touch with a network of feminists and activists, both in and outside of CUPE.

In the labour movement these were years of growing feminist activism. Working women were organizing, sometimes within the mainstream and sometimes on their own. Hartman was aware and supportive of both these efforts. She attended a long list of women's movement meetings and conferences – usually speaking or chairing a session – including CLC's 1976 Conference on Women Trade Unionists and the first Ontario NDP Women's Committee conference in 1979. She wrote articles for magazines and women's anthologies such as Gwen Matheson's *Women in the Canadian Mosaic*, and sent money to women's causes. She supported the work of Organized Working Women, which had been set up in 1976 to advance women's issues in the trade union movement and legitimize demands for daycare, equal pay for work of equal value and maternity leave, and to provide women a place to learn to be leaders. Two years later, OWW organizer Deirdre Gallagher recalled the beginning: "International Women's Year did trigger people's consciousness. CUPE came out with a self-evaluation on women's positions which showed the hierarchy of male domination. Then Grace Hartman, president of CUPE, made a speech called 'There Is So Much To Be Done,' talking about how women's issues must be fought by the trade union movement. Women's issues were still not being taken up. There was a contradiction between the trade union's espousal of equality and the practice of it." The issue had been raised, the politics analysed and the campaign for gender equality launched. Now it was time for the hard effort and the committee work. For Hartman there was a CLC Women's Committee – at last – and she advanced the cause in international circles too, mainly through Public Service International (PSI) on whose executive she served (the first woman, again) as Stan Little had before her. As early as 1968 she attended the third world conference on "Problems of Working Women" in Düsseldorf, Germany, representing the CLC. Hartman did not, in other words, retire to eat worms when she realized the CLC labour barons weren't going to invite her around to join their golf game, a point she made once when talking about how she adjusted to the marginalization – as a woman, a leftie and a public employee – on the CLC council.

One of the myths that has persisted longer than most is that women are too emotional, that they tend to burst into tears in the board room. It seems more likely that any woman who has fought her way to the top in a society like ours (in which it takes more skill, more energy, more qualifications and more determination for a woman to reach that level than it does for a man) will have few tears left by the time she gets there. In any case, better she burst into tears under stress than have a heart attack behind her executive desk." Hartman wrote that in her chapter on "Women and the Unions" for the Matheson book. She might have added that while displays of distress around a committee table may be beneath contempt in male society, she hadn't found displays of temper much of an improvement. Hartman had worked with the best of the worst: fiery union leaders who talked hard, fast and nasty. Stan Little's outbursts and Dennis McDermott's flights of rhetorical overkill come to mind. Stress is par for the course, although not all of it is negative. Likewise, leadership has its unsavory side, unpleasant tasks that have to be done. For Hartman, negotiations with staff unions led in the category of tricky situations that had to be faced. Internal disputes, of course, are never agreeable, especially when they involve an audit or a local being put under administration.

In the late seventies there had been a major dispute with Local 52, the 2,500 Edmonton inside workers who declared they were being underserviced and overtaxed by CUPE. They held out for a rebate (an old refrain) and then in the spring of 1978 voted to disaffiliate. "I feel genuinely sick tonight," Ed McAllister said when the meeting voted to bar him entrance. He had gone as Hartman's emissary to explain the national union's action in sending in an audit team and opposing the breakaway. There were other large Alberta locals which shared 52's point of view and had also made moves to pull out. Not that criticism of national office was unique to Alberta. CUPE's decentralized structure and hallowed tradition of local autonomy made this sort of tension inevitable. Besides, issues of money usually boil down to issues of staff: who appoints them, how the division of labour between regional and national office is managed, what the appropriate public and political roles are. Conflicts recurred, both bureaucratic and political, and when things got tense, Hartman would head out to the hot spot herself if she could. It was a matter of principle that national officers be available to speak to members during these kinds of disputes. So in March 1979 she went to Lethbridge to address the Alberta Division convention. Two weeks earlier the Royal Alexandra Hospital local in Edmonton had disaffiliated, and she referred to its going as unhappy. Her call for unity was an appeal to recognize the value – including the dollar value – of being CUPE at the bargaining table, and the cost to workers of forgoing the protection of numbers.

Unpalatable, too, were turns in the political tides that put her in opposition to former friends, like the NDP governments of Saskatchewan and Manitoba which both acceded to passing anti-inflation legislation. Eventually Grace Hartman had to speak out. "Having two NDP governments co-operate with the Liberals was quite traumatic. I was invited to speak at a rally in Regina and I went to see [Premier Allan] Blakeney first. We had quite a long meeting and he was adamant that he could not opt out. I said that it was going to hurt me but I was going to have to condemn his position. He accepted that I'd have to do that, but I don't think the other ministers present thought I would. However, we'd had a strategy session back at the office and that was what we had decided." In Winnipeg, Ed Schreyer's reception was very different. Not only did he dodge the point of the discussion, saying he'd be announcing something soon, he also found the meeting with Hartman excessively awkward. Grace described it: "I had the CUPE vice-president from Winnipeg and my executive assistant with me, both men, and I found I was asking him questions and *he* was answering either of the two men."

Then there was personal stuff. Stories cranked out by the rumour mill every now and then about the alleged Hartman/Carr rivalry always rankled. So did the red baiting. There were always a few people around carrying red paint, who would turn up to do a bit of splashing: a bid to get elected to a labour council committee in the very early sixties queered; the fake letter on Communist Party letterhead, implying Hartman's continued connection, which circulated at one convention; the allegations aired by one CUPE staffer in 1967 about the national secretary treasurer's loyalties. They may seem silly now, but in the mid-sixties, with the pro- and anti-Vietnam wars in full swing in Canada and the U.S., and Cold War Colonel Blimps in charge of the very real military-industrial complex, political labelling was a threatening practice. When the Voice of Women sent a delegation to meet with Russian women in Moscow in 1966, Kay Macpherson was grilled by reporters about being a Communist. Hartman must have often wondered when and how her radical youth might be served up to her. In 1967, when the Royal Commission on the Status of Women was appointed, she learned just how the authorities viewed her: "Feet too firmly planted in the Left" was the reason Judy LaMarsh gave to explain why she had not been named to the Commission, even though several groups, including the CLC, had put her name forward. The government preferred to have *no* representation from labour rather than Mrs. Hartman, apparently.

In 1977 she was brought up short by two stories which broke about CUPE and spying. In August, Lawrence Martin and Victor Malarek reported in the *Globe and Mail* that the government was keeping a trade union blacklist. One such list, naming some civil servants, had become public in January, but the government had sworn no others existed. Now Colonel Robin Bourne, head of the Police and Security Analysis Branch of the solicitor general's department, confirmed that other lists and reports had been compiled and sent to cabinet ministers. Bourne said members of the Canadian Union of Public Employees, the National Farmers' Union and the Indian Association of Alberta were named, and another source said that one list took "a special whack" at CUPE. Hartman wrote Solicitor General Francis Fox the same day: "The members of my Union woke up this morning to find themselves branded as security risks by their government. They don't know how their government collected this information, or why, or when or how it's being used. All they know is that some mysterious Colonel in some equally mysterious branch of your Department has waved a blacklist of names and organizations at them." She had ten very specific questions and was insistent about answers. Fox's reply quoted the mandate of the Branch at length (as if it explained anything) while denying the existence of any list of trade unionists whom the government was keeping under surveillance. He was vague all the same as to the possibility some labour leaders were being investigated. Finally, when pushed to clarify who was telling the truth, Robin Bourne or himself, Fox fell back to claiming that the newspaper had got it wrong in the first place.

It didn't end there. In November the news media again were agog over the story that the Armed Forces was maintaining "a domestic network of informants and agents to supply detailed reports of union activities to the federal government." The Canadian Press item included the information that, on the basis of intelligence reports from the military and the RCMP, the Bourne group had considered a plan "to distribute adverse information about Mrs. Hartman to prevent her from getting elected as head of CUPE in 1975." Hartman, the report continued, "was considered a radical by military intelligence and the 230,000 member union was regarded as critical as it represents workers in essential services such as hospitals." This time Hartman held a press conference and announced she was asking to meet with the prime minister. "Press reports indicate that information gathered about CUPE's bargaining strategy was fed directly to the federal cabinet and employers. These allegations lend credibility to our long-standing claim that the government is NOT a neutral third party in labour-management relations but actively provides information on union activities to employers." Trudeau never responded. It had not escaped Hartman's notice (or the journalists') that the unions mentioned – CUPE, the Québec Federation of Labour, the Confederation of National Trade Unions – were all involved in Québec's Common Front Strike of 1972.

It was Wilfred List, though, who popped the obvious question; did she have a past worth investigating? List reported that Hartman at first denied having ties to the Communist Party, and then conceded that she had been a member of a Communist youth group. This, List reasoned, might explain the security branch's interest – which the headline duly translated as: "Are the old ties to the Communists hurting her?" It was a question Grace Hartman was certainly asking herself, and it was the kind of headline that makes your heart sink to your knees. She knew what her history on the left meant; she knew the record of the Canadian government when it came to unions and workers' rights, and police interference in trade union affairs. She was not surprised that they had a file on her. She was staggered, though, to hear that dirty tricks had been contemplated to stop her election in 1975. Did they think she was *that* dangerous? Be that as it may, it was time for her to consider just how loudly her low-level involvement with activist movements and the Young Communist League in the thirties and forties might be played in the present tense. What would she do if it were used to compromise or intimidate CUPE and blunt its gathering influence and militancy?

Between these two news stories, the 1977 CUPE convention took place in Vancouver and Hartman was re-elected by acclamation with the slogan, "ONE GREAT TERM DESERVES ANOTHER." The fortuitous timing, of course, didn't mean the danger had gone, and Grace felt it prudent to put on the record what she figured the RCMP and their pals already knew; there is safety in having everyone travelling on the same information. She may also have figured the climate was auspicious, given that the RCMP was itself under public investigation by the McDonald Commission for illegal activities, while a whole generation of sixties protesters with "pasts worth investigating" were then moving into responsible jobs. But she worried. "A lot of the staff came to me telling me they were sure someone had been into their homes or hotel rooms. Nothing would be missing but things had been disturbed." It had happened to Hartman too, on more than one occasion. She hadn't dismissed the incidents, but she was always careful never to say anything on the telephone she didn't want the force to know. And she wondered about CUPE. "It sent shock waves through the organization. A lot of people were afraid, curious about why the RCMP would want to keep an eye on what CUPE was doing. They were upset and didn't know what to think. Then I was accused of being a left-winger. I thought that might have a real impact on me ... but it didn't."

Nevertheless, it played into another narrative gathering shape just then. In May 1978, Dennis McDermott was elected president of the CLC, bringing from his post at the UAW (where he was succeeded by Bob White) his combative style and reputation as the "fastest lip in the labour movement." When elected he promised labour a higher profile which, if nothing else, his fondness for flowery open-necked shirts, gold chains, and diamond rings guaranteed. He dressed in that laidback "syndicate chic" style popular then, effeminate anathema to the old labour leader "Mustache Pete" types. The effect was more mod than sober. (Interestingly, McDermott's garb attracted far more commentary than any woman in the labour movement's ever did.) However, McDermott was not the main event at the convention; that was due to the vote on Québec's right to self-determination. This was a debate Hartman and CUPE participated in heartily and worked to get passed – which it was.

The unofficial opposition at this convention was the Canadian Union of Postal Workers (CUPW), another public sector union. The postal workers and their president, Jean-Claude Parrot, had come to the convention with their own "Program of Action for the Labour Movement" to compete against the Congress executive's tepid policy statement. It naturally drew out debate, particularly as it involved another kick at tripartism. McDermott denounced CUPW's contribution as "negative rhetoric," calling Parrot "about as popular as the advance man for the Asian Flu." Subsequently, McDermott announced through Wilfred List's column that the opposition to the executive's policies was "the work of Communists, a small assortment of Maoists and Trotskyists ... and CUPW, the new Bible thumpers of Labour." Before the year was out, CUPW had gone out on legal strike and been instantaneously legislated back to work by the federal government, but had continued on illegally for several days with Parrot's encouragement, winning him a contempt of court charge and thirty days in jail. The CLC executive was miffed that CUPW ignored its advice, acting without consultation in defiance of the law. More to the point, it considered the course of action suicidal because it was a strategy requiring the possibility of a general strike to back it up. McDermott called it "folly of the worst kind" while explaining, when someone thought to ask, that the Day of Protest walkout was different, though admittedly no less flagrant a violation of the law. "But it had to be done and I thought it could be," he said. Hartman, who rarely missed a meeting in her life, missed the executive council meeting which took the decision not to support the CUPW strike. She would have spoken against it, and did so when it was rehashed later, for she knew how it would be read by her membership. "The first reaction was to get out of the Congress. We were uneasy. We felt that if the Congress let the postal workers down, that didn't say much for what they would do when we public servants were out against the government. The postal workers may have made mistakes in judgment but that's no reason for abandoning them during the strike and not supporting them publicly when they were under attack by government and the RCMP," she said (referring to the raids on CUPW offices and interrogation of CUPW staff by the Mounties during the strike). McDermott retaliated with more pointed remarks about lefties and the "ideological ego-trippers" in CUPW. The lines were drawn, the battle positions were set.

In 1979 CUPE surpassed its own record for unruly and controversial conventions. Democracy in full bloom or leadership in chaos depending on your point of view. For presiding President Hartman it was the convention from hell. From the opening gavel the place was in an uproar as the 1,000 delegates refused at times to go along with even routine motions of convention business. At the end of the first day, Harry Greene (a former CUPE general vice-president and president of the BC Division) introduced a motion of privilege calling for convention committees in the future to be made up of rank-and-file delegates without representation from the national executive board. It carried – which spoke volumes about the disaffection between rank-and-file and leadership. On Tuesday a dues rebate proposal was argued and rejected, and a per capita tax hike debated and passed with the customary ill-humour. On Wednesday evening the delegates passed two resolutions; one expressed unwavering support for CUPW and harshly criticized the CLC leadership for its betrayal of the postal workers' struggle. The second one called on the union to request Brother McDermott's resignation. The Resolutions Committee was reluctant, recommending non-concurrence and citing the existence of "a democratic process in the termination of a CLC president," but the delegates persisted and the motion passed one vote short of unanimity.

The delegates were bloody minded that week in October in Québec City. Feeling the union establishment was trying to control too much, they seized the agenda of the convention and took what Hartman herself called the "membership's day in court" right down the line, sorely trying her grip on Robert's Rules of Order. "It was at a night session – the last CUPE ever had, I think, as a lot of people either go off or drink their supper – and the most raucous I ever chaired. I was absolutely exhausted by the time we finished." This was the part of the proceedings everyone talked about at the time and remembers today. Clearly the CUPW discussion was a lightning rod for the emotions of the moment, but it also touched on the deep-seated fear and frustration of the delegates. In 1979 CUPE members were hurting. Their wages were under controls, privatization was eroding the public service and eradicating jobs, and many delegates simply felt the union's response was inadequate. So they pushed.

That Wednesday night session they also debated a resolution dealing with health care workers and the need for a full-time co-ordinator for the sector. Delegates representing hospital and nursing home workers had come to the convention organized. Armed with arguments, for the second time since Monday they fended off a resolution which fudged the issue of a co-ordinator, and sent it back to the Resolutions Committee for further details. The following morning a motion to review the power and practice of convention committees, considering their potential for constraining the free discussion and voting at convention, was debated and although defeated, served further notice as to the temper of the delegates.

Hartman had not been expecting this level of anger and militancy from the membership. It was clear that the program of constitutional reforms she and her colleagues had presented to the convention would not suffice. After the third day, Gil Levine was charged with producing an Action Program. "I pulled together the research staff who were present and we worked through the night, putting together a ten-point Action Program which was presented to the president by ten o'clock the next morning." When it was proposed to the delegates on Friday morning it was roundly endorsed, bringing the union together for the first time at the convention and saving the day or, as Levine figures, "Grace's hide." A hard-hitting, six-page document, the action plan called for a coalition of public sector unions to take the offensive with government, employers and agencies who legislate and administer restraints on unions. It addressed cutbacks, contracting out, nursing homes, affirmative action and CUPE's role in the CLC: "The public sector and its workers are under attack in every part of Canada. Public employees have been the victims of lay-offs, the gutting of collective agreements, wage control legislation, cuts in the services they perform, speed-ups, and a general deterioration in terms and conditions of employment. In the face of these unprecedented attacks, CUPE has been forced to take a defensive stance in order to protect the rights and benefits it has won in the past. However, the time has now come for CUPE to do more than merely defend the status quo. CUPE is serving notice that from now on it will take the offensive."

Julie (Griffin) Davis, a CUPE staff rep with the library locals in Toronto in 1979 (recruited for a staff position in 1975 as part of Grace Hartman's International Women's Year project), was on the sidelines watching the drama unfold from the first morning. "A group of people had decided, enough of this nonsense of the national union appointing a Resolutions Committee, that the convention would be put on hold until a proper one was elected. Grace let that debate play itself out and finally said, 'Alright, I'll tell you what. If you vote to adjourn this convention, it will be adjourned, but for two years. That's my ruling, and that's what I'll do.' It was only about 9:30 in the morning and needless to say the convention wasn't adjourned. Grace was quite amazing, actually. She was never combative, but when pushed as she was that morning and throughout the convention she planted her feet and pulled herself up – all five

Rusins cartoon in the Ottawa Citizen *depicting the Hartman-McDermott skirmish after CUPE delegates to the 1979 convention demanded the CLC president's resignation.*

feet, one inch of her." What Davis saw as adeptness in Hartman's handling of the situation, others preferred to read as indecision; what some took for democracy in action, others saw as the leader losing control. Undoubtedly the entire week was a test of Hartman's leadership and her mettle, in this case her ability to weather broadside attacks without taking them personally. The assessments diverge roughly along gender lines, perhaps reflecting different cultural approaches to the exercise of power.

As the week progressed it became apparent that the customary visit from the CLC president could be disastrous, and Ed McAllister was detailed to disinvite Dennis McDermott. "The Québec members had promised to turn their chairs to face the back 'when the son-of-a-bitch comes into the hall, and if that doesn't shut him up we'll get up and walk out.' I called McDermott's assistant and explained we had a wildcat convention. I said McDermott would wind up being publicly embarrassed if he came. He's going to be mad, I was told." McDermott was mad as a scalded cat. He immediately began sounding off to the press about CUPE being on an "emotional binge," and the resolutions against the CLC being evidence of ultra-leftists taking over the union. He dismissed the criticism of himself, sneering at Hartman as a "lightweight." On Thursday, October 18, the day he had been scheduled to address the convention, the pair spoke to Barbara Frum on CBC Radio's "As it Happens." Hartman played down the split, emphasizing instead the message the delegates were sending, "He doesn't understand the frustration of our members, or what they're going through with the cutbacks in social services. Public sector workers have probably lost more than any other group under the AIB. And they don't feel the CLC is sensitive enough to their problems." McDermott had nothing nice to say whatsoever.

FRUM: You think Grace Hartman's let the troops out of line?

McDERMOTT: I think so, yes.

FRUM: She's got a mandate to push you.

McDERMOTT: Well, let her push. I'm not worried about that. This is one affiliate among many.

FRUM: They are the biggest, though.

McDERMOTT: They are the biggest but not the highest regarded. They're not held in high regard in the labour movement.

FRUM: I think the suggestion [of the CUPE delegates] is that they don't like your act. They think you're too fancy.

McDERMOTT: Well, I've faced that criticism before. So I guess I'll go to China and buy myself a proletarian suit and see if that will satisfy them.

McDermott's response was to go on the offensive in an effort to isolate CUPE and Grace Hartman. Hartman initially attempted to use the CLC resolution to raise the cause of public sector issues. McDermott was having none of that, though. To him it was a power struggle, pure and simple, and he took CUPE's reproach as an insult to his integrity. Hartman went on from the CUPE convention to a meeting of the CLC executive council in Halifax, dreading the confrontation she knew was coming. There are all kinds of stories about that wild executive meeting, featuring Dennis McDermott in a Mao cap complete with red star, taunting Hartman. The two other women in the room – Shirley Carr and Shereen Bowditch, the secretary to the executive council who was attending her first meeting and taking minutes – remember the tirade, McDermott lunging for Hartman with all the invective he could muster. Ed McAllister to this day regrets missing the meeting. "Look, I couldn't beat a punching bag, but I'd have gone over the table after McDermott if he'd done that to me. So would those other fellows; he'd never have tried that on any of them because they would have walked out and withheld their per capita until there was an apology." Obviously McDermott was counting on Hartman not to respond like the fellows. Either she would splutter a response or get up and walk out. Maybe he imagined she'd crumble before his eyes. He never questioned his right to call her on the carpet, though, and no one there (including Grace) objected to his behaviour. "It was really quite horrible," recalls Shereen Bowditch. "He went on and on, and she defended herself only saying that CUPE had a lot of young activists who had questions to ask and the right to debate issues according to the union's structure. He'd say 'I'd have been able to stop it.' To be honest, I don't think they understood CUPE then, or how it might be possible that Grace could not stop the debate – or didn't want to. In any case, according to their code Hartman had made a grave error; the guys look after each other, and she hadn't."

It was nothing new for McDermott to be on Grace's case at meetings; he was always after her, Bowditch remembers, and along with the other men on council would "pull out the left stuff every time they didn't like something. It was really bad." McDermott behaved as if betrayed and seemed to want a retraction, some sort of statement of support from CUPE. "She never said she wouldn't; she never said she would." McDermott remembers only the fight. "I thought she should be doing more than going around the country giving bullshit leadership. We had a knock-out fight. I remember a private session after with Shirley Carr and Grace and being accused of screaming sexist remarks but it was about leadership not gender. The hat was pure accident. Someone gave it to me in the airport." Hartman's refusal to fight was perplexing to some, especially those who could only understand the refusal to argue back as a refusal to stand up for oneself or worse, as acquiescence. But Ed McAllister understood the reaction. "She did the Grace Thing and that is shut down. McDermott could shoot all day and he'd get no response from her."

According to Grace Hartman's recollection, "We went into the meeting and Dennis wanted to know what the hell happened at the CUPE convention, so I told him. And, of course, he started in, 'You weren't controlling the delegates if you let them get away with that' ... We discussed it. I thought we had an understanding, that it was over and done with. The next morning when I walked into the full council meeting I could feel the icicles. 'I think we have to be on our guard today,' Shirley said. Dennis came into the meeting – I remember it well – wearing dark slacks, a light blue short-sleeved shirt, open down the chest, and a little Mao cap with a red star on it. He turned to me and said something like, 'If you can't beat 'em, why not join 'em?' The meeting was hardly started when my friend John Fryer [NUPGE] took the first crack at me, then the Woodworkers [Jack Munro], then the Steelworkers [Lynn Williams]. Finally I said, in less polite words, 'Look you guys. I don't have to defend my union to any of you. I explained what happened. If you want to go on talking about it, be my guest but I'm finished.' " Looking back on it, Shirley Carr speculates about Hartman's response, "I don't know if Grace was being smart, or if she was afraid, or if she just thought, what's the use? I'm not going to lower myself to that level. I'd say women in those situations have many times experienced all three, but I'm sure the last one is most common." The council went on to reaffirm its unqualified support of McDermott, and Grace Hartman voted along with the rest of them, which the press noted with thinly disguised amazement. And to clear the air, another vote condemning the CUPW strike was taken. "Of course I opposed it. Some of the executive members were really rough on me during that discussion, but I'd made up my mind I was going to stand back from it all. I didn't feel I had to defend anything." She departed before the scheduled press conference, and when stopped by a CBC reporter decided to say something less diplomatic than usual. "Instead of getting so excited Dennis should be asking what he's done wrong."

In the month following the CUPE convention, two memos went out from national office. One was a searing reprimand from the president to senior staff who attended the convention, the other a letter to the CLC executive over the twin signatures of Grace Hartman and Kealey Cummings, national secretary treasurer. Obviously responding to widespread speculation about a split in the labour movement, and the rumours about "Marxists" in CUPE, the letter read in part, "We will make every effort to ensure that CUPE members actively support the union's political, social and economic policy as laid down by our convention, national executive board and elected leadership. As with other unions, CUPE is not unique in keeping a watchful eye on forces that seek to destroy the democratic nature of the Canadian labour movement. And we will not allow our union to fall into the hands of anti-democratic forces – be they of the ultra-right or the ultra-left." The letter was a gesture of appeasement, the closest thing to a retraction Dennis McDermott was going to get, but it did seem to dignify his notion that a small group of radicals had been responsible for the turmoil at the convention. McDermott fixed on one group called the Marxist-Leninist Organization of Canada In Struggle (In Struggle, for short), which was present at the convention distributing pamphlets bearing the slogan "Dump McDermott." In the sober light of day, few could seriously suggest that this tiny band was responsible for one thousand minus one delegates voting to ask Dennis McDermott for his resignation. Hartman was certainly aware of the presence of what she called a "small but vocal ultra-left" in CUPE, and of the organized opposition that took place at the convention and which she spotted from her perch on the podium. She also understood that the discontent and the frustration with the enforced injustice of wage controls ran wide and deep in the membership, as did the desire for action. And she figured this is what the activists tapped into. Kealey Cummings blamed Harry Greene for letting the genii out of the bottle with his motion pitting NEB members against the rank and file. "Lo and behold a former general vice-president gets up and says this damn thing is dominated by the executive, this [the Constitution Committee] isn't a member's committee and strings are being pulled at the top ... So, the convention starts to bubble." Greene was part of a left caucus at the convention, but there was more than one that year, just as there were groups outside the left caucusing, some more formally than others, to press their agendas. But Cummings's point about the convention having a life of its own is well taken, for a convention, especially a CUPE convention, develops a character and has moods. Over the five days you can feel its momentum ebb and flow, and you can understand how capricious these changes must feel to those running the show.

One reading of the CUPE letter to the CLC – Hartman's soft-pedalling of the resignation motion (a slap on the wrist she called it), and her insistence that CUPE did not want a split with the House of Labour – is that she bowed to McDermott's ire and pulled back from the attack. She was, of course, doing what she was elected to do – and at that 1979 convention she was re-elected for a third term – which is to interpret the will of the membership between conventions. The convention resolution did not instruct her to withdraw from the CLC or fight a verbal duel to the death with McDermott. Hartman emerged from the CUPE convention with fighting words suggesting McDermott might have to defend his leadership, and she may indeed have contemplated a public sector coalition mounting such a challenge. But this coalition did not materialize, and few thought it could or would. Yet the anticipation of such a challenge may explain the vehemence of McDermott's counterattack, and the closing of ranks against any criticism. McDermott had so personalized the conflict, in any case, that there was no percentage in continuing the conversation; no one was listening. Better to deflect attention back to the issues, and to taking care of business in her own back yard for the time being.

The irony of the whole situation was not lost on Grace Hartman. Finding herself up on the podium being berated by radicals, treated as a slow-moving reactionary one day and a loonie leftie the next, treading close to the line of red baiting herself when declaring her lack of sympathy for some of the tactics of her members. (Some time later, in private, she would speak admiringly of Judy Darcy, one of the organizers of that fight from the floor, saying Darcy reminded her of herself when she was young.) Hartman was steering a middle course, obviously. She may also have been worrying about the Mounties again, as earlier in the year there had been new revelations about a "labour liaison group" in the Security Division of the RCMP in British Columbia (which the Mounties claimed was not intelligence gathering but "like any other community liaison group") and reports that some friendly RCMP constables had turned up at a CUPE Christmas party in Vancouver. An enterprising journalist dug up Allan Millard, Stan Little's former executive assistant, who

Grace Hartman survives the convention from hell to win re-election as president of CUPE. Stan Little (right) announces the election result as Joe Hartman congratulates Grace and Kealey Cummings (left) looks on.

put his allegations about Little's secret meetings with the RCMP on the record. Little called it bunk, but nonetheless admitted he had had occasional conversations with the RCMP. He still denies any discussions about CUPE staff or officers took place, though he acknowledges the consultation over Gil Levine with Bob Rintoul. In January 1980 Hartman felt it necessary to send off a memo directing staff to avoid any situation where they might be used as a source of information for the RCMP unless required by subpoena or writ.

Grace Hartman's memo to senior staff a month after the convention had two items on it: "A statement from me which is not debatable" and a discussion about assignments on the Action Program. It was the first part that blistered. Hartman described the convention as the most destructive in CUPE's history and vowed that, in the future, the "lunatic Left will have much more difficulty pulling strings from the visitor's area ... I have had about 100 complaints from staff and members about what was going on." She laid into the perpetrators and laid out her position, beginning with: "From this day on there will be no more political involvement in this organization by any members of the senior staff that are at odds with CUPE policy as laid down." And ending with: "I do not intend to sit idly by and let anyone destroy this union so they can rebuild it closer to their heart's desire. Everyone should remember that they get their pay cheques from CUPE, not the individual members of the same, and that the signatures on those cheques are Grace Hartman and Kealey Cummings – and we are the ones who will run this union." In between she made it clear staff were not to speak for the union or go to conventions to plant resolutions or take on elected people. Which is what she obviously felt had gone on. Reading between the lines of this decree, and the directive to staff across the country to refer all media queries to national office, you can recognize an attempt to curb internal dissension and control the damage. The staff involved undoubtedly resented the move as they were being told, in effect, they were playing politics out of turn.

Hartman seems to have blamed Gil Levine above all, and at this moment the two had a serious parting of the ways. Although they never actually spoke about it, Levine is certain she thought he was behind the convention uprising. "I certainly didn't oppose it. But I was not, as she said, pulling the strings from the back of the convention hall, which would have been an impossible feat in any case." The membership was hurting and looking for leadership, and Levine had suggested a program of action some months prior to the convention. "She didn't think it necessary and instead went forward with a series of 'housekeeping' amendments to the CUPE constitution as Ed McAllister advised. I think she needed a scapegoat for everything that went wrong at that convention." Levine is bitter about Hartman's reaction to the outcome of the 1979 convention, particularly the way she seemed to take up the chant of the anti-leftists, using it to placate McDermott. Hartman herself would say some years later, "When I say left, I'm not talking about the real left. I don't have problems with Communists. I have a problem with the ultra-left because I don't know where they are coming from, and sometimes it's the extreme right." She made distinctions. And one might speculate that if Grace Hartman was spooked, it was more likely by the activities of the RCMP, or by the antagonism of McDermott and the Boys which forced her to imagine what a real split with the House of Labour might be like, than by any ultra-left grouplet in the ranks of the membership. Levine and others perceived her disciplinary actions as red baiting, nonetheless. The rupture was permanent and it meant that the friendship between Grace Hartman and Gil Levine ended, and the political relationship chilled too. Inevitably this hurt Hartman, for it affected the level of communication, consultation and trust between her office and the research department at a time when the membership especially needed its services, and it boded ill for the hospital workers' strike looming in Ontario.

The image is indelible. A picket line outside Toronto's Riverdale Hospital during the 1981 strike. Cold, snow blowing, people bundled in thick clothing, stamping at the pavement as they walk. At shift change, non-striking maintenance workers approach the line. They are large men, but the nursing attendants on the line are large too. The men test the women, walk up towards them, slow, turn and advance again. When they don't stop, the women grab for them. It doesn't last long. There's some pushing and tussling before the guys disengage themselves and retreat at a clip. Couldn't get through the line, they tell the administration – threat of imminent physical danger and all that. Up close, you could see something else was happening. There was no belligerent body language, no one was getting cursed out, only muffled laughter. The women, it seems, were tickling their adversaries.

There are myriad such stories from the strike. Although it lasted a scant eight days, it affected thousands of workers and shook up the union. At its height, fifty-four locals and 14,000 Ontario CUPE hospital members were out, most of them women, many of them immigrants and the vast majority inexperienced with strike action. The stories reflect the courage and the confusion: neophyte strikers calling around to find a CUPE manual which would explain how to set up a picket line; women overcoming fear and the natural hesitation about getting involved. One young clerical worker crosses the picket line as her husband, looking on, tells her what to do. Two hours later she bursts from the building in tears. "I couldn't, I just couldn't. All my friends, my God, and me! I wanted to strike too. When I realized that, I left to join my side. My husband's a good man but he doesn't think I know what I'm doing," she said afterwards. The police show up unannounced at the home of one Toronto activist who hides inside with the lights out and a candle burning, aware that she is being intimidated yet fearful of the uniforms. "I'd never been in trouble before, and I was scared. I didn't answer the door. I remember just sitting crying and wondering, what next?" Isolated on picket duty, without resources or information about what was happening, an orderly in Hamilton is dispirited by the nightly TV footage of unpicketed hospitals. "Even our own president didn't know if Toronto had given up. I know I found it hard to take." For the workers involved, the strike was by turns exhilarating and disillusioning. For some it was transformative, as the experience of taking action against unjust conditions, and doing so in the teeth of the law, on one's own behalf together with others, often is. Others saw it as a lost opportunity marred by divided leadership. A few just regarded it as a lost cause. Valiant or foolhardy, the strike was controversial in 1981 and still is. Fourteen years later there is no consensus about whether it ended in victory or defeat.

It was, above all, a spontaneous action initiated by workers and local leaders who were well and truly at the end of their rope with the poor conditions and low pay. And it was undertaken largely on their own, without staff support. Yet these workers were not the sort usually credited with the gumption and commitment for radical action. They were women and immigrants in a high-turnover, bottom-of-the-industry workforce. The militance of an historically placable membership may have astounded the experts, and the turnout on the picket lines may have exceeded all expectations, but if ever a group of citizens was victimized by bad law, the hospital workers were that. The Hospital Labour Disputes Arbitration Act (HLDAA) had cast a pall over collective bargaining in the sixteen years of its existence, dragging salaries farther and farther below a living wage. In 1974 a concerted effort, backed by the threat of a strike, had actually brought the hospitals back to the bargaining table where they agreed to a substantial wage increase, but conditions had barely improved. Wage controls only aggravated the problem so that, by 1980, salary increases were running 20 percent behind the cost of living. Where once Ontario hospital workers had been earning 50 cents more an hour than their counterparts in BC, they were now earning $2.00 less; they had substandard holiday and sick leave provisions, no coverage of part-time workers and no monitoring of workloads which were escalating with the cutbacks. Add to this the generally derogatory attitude of hospital administrators towards the work itself and the people who do it (the notion that orderlies and nursing assistants do work which is mean and menial and possess the brainpower to match), and it's easy to understand where the fury and determination came from. Easy to see that a showdown, sooner or later, was inevitable.

Within CUPE, the hospital workers were relatively recent arrivals. In comparison with municipal and hydro workers who dominated the union, they were an underappreciated minority who had never figured largely in its national affairs, though they had registered dissatisfaction with national office often enough. In 1979 their complaints reached the floor of the convention in the form of the motion to hire an Ontario hospital co-ordinator. Resolution 32 was one reason why 180 resolutions were left over that year for the NEB to deal with. It took three rounds of debate and two revisions before the health care workers got what they wanted.

WHEREAS nearly 25,000 Ontario CUPE members are employed in the health care field; and WHEREAS *the majority of health care workers are employed by hospitals and homes for the aged where they are a target group for government funding cutbacks; and WHEREAS there is a great need to effectively co-ordinate groups of health care workers to fight cutbacks, achieve the right to strike and fight archaic labour legislation; THEREFORE BE IT RESOLVED that CUPE shall continue to support health care workers in their special struggles; and BE IT FURTHER RESOLVED that a permanent, full-time co-ordinator for health care workers in Ontario be immediately appointed; and BE IT FURTHER RESOLVED that the same consideration be given by the National Officers to the other provinces that are experiencing problems in this area.*

No doubt the resistance of some of the delegates to the proposal had to do with the fear of separate sectoral councils wielding undue power within the union. However, the health care workers prevailed, putting everyone on notice that they were not pleased with the status quo. At the same time, there was a movement within the membership to renew the fight against restrictions on the right to strike. At the 1979 convention a motion was passed committing CUPE to set up a common front within the labour movement to give support to any unions or locals fighting anti-strike legislation. And the Action Program outlined a comprehensive campaign to end discriminatory legislation against public employees and anti-unions laws generally.

Despite all this, the hospital strike caught the CUPE leadership by surprise. How ironic, then, that the Ontario Hospital Association (OHA) took the assertiveness and solidarity of the workers as evidence of a conspiracy on CUPE's part to avoid negotiations in the period leading up to the strike. "There had to be pre-planning," said the OHA's executive director, George Campbell. "They [the strikers] came out like gangbusters overnight." In fact, CUPE was anything but prepared.

The bare bones of the story are these: in the late summer of 1980, the Central Bargaining Committee for CUPE's 16,000 members in sixty-five hospitals across Ontario come to a tentative agreement with the OHA. The union had asked for an increase of $2.00 an hour, a cost of living clause and a one-year contract, but the negotiators settle for a 65 cent an hour increase across the board in each year of a two-year contract. To hospital workers averaging $6.64 an hour this represents a 9.8 percent increase in the first year and 8.9 percent in the second, well below the existing rate of inflation which is running at 10 percent. The morning after the memorandum of agreement is signed, a meeting of CUPE hospital local presidents looks it over and votes it down. Later in October, over 90 percent of the membership also rejects it. By early December talks are stalled; the two parties are ordered to proceed to arbitration in accordance with the HLDAA. At this point, in a largely symbolic gesture, CUPE refuses to go along with the lengthy arbitration process and declines to appoint a representative. (Terry Meagher is eventually appointed by the minister of Labour on their behalf.) According to Campbell, "This was when, in our view, CUPE started to step outside the law."

On January 6, 1981, Grace Hartman announces a strike vote for January 15; 61 percent of the membership votes, three quarters in favour of striking. The OHA refuses to bargain while being "blackmailed" and applies to the Ontario Labour Relations Board for a cease-and-desist order. On January 21 the OLRB orders a halt to strike preparations and calls for the two sides to meet again, with mediation. CUPE's executive board and Grace Hartman publicly agree to comply. A mediator is appointed; his efforts over the weekend of January 24/25 come to naught and the strike begins in the early morning hours of January 26. Now, finally, the minister of Labour, Robert Elgie, insists the parties come to the table to negotiate – while the attorney general, Roy McMurtry, applies to the Supreme Court of Ontario for an *ex parte* injunction against the strike, and an OLRB back-to-work order.

On January 30 the injunction is granted. Grace Hartman affirms her unqualified support for the workers and sends a message to Premier William Davis, urging him to personally instruct the OHA to begin serious negotiations. "It should be made very clear that the

Grace Hartman at the Hamilton hospital workers rally, Teamsters Hall, February 1, 1981.

Supreme Court Order will not stampede workers back on the job ... It is unfortunate that the Courts have now been injected into the dispute ... and ironic that one part of your government (the ministry of Labour) wants to solve the dispute through negotiations while another part (the attorney general's office) wants to solve it through court action. The hospital workers do not want to prolong this dispute but their union will not order them to comply with an unjust law when a negotiated settlement could reasonably be achieved. The injunction is not being used to help patients. It is being used to intimidate workers." Mediation breaks off. The following day

McMurtry threatens to prosecute the union, both leaders and members.

No doubt this was the turning point in the strike, the point of no return for CUPE. It was the place where Jean-Claude Parrot had stood with CUPW in 1978, contemplating a face-off with the federal government. Even though CUPE had support and was not isolated from the labour movement as the postal workers had been, the stakes for the membership were equally high. There had been talk of $1,000-a-day fines and charging the workers with damages. For its part, the OHA had come to the table in a surly mood. This round they were not going to be snookered by strike threats; they were going to dig in their heels and insist the province enforce the law. In effect, the OHA was calling the government's bluff as well as CUPE's and, in the days leading up to the strike, it stonewalled the negotiation process while hospitals around the province posted warnings and threatened action against any workers who dared participate in a strike. When the attorney general intervened to obtain the injunction ordering the workers back, he was unmistakably taking the OHA's side, something untoward for even if the province pays for health care, it is not the employer in this case. It was obvious to all that the strong arm of the state was being flexed in the faces of the strikers. Hartman could recognize a brick wall when she saw one.

The government was obdurate and Roy McMurtry was taking no prisoners. He made speeches about lawlessness and innocent hospital workers being "swept away by leaders who portray their cause as being more important than respect for the law." Grace Hartman had no reason to believe that in a head-to-head confrontation the Ontario government would care about cracking a few skulls, metaphorically or physically. There was no history on its part of generosity or respect for the men and women doing society's dirty work on the wards, in the laundries, kitchens and basements of hospitals. Her own tale of the strike was a tale of weighing the probable consequences. "I had some real worries when they issued the back-to-work order. I didn't say to the workers, 'Go back to work.' First of all they wouldn't have; they were really solid at the time. Secondly, I had no authority under the CUPE constitution to do that. At the same time I couldn't really tell them to stay out because they could have lost their bargaining rights, and, above all else, I didn't want the government moving to revoke those rights." Hartman's public statements, carefully lawyered, tread adroitly along the edge of legality. The workers, she said, had made every effort to settle the dispute but the OHA had chosen to ignore the collective bargaining process. "Having complied completely with the Labour Board's order, I had confidence that this would be recognized as our earnest desire to get back to the bargaining table ... If the employer is willing ... we can reach an agreement today," she said on January 26, the first day of the strike. The situation demanded she sound compliant even while encouraging the strikers. "There is no doubt that Ontario hospital workers deserve fair treatment. As national president of their union, I fully support their efforts to bring this about."

In early January, as the strike loomed, Hartman had gone on the road to talk up the cause of hospital workers with CUPE locals and the public. She returned to Toronto mid-month to join the negotiating team in residence at the Holiday Inn, keeping her head down, visiting picket lines at night. It was not until the press conference on January 30 that she came out for defying McMurtry's injunction.

REPORTER: Just to clarify something. You say that you're not telling the workers to go back to work. Are you then advising them to stay on the picket line?

GRACE HARTMAN: Those are decisions they have to make knowing the consequences. With this union, I cannot order them back to work.

REPORTER: What can you advise them in the interest of the union and of their bargaining?

GRACE HARTMAN: I can advise them to keep fighting.

REPORTER: So you are advising them to stay on the line?

GRACE HARTMAN: To let their conscience be their guide.

REPORTER: That's a rough choice. I mean, you're not telling them to stay on the line; you're not telling them to go back to work. Where do they stand?

GRACE HARTMAN: We're supporting them.

REPORTER: You're supporting them? The question is are you leading them?

GRACE HARTMAN: We're leading them.

REPORTER: What do you advise? Clearly!

GRACE HARTMAN: To stay on the picket line.

Hartman's fear had nothing to do with the morality of the act but with its impact on workers, with what might happen if the government decided to get aggressive, if workers were fired *en masse*, for instance. She had not leapt at the strike call, or stepped in immediately to lead it. Partly this was due to the peculiarities of CUPE's structure, which places responsibility for collective bargaining firmly in the hands of the local unions. A strike is not the president's to call, or hers to lead necessarily, and there is no protocol for her involvement. At the best of times it is not always obvious when a dispute has reached crisis proportions and the national officers should become involved. Part of the problem was that the lines of internal communication got perilously tangled in the months leading up to the strike, as a split developed between and among staff and the hospital workers. In the middle was the Ontario Regional director, Pat O'Keeffe, who was opposed to the strike and who advised Hartman all the way along that it couldn't possibly fly. "I didn't think they could win the strike and I thought it would be bad for the rank and file if in fact they lost it. I wanted to bluff it out without going on strike ... which you could do if you had the ministry of Labour on your side and you were skillful." The "they" O'Keeffe referred to were local activists who had emerged as leaders: Paul Barry (Bargaining Committee rep for Region Four and president of Local 906 in Ajax), Cathy McQuarrie (chairperson of the Health Care Workers Coordinating Committee) and Patrick Kenny (rep for Region Three and president of Local 1144 in Toronto), among others. O'Keeffe had little patience with their militance and tended to dismiss them as nay-sayers and lefties "gunning for a confrontation," underestimating both the support they had among the membership and the frustration of the rank and file. As a result, there was no preparation for a strike and no co-ordination or strategy in place when it broke.

Few people, least of all Pat O'Keeffe, were anxious to go on illegal strike, but from the perspective of the workers they had hardly anything to lose by then. As Paul Barry describes it, "I think the notion of an illegal strike started to gel as soon as the tentative agreement was rejected. It was firmly established in case law under the HLDAA that arbitrators do not tinker with proposed settlements unless there is substantive reason such as new circumstances or a fatal flaw somewhere. Moreover, the OHA had made it clear to us in a face-to-face meeting that a circle had been drawn around the package and there would be no expansion of the total effect of the offer. We could roll over and die. In that process the workers had no democratic right to reject a settlement, no right even to give their leaders a reality check on the offer."

It was not until the eve of the strike, though, that Barry and his colleagues became aware of how O'Keeffe was counselling Grace Hartman. "Pat had seemed supportive when we were still in the process of trying to get a deal, but when the OHA stonewalled and the time came for us to put our picket signs where our mouths were, it became clear he was not. We were in a meeting, Grace Hartman in the room, and Pat reiterated what I presume he had been telling her, that a strike would put the whole union in jeopardy – and Grace was not contradicting him. We realized then that she had not been getting the whole picture." The regional director is typically more of a player and closer to strike action than anyone at national office, the president included. Gainsaying his advice or interfering with his handling of an action is not done lightly. The situation was further complicated for Hartman by the rift that had developed between O'Keeffe and some staff in national office. Early in the fall, Gil Levine had produced a critical analysis of the tentative agreement which was particularly scathing about the OHA's proposal to eliminate the standard hospital sick leave plan and replace it with an insurance disability plan which would reduce the workers' benefits. He made sure his report got to those local union leaders who could use it. Lofty MacMillan was also working openly with rank-and-file members who opposed the deal, and he had attended strategy meetings in Toronto. O'Keeffe regarded this as insubordinate interference if not incitement to riot, and wrote President Hartman demanding she restrain the pair of them. It appears the strikers were also appealing to Hartman for intervention, but they were asking her to restrain O'Keeffe.

For about a week in mid-January, however, Levine and MacMillan were "muzzled." MacMillan recounts the story and its dénouement with some glee. "Pat O'Keeffe led her down some terrible paths in that strike. We had the troops, we had prepared them, but he wasn't with us. When she grounded Gil and I she took Pat O'Keeffe's word over ours. News travelled quickly that we weren't allowed to take part in the January 11 rally in Ottawa [the Ottawa District Labour Council, which organized it, reported that eighty unions and organizations, and 15,000 people contributed]. A group of members landed in on national office to demand the ban be lifted. They told me either Gil and I would be at the rally on Sunday or pickets would go up around the office. Then they went down the hall to say the same thing to Grace. McAllister phoned me later and told me, 'You're out of the den.'" MacMillan only regrets the length of time it took Hartman to come in on-side in the strike. Along with Levine and O'Keeffe, he remains extremely negative about her role in it. All three of them speak of her as being a victim of the other guy's manipulation. "I knew and she knew that the balloting in the hospital strike was fraudulent; it was run by the people who wanted a strike," says O'Keeffe. "She was getting advice and doing nothing. I was advised by her that I should fire Brown and LeBel [the staffers who had signed the proposed settlement] but I couldn't do it. MacMillan put her up to it, I think ... Grace was just a follower and not a very good follower at that."

The strikers, caught between rival staff groups, were on their own and felt let down by all sides. McQuarrie, Barry, Kenny and the others had locked horns with O'Keeffe before. They had been angered when he hired Bill Brown as the hospital co-ordinator over their choice, Peter Douglas, who had been working in the field in Hamilton. (Brown and assistant director Giles LeBel were the staff reps on the negotiating committee. O'Keeffe says now that Brown let him down by signing the proposed settlement without Patrick Kenny's agreement, something he had specifically charged Brown not to do.) Once the strike was enjoined, O'Keeffe left instructions for staff to give it their priority and then absented himself from the scene. The strikers and their supporters were angry, feeling he first had undermined what they were trying to do by campaigning for acceptance of the settlement, and then, when the strike came, had abandoned ship. Some staff were disturbed by the initial orders to do nothing and helped out anyway, attending demonstrations, doing picket duty. For them it was a question of elementary solidarity, and their defiance became a badge of honour. When the strike was over, the members let the regional director know of their displeasure in no uncertain terms – by picketing his office. At the May convention of the Ontario Division in Windsor, the Central Bargaining Committee report criticized the national leadership for complying with the OLRB order, and delegates registered their aggravation with O'Keeffe by calling for his head. Pat Kenny accused Grace Hartman of knitting through negotiations and, along with others, called for a motion of censure against her and Lucie Nicholson, Ontario Division president. This was defeated, as was the motion to dismiss O'Keeffe, but Kenny was right about the knitting; Hartman completed a sweater for Joe and half of one for Bob while she and her colleagues waited through the long pauses between sessions as the mediators did their shuttle diplomacy between hotels. (Would he have been as acerbic if she'd been down in the bar drinking?)

If Grace Hartman was dealing with internal divisions and complex legal and political situations, she was also facing public opinion that was fraught. At rock bottom was the sort of thinking expressed in a

Toronto *Sun* editorial in 1979: "CUPE is what could kindly be termed as a parasite union. That is it doesn't represent the productive workers of society but those who feed off government and the public purse. They have a different view of the world and don't have the same link with reality as those who get their fingernails dirty and who sweat on the job and who produce the goods which keep our society functioning." Sitting in a hushed radio studio, Betty Kennedy read that incredible passage in a deep-pile broadloom voice to match the privilege of CFRB's audience, and asked Hartman what she thought. "People need the services we provide, like getting water when you turn on the tap," Hartman patiently reminded the listeners. "People have to weigh the value of schools and hospitals against TVs and refrigerators but that doesn't mean public employees do not deserve fair wages and good working conditions and some dignity on the job."

As the hospital strike deadline approached, CUPE mounted a counter publicity campaign, making the case that cutbacks were eroding the quality of health care because workers were having to do the jobs of one and a half people and everyone was suffering. "Dear Ontario. Who cares about Patient Care? ... Our Hospitals are in Critical Condition and We're All Paying for it," explained the posters and ads. It appeared to have some effect. Although there were still many citizens eager to defend the hospitals and vilify the strikers for victimizing the ill and the elderly, there was less vitriol and more sympathy expressed in letters to the editor than in earlier public sector strikes, by the postal workers, for example. The media proffered the odd comment about the illogic of declaring some workers in hospitals essential and others not, of allowing doctors to strike (and extra bill if they thought the province wasn't paying them enough) but prohibiting nursing assistants the same privilege. A few reporters even questioned the rationale of criminalizing action that would be perfectly legal in eight provinces and most democratic countries.

"The strike of the Ontario hospital workers should be viewed in its proper perspective. The threat to this union by big government has never been more evident and I feel it is accurate to say that our continued existence as a union, in the sense that we know it, hung in the balance for several days. That isn't intended as a dramatic statement, but a simple matter of fact. The venom generated by an unholy combination of the Tory government, the Ontario Hospital Association and individual hospital administrators was difficult to ignore." Grace Hartman thus reported to the CUPE national executive board meeting in February. As January had faded into February, with the machinery of state in gear and no settlement in sight, CUPE secretly approached the OHA with a proposal for a return to work if there were no reprisals and the hospitals undertook to commence negotiations at once. The OHA, of course, felt it didn't have to concede the time of day. It refused any conditions and sat back to wait while provincial police were dispatched to the picket lines to take photographs, read the riot act and threaten strikers with arrest. In the face of criminal charges and a vengeful employer, the strike disintegrated. Hamilton and Sudbury locals held out until February 4, by which time reprisals were already taking their toll: more than 3,400 suspensions – totalling 8,646 days – 5,500 letters of reprimand and 34 dismissals, though all of these latter were successfully grieved. With the strike over, there was no choice for the union but to go to arbitration.

On February 3 Hartman was interviewed by Joe Coté on CBC Toronto's early morning radio program "Metro Morning." Having conceded defeat in the strike, she was quoted as giving two reasons for it: the reign of terror conducted by the Ontario Provincial Police (OPP) and the intimidation by Attorney General Roy McMurtry. Coté rejoined, asking if the province and police "weren't just doing their jobs?" Why did the workers choose an illegal strike? With a touch of weary sadness in her voice, Hartman replied. "We've tried everything, all the established processes; nothing worked. The workers decided the route they would take and it was not decided easily or irresponsibly. It was decided out of sheer frustration and the desire to get a fair deal just once. Instead of using its clout with the OHA to bring about a negotiated settlement, the province has let the OHA run out of control. It seems the province can bring the heavy hand of the law against the workers but can't get the hospitals back to the bargaining table. There is something one-sided in the justice here." So easy to pick on the little guys, she pointed out, making it powerfully clear how contemptible she found the display of brute power.

It took labour columnist Ed Finn to point out that while the hospital workers were going to the wall for a few extra cents an hour, Ontario doctors had been awarded a cool 14 percent hike in their fees. What was so galling was the fact that Paul Weiler, the arbitrator in the CUPE/OHA dispute, was himself a fact-finder in the negotiations between the Ontario Medical Association and the government which had given the doctors an extra $12,000 a year in May. When it came to the hospital workers' award in June, Weiler was mean and measly – 80 cents per hour increase in year one, 85 cents in year two, just 20 cents an hour more than was in the original tentative agreement. "It's hard to escape the feeling that Weiler's award was in fact just one of a series of punishments assessed against the hospital workers for daring to go on strike," wrote Finn. "It could be interpreted as a message to the workers that a strike will gain them nothing more than they would get from hospitals without a strike. A great injustice has been done." Finn's point is true if not strictly accurate, for the strike did win an increase, minuscule though it was.

The strike was a wake-up call, and provided the focus and pretext for a reorganization which quite definitively changed the status of hospital workers within the union and within the sector. In its aftermath, President Hartman moved to bring people back together. At the suggestion of senior staff, the Central Bargaining Committee was detailed to hold meetings throughout the province, and four men from national office were assigned to it: Levine, MacMillan, Randy Sykes (research officer in charge of hospital workers sector) and Fred Tabachnick (CUPE's PR director). Paul Barry was also drafted to the project, which had the task of assessing the structure and the process of hospital bargaining in Ontario and making recommendations. Hearings were held in major centres and the resulting report proposed a new structure which became the Ontario Council of Hospital Unions. The new organization was constituted to give the membership greater control over the bargaining process, addressing the conflict between members and staff which had plagued the hospital strike.

Grace Hartman was right about the "continued existence of the union as we know it" having hung in the balance during the strike. But it wasn't only because of a recalcitrant OHA backed by an interested government; the internal strife was debilitating and could only compromise the union's effectiveness, especially in a time of crisis. But while the upper echelons of the union had vacillated, the members knew what they wanted. With real nerve they took over and occupied the vacuum. The main fault of the organization was in not seeing it coming, in not being there with support in time. Hartman discovered in the process that she was out of touch with this sector of the membership and that she was not hearing the advice she needed. In the end she listened to instinct and went with the workers.

Sunday night, February 1, at the Teamsters Hall in Hamilton. A rally organized by the Labour Council for the hospital workers is in full swing. The place is packed and spirits buoyant as a dozen speakers deliver greetings and support from the Steelworkers, United Electrical Workers, Communications Workers, Canadian Food and Allied Workers among other labour organizations, and as NDP politicians pour out their congratulations and their own condemnations of Davis and the Ontario Tories. Local strike organizers Jim Connally and Liz Brocklin speak, and then Grace Hartman is introduced to wild applause. In the audience is one Constable G.

Desjardins wearing a bodypack, planted there by OPP Intelligence to record every word being said.

> Thank you for [unintelligible] (LOUD CHEERS AND CLAPPING). Thank you very much for that response. I want to say congratulations to you for the fight you are putting up. And thank you for coming out here on a Sunday. I know Sundays don't mean much when you're on strike ... I think that this hospital strike in 1981 is going to be a milestone in the history of the Canadian labour movement. (CLAPPING, CHEERS) It's a struggle for some basic human rights. We're not asking a hell of a lot in this struggle. And we have to continue it; it's important that we continue it for our own dignity as workers. Because if we lie down and take it, at this point, they will exploit us in ways that we haven't even thought about yet.

Hartman speaks of the arrogance of hospital administrators and the intransigence of government and declares herself "the proudest union leader in the country when I look out over a crowd like this. I am sure I am safe in saying that there are many workers in this country who will thank you when this is all over. And I am sure we will see justice down the road." She concludes to "GREAT CHEERING AND LOUD APPLAUSE" – and is given a standing ovation.

This moment was the high point in the hospital strike for Grace Hartman, the moment when there were no more uncertainties, public or private, about the strike and her leadership. She knew by then that the workers would not prevail this time; she guessed she and others would end up in jail. And she wouldn't put money on the arbitration award. Yet she knew in her heart that the workers had won something important. Some recognition, and affirmation of their importance and their dignity.

Grace Hartman on her way into court with Maureen Namaro-Martin and Susan Brooks, June 1981. Namaro-Martin was given a suspended sentence and Brooks was fined $200 for their part in the strike.

6

A Rose and Barbed Wire

I t was hot that June, temperatures reaching for the mid-twenties. The forecast called for a partly cloudy day, but it was clear and bright the Thursday morning Grace Hartman walked down University Avenue into provincial court with eighteen other co-accused CUPE members and staff. All were charged with contempt of court for refusing to comply with the order to end the strike, for staying on the picket line after the injunction or for counselling others to break the law, and all were convicted. Stylish as always, Hartman arrived wearing a creamy linen skirt with two matching blouses, one sleeveless and delicately embroidered along the neckline, the other a georgette shirt. She smiled jauntily and gestured at the cameras as she went by with hospital workers Maureen Namaro-Martin and Susan Brooks, the three of them looking like a trio of ordinary working women heading over to Simpsons for a spot of shopping on their coffee break.

Inside the courtroom the mood was somber and grew somnolent as the hearing stretched through the afternoon. The lawyers droned, spectators fidgeted, defendants wilted. Finally the proceedings came to the sentencing. Grace Hartman was first up. She read a prepared statement into the record which said in part, "By our plea of guilty we have recognized the effect of our actions which we understand is expressed in legal terms as contempt of court. But we must say on behalf of all hospital workers that society cannot continue to treat hospital workers with contempt." She emphasized that the union's intent was not to encourage disrespect for the law, and asked that the workers' situation be considered a mitigating factor. Had her defence been rhetorical, she could have added that what Ontario hospital workers did when they walked off the job was not illegal in most of Canada. She could have remonstrated (as she did later to the press) about the difficulty she had explaining to Ontario hospital workers why they were denied the right to strike while the province's 2,500 hospital doctors weren't – and had struck barely three months before CUPE members went out – or why they were designated essential workers but not paid an essential wage.

The crown asked for thirty to sixty days. Mr. Justice William Parker, the associate chief justice of the Ontario Supreme Court, looked down at the short pale figure before him and imposed forty-five days, citing the need for deterrents against actions such as hers. The courtroom was suddenly bristling with attention. Two matrons took Hartman by the arms and headed out with her through a side door, but the judge stopped them and told them to wait until all the sentences had been handed down. He gave Lucie Nicholson (president of CUPE's Ontario Division) and Raymond Arsenault (a CUPE staff representative in Ottawa) fifteen days each, and fined or gave suspended sentences to everyone else. Then Nicholson and Hartman were whisked away, touching hands with other CUPE members across the barrier as they left.

Grace had come to court prepared, with her convictions in place and a suitcase packed for jail. A great deal of time had been spent preparing the statement, which was supposed to be an apology, but Hartman had refused to say outright that she and the strikers were wrong, and the judge was annoyed. "The court wanted her to eat crow," remembers Michael Mitchell, the lawyer who advised her, and jail was a foregone conclusion. Going to jail, of course, is not nice and is not meant to be. The process is intended to intimidate and Hartman must have also felt the ineffectualness of the workers' plea acutely. So, too, she must have felt her own insignificance standing, a lone individual, before the court. Grace Hartman the president of CUPE may have been sentenced to forty-five days in jail, but Grace Hartman the sixty-two-year-old woman did the time. At first she thought they might handcuff her and Lucie, and at just the thought of it, after that endless day spent politely taking her licks for defying the system, Grace kicked up a fuss. "No we're not going to put handcuffs on you," the matron replied. "And yes you are going in a Black Maria only it's painted orange." Hartman and Nicholson were loaded into the back and, upon hearing thumps and knocks on the side, looked out the little side window to see a couple of CUPE staff guys – "one a great big bear of a guy and he's crying like a baby," Hartman recalled.

Alone in the back, the drive to Toronto's West Detention Centre was intimidating; the reception at the centre was worse. Forced to strip on arrival, Grace Hartman had to sit around while the staff went madly searching for jeans to fit her. A small man's size was eventually located, which she had to wear without a belt, keeping her hands in her pockets to hold them up. It was after dinner by then and neither woman had eaten. The guards offered the standard evening snack of sweet cake and over-sugared coffee (meant for women coming off drugs and given to everyone). As the attorney general had ordered they be segregated from the other prisoners, they were stuck in a huge, empty twenty-unit holding tank. "At this point we didn't want to be separated. They had put us in the dirtiest hole. I remember Lucie saying that she wouldn't stand on the toilet to pee. The guard let us drag a mattress from the cell next door for the upper bunk. It was a horrible night. I couldn't stand the clanking doors. The next day we had to go for a medical exam and, being men's day, we had to pass through a room of guys who all whistled and shouted. I said to Lucy I didn't know if I could spend forty-five days in such a place. She felt the same. Then they made us clean up a huge room and wash toilets. At lunch I remember we had a banana because the guard who brought it tossed it through the bars saying, 'Here's your dessert.' "

The courtroom had not been packed the day of the sentencing. Some people assumed the place would be mobbed and stayed away; others apparently assumed nothing much would happen, that the system wouldn't be so daft as to jail a bunch of women and make a martyr of somebody's grandmother. Some support from the labour movement was there, particularly from public sector unions, but it seemed low key. Senior leaders were not in evidence, not even Jean-Claude Parrot, which disappointed Hartman. Of course there was a lingering ambivalence about the strike within the movement, as well as an inability on the part of some to imagine a woman in the role of jailed leader, an assumption that the justice system would not take Hartman any more seriously than they did. Forgetting Annie Buller and Jeanne Corbin (sentenced to a year in jail for her involvement in the Noranda strike of 1934) and all the other heroic women who had served time, they supposed her age or her gender would get her off. The reaction to news of the stiff jail sentences was immediate, unrestrained and echoed through the union movement. People were truly shocked. "That's not justice. That's a vendetta," declared Jean-Claude Parrot. Others (Cliff Pilkey of the Ontario Federation of Labour, Wally Majesky of the Metro Toronto Labour Council, and Sean O'Flynn of the Ontario Public Service Employees Union, who had been jailed himself for illegal strike action) called it class discrimination and pointed to the rich man's justice being dispensed in another courtroom the same day Hartman was dispatched to prison. Three senior K-Mart Canada Ltd. executives were sentenced with a rap on the knuckles for conspiring with a private investigating firm to thwart union organizing by the International Brotherhood of Teamsters. Describing the defendants as misguided, the judge issued immediate and conditional discharges – so they'd not have criminal records – and gave them a year's probation. No question of the executives serving time as a deterrent to others. Pilkey called it one law for agents of capitalism and another for the agents of labour. The judge in the CUPE case did not recommend Hartman and Nicholson for the immediate temporary-absence program, which meant he intended that they experience prison. It was a moot point anyway, as all three CUPE prisoners decided not to seek benefit of any kind. The one-third time off for good behaviour was automatic, however, so Nicholson walked after ten days, characterizing the experience as "nerve-wracking, degrading and scary."

The day a union leader goes to jail is a moment for acknowledging the role illegal actions have played in the history of labour. Said Kealey Cummings, acting president while Hartman was on Leave of Absence ("for criminal activity," according to the official form), "If people had not confronted the established order, we would not have many of the rights we take for granted today." It is a moment also to reflect on the significance of jail terms to labour generally. "If this aggressive policy of seeking jail terms for trade union members on every occasion goes unchallenged, conditions in Ontario will soon become as undemocratic as Chile and Argentina where free trade unions have been outlawed," warned Bob White of the UAW. Ironically, Lech Walesa and the *Solidarnosc* movement in Poland were hot subjects in international news at the time, but the mainstream media failed to draw any comparison between the Polish workers' peaceful struggle against unjust and unacceptable laws in Eastern Europe and the hospital workers' protest in Ontario. Grace Hartman was disparaged for "leading CUPE down the road to anarchy" by the same editorial writers and politicians who hailed Walesa for doing the exact same thing. The juxtaposition of these events was extraordinarily revealing; right-wing columnists like Larry Solway in the Toronto *Star* felt compelled to go into print declaring (three times to make sure) that there was no such thing as a law for the rich and one for the poor.

By mid-summer the pattern of hospital administration reprisals against the workers was becoming evident as well. In the case of one hospital, Perley Hospital in Ottawa, thirty-eight members, none of whom had crossed the picket line, were laid off without regard to seniority while four junior employees who had worked through the strike were kept on. The local president and vice-president, Michael Hurley and Sheila Casey, were fired as were six part-time employees who had participated. CUPE laid a complaint with the Labour Relations Board. It was summarily rejected. Workers fired for going on illegal strike put themselves beyond the act, they were told; CUPE had not proven the case of an unlawful lockout. (This left the fired workers with the grievance procedure of the collective agreement.) Together the government, the ministry of Labour, the judiciary, the OLRB, the hospitals and the OHA constituted an implacable front, one powerful enough to avoid having to acknowledge the truth of their collusion. Premier Davis wrote to the general secretary of the International Confederation of Free Trade Unions in Brussels, "I believe it is quite unfair to suggest that this incident reflects an 'anti-labour' attitude on the part of this administration. Indeed ... the very conduct of the persons involved served to remove this matter into an arena – the judicial process – over which this Government has no direct control."

It would have been hard for the labour movement to ignore the jailings. But the very vehemence of its reaction tended to expose the tepid support given the strike while it was on. In March, John B. Lang, secretary treasurer of the Confederation of Canadian Unions, had written Hartman a note in which he lamented "the low level of response from the labour movement generally to the attack on the hospital workers especially when the issues involved are so fundamental to the growth and strength of the trade unions in the province." Now the outpouring of support came in abundance, from across the country and around the world. Letters, telegrams – and roses. After a day, Hartman and Nicholson had been taken to the Vanier Detention Centre in Brampton, a facility for women serving sentences under two years, which was somewhat less disagreeable than Toronto's West Detention Centre. Though they were locked in at night, they were not constantly accompanied. The media was there in full force when the two women were brought in – through the service entrance at the rear. Thereafter, supporters regularly made the trek to Brampton to wave from the sidewalk to the prisoners in the jail yard. They came from all over, even the United States where CUPE's sister union, the American Federation of State, County and Municipal Employees, organized several trips to join the vigil outside the Canadian jail. Every evening buses would arrive and disgorge unionists, each carrying a single red rose. They would file silently back and forth in front of the building for half an hour or so. No speeches were made, no placards carried. As they left, someone would gather up the flowers and hand them to a guard for delivery to Grace Hartman. "Give us Bread, but give us Roses, too."

Life in the slammer involved mopping floors, doing laundry and kitchen duty, and following rules: remembering only to sit on the benches in front of the Activity Building between one and two, and four and six in the afternoons; being careful never to wear "items of personal clothing which can be seen through without the wearing of proper under-garments"; attending compulsory movies like *The Bad News Bears in Japan*; watching the young women (most of the inmates were well under thirty) play volleyball. One day in the laundry, Grace and Lucie were given clean clothing to fold – including the socks and the underwear of the male prisoners down the street. "No way" they both protested. "The man in charge was a very interesting person, a Jamaican who was very active in the Black community here; civil rights type of person. He came and put his arm around me and said, 'Grace, please, not in my department!' I said, 'I am not going to fold their underwear; let them do it themselves.' 'OK,' he said, and gave us towels and facecloths instead."

It took a while for the other inmates to figure out how to treat Hartman and Nicholson. They knew the older women's faces from TV, "but once they saw our names on the duty roster just the same as theirs, they sort of accepted us," Grace remembered. Getting to know them was getting to see a side of life she wasn't used to. "There were kids as young as sixteen. Most were in for break and enter, assault or drugs. And I was amazed. I'm not being chauvinistic, but most of those women were in for some reason that related back to a man. Three of them on drug charges; some guy promised them money to bring something back from Jamaica, or, in one woman's case, offered to switch suitcases at Immigration because hers was heavier. She came to visit her children at Christmas and had yet to see them. It drove me crazy listening to them. I think there is an awful lot unfair in the way judges mete out sentences." In interviews following her release, Hartman spoke about her discovery in jail that not only is there one law for the rich and one for the poor, but there is one for men and another for women. She told a CBC "Morning-side" audience about a woman she knew at Vanier who had been given four months on a second impaired driving conviction, and compared her sentence to that of CTV news anchor Harvey Kirck, convicted of the same thing and given fourteen days in a halfway house. The woman lost her job; Kirck didn't miss a newscast. Many of the inmates befriended Grace, talked to her about their troubles and wrote her after she got out. "It was great hearing from you. Everyone wanted to know how you were doing so I let them read your letter ... Boy, the morning you left was exciting. We lined up at the TV window and watched the crowd and the mad dash and then watched the news and saw you again. Right on Gracie! You must have been exhausted by nightfall," wrote Minty in a small, neat (all dots small zeros) hand.

All of these are responses we might have expected from Grace Hartman. What she didn't talk much about was how it affected her physically and emotionally. The knowledge that, once locked in for the night you were stuck until someone let you out again in the morning, was seriously disturbing to her. And she admitted the hardship of doing without Lucie for the last twenty days of her term. She didn't mention how bizarre it felt to be suddenly and completely dependent on the good will of others. She didn't talk about the fear, or the anger aroused by the attempt to cow her defiance. (Surely she thought back to her words to Fred Gardiner about front-line workers at the Don Jail back in 1961.) It was naturally hard for her (as it is for most everyone) to stay out of authority's way. People don't assume subservience along with the "joint garb" the system issues. "I got into a hassle with the psychiatrist who called one of the young women a troublesome broad. I said to him, 'Doesn't do much good does it, talking to people like that.' 'People get themselves thrown in here and then they want to tell us how to run the place,' he snorted at me." Management at Vanier must have worried about having someone like Hartman around the inmates and the staff. Who might she counsel to strike next? Ed McAllister went in twice a week to see her, to take letters and papers for her signature. "They mistreated Grace. They had her cleaning floors in the mess hall, down on knees which were arthritic and she was too old for that. I couldn't say anything to the warden or Grace would pay, I knew. She had the guts of a burglar, Grace had. She'd fight a bear with a switch, and she never complained." So Grace Hartman did not receive any special treatment. It was contempt as usual.

The response to Hartman's public ordeal was sympathetic, for all the self-justification of officialdom. Former opponents and many citizens looked at her with a different eye. "Rather than raise public respect for the rule of law and confidence in the prevention of anarchy, I suspect the jail term has raised respect for Mrs. Hartman. She has gained admiration for the dignified sincerity with which she accepted her punishment while vowing to continue the battle against what she and her large membership perceive to be an unjust law," wrote *Globe and Mail* columnist Hugh Winsor. Whatever her reputation up until then, it was enhanced by the prison term in both directions. It absolutely guaranteed that the strike would go into the history books – legal, labour, as well as women's history. It also meant that Grace Hartman had joined the illustrious club of labour leaders who've been thrown into jail for defending their members' rights. So wrote Ed Finn in a column remembering a few of the men (J.S. Woodsworth, A.A. Heaps, Louis Laberge, Sean O'Flynn,

A Hartman family portrait taken the day Grace was released from jail.
Joe Hartman stands beside Grace, sons Bob and Warren stand behind,
and grandson Danny in front.

Paddy Neale, Jean-Claude Parrot) who'd so distinguished themselves. The added notoriety of a jail term, and the ensuing public sympathy, infuriated others. Hospital administrators curse Grace Hartman's name as if the strike happened last winter, and still talk of her as evil incarnate and the source of all their travails. "Ach," grouses one hospital administrator in a sharp Scottish burr, "I left England to get away from people like her!"

For that matter, some of the strikers were dubious of her stepping in to take the limelight. Pat Kenny criticized the logic of the process. "In the union movement it's the members who are boss and the leaders are supposed to do what the members tell them. Hospital workers made the decision to go on strike, and by not asking us to return to work Grace Hartman was just doing the job we elected her to do. Now she has to go to jail because some stupid judge doesn't understand that." And understandably, those who believe her leadership in the strike was too little, too late were cynical about the media circus the prison term generated, as well as Hartman's motives. The opportunism of the politician, the egotism of a retiring warlord; they wonder. "If she was in jail it should have been for betraying the workers," is the harshest judgment. But clearly it was the right thing to do, and what Hartman herself asked of the crown attorney. She insisted she serve the time and have the record rather than any members, which is what she figured she was elected to do and paid her good salary for. To most people, CUPE members, workers inside and outside the labour movement, and all sorts of other Canadians as well, she became a hero.

The scene takes place in the chambers of the speaker of the Manitoba Legislature, amid the opulence of prairie colonial architecture and British parliamentary tradition. It is May 8, 1986. The thirty-third session has just been opened by the lieutenant governor with customary ceremony; the new speaker feigning resistance while being strong-armed by the premier and the Opposition leader for presentation to the Queen's representative. A reception is taking place upstairs where a crowd is celebrating with noisy excitement over punch and fruit juice. For the first time ever the new speaker is a woman, Myrna Phillips, an MLA from Winnipeg who was one of several women elected in 1981 when Howard Pawley and the NDP formed the government. That isn't all. The speaker is a woman, but so is the lieutenant governor *and* so is the Opposition leader. (The Conservative caucus refused to endorse Phillips as speaker, citing her "strident partisanship," so the newly elected Liberal leader, Sharon Carstairs, leapt at the chance.)

All sorts of people have come to celebrate; women from across the province and the country, women and men from all parties. It seems to many that women are finally beginning to show signs of achieving critical mass in the political process. It is an occasion to applaud the spirit, and tenacity, of women in politics. For a few hours this inspires a sense of solidarity which crosses party lines, ruffling the restrained atmosphere. Myrna Phillips is the sort of politician who would do that in any case, and it is said by more than one wag that making her speaker was one way for the premier to keep a lid on her strong opinions. A strong-minded woman, known for her warmth and wit (and for offering to blowtorch the balls off the bronze buffalos standing in the Legislature's main foyer), she enjoys taking over an office so steeped in male decorum. She's already started with the walls, tacking up political posters and displaying women's art. As the crowd flows around her, nodding and congratulating her, she proudly directs visitors to the holy of holies, the speaker's private loo. There behind the door is a giant poster of Grace Hartman behind bars, with the slogan, "Fighting for Workers' Rights is a Woman's Job."

*

For Grace Hartman, the Ontario hospital strike was both the crucible and the climax of her union career. She was easily re-elected at the CUPE convention the following autumn, and served another term as president before retiring. Whatever outstanding criticisms the membership may have had of her and national office paled beside the injustice of the prison term she'd served and its public impact. Her time in jail was taken as a statement of commitment to the workers, and of the justice of the strikers' cause. Circumstance had turned her incarceration into an international event which worked to political advantage. Nonetheless, the whole affair had been hard on the union; many members had lost faith and there was serious healing work to do. When the report of the hospital workers' Central Bargaining Committee was completed, Grace Hartman telephoned Julie Davis. "It was a Sunday afternoon. I had been on the periphery of the strike as I didn't have any hospital locals. Grace called and asked, 'Are you sitting down? I need to have a long chat with you.' She wanted me to switch jobs, to leave a situation where everything was working well to take on something uncertain. Centralized bargaining had so far failed to recognize the really poor working conditions and the lack of uniformity in hospitals across the province. CUPE had let things bump along, and in the wake of the strike set out to create a structure that would be more receptive to the needs of hospital workers."

This time around the president hand-picked the new co-ordinator. "I thought the people who were co-ordinating the bargaining and the strike had worn out their welcome and I felt the situation called for a new person. Julie Davis had co-ordinated the bargaining for library groups in Toronto, and I don't know if they were unique, but those library workers used to be real conservatives in the labour movement and all of a sudden they became quite radical. Davis had got some really good contracts for them, the first maternity leave for part-time workers, for example. I just felt she was the one to do the job. Then I had to do the political manoeuvering so that I wasn't stepping on anybody's toes. I wanted her and I wanted her to want to do it, and I also wanted the other staff who had been doing the work to go on to other things without feeling shunted aside."

In the end, Hartman was right about the strike; it was a milestone. It also became a symbol of working women's resistance, and of the gutsy fight people on the lowest rungs of the economic ladder are able to put up when they have a mind to. The strike created an icon for women, the image of Unrepentant Womanhood behind bars, of Grace Hartman on her knees washing prison floors for Roy McMurtry and for the right of hospital workers to strike. Even Hartman's telephone call to Julie Davis was symbolic in its way, for when she was first elected president of CUPE there were no Julie Davises for her to call upon. Her experience as a leader was, particularly in the early years, one of isolation; she had cohorts and collaborators among the men she worked with, and friends certainly, but no network of women confidantes as many feminist activists and politicians have today. It was lonely in those days at the top – there were a lot of nights alone doing needlework in hotel rooms while the men were off doing the town – and Hartman must have taken enormous satisfaction when the efforts at advancing women in the union began to pay off, when she was able to actually see her generation's legacy pass to the next. Davis had become active in the union movement at Madeleine Parent's instigation, and had been persuaded by Grace Hartman to try for a rep's position in the mid-seventies. She was one of many union women whose careers Hartman guided and encouraged.

The world these women came of age in was already changed, the style and political approach of feminism affected by the shifting mores of the counterculture. Hartman's generation of women did not engage in the sexual revolution or burn their bras; they were political activists and feminists to the core, but their outward affect as women was traditional. You could take a Grace Hartman or a Madeleine Parent out of the union office or off the picket line any day of the week, put them in Rideau Hall for tea with the Queen, and they would look the part – which is to say, appropriately dressed and exquisitely groomed. Like Parent, Hartman took professional pride in looking correct, considering it part of the job to dress with respect for the people she represented. Every week there was a trip to the hairdresser and a manicure, and when she gave up trying to find time to sew her own clothes, there were excursions to the dressmaker. Through the years the hairstyles changed, as did the eyeglasses and the outfits, and at a certain point she made a "decision not to go gray" as son Warren puts it. She paid attention to fashion but more and more as a matter of accommodation. She had to look serious, she had to look mainstream. When she turned up at the 1971 convention dressed in a purple pantsuit, large-collared flow-ered shirt, knee-length veston and hair piled in large curls on her head, you can be sure scores of women went to work looking exactly like that every day. And those women, women who thought of themselves as ordinary working women, were the women who iden-tified with Grace Hartman. She was, as Shereen Bowditch (Hart-man's secretary during her last term at CUPE) says, ahead of her time but not so far ahead that those members who earned $6.75 an hour couldn't look at her and see themselves. She wasn't slick or pretentious. She was a working woman who looked the part and she took care the image never strayed from that.

Grace had a personality that attracted people, not the kind that dominates the room but one which impresses with steadiness and quiet. Some called it charisma, others warmth, others genuine car-ing. Cynthia Wishert tells her story, "I hadn't been long as a rep in Newfoundland and I was in Ottawa for meetings. I came by her office, the door was open and she called me in. Then she arranged for some tea and asked me how things were going. I had my big smile on but when I looked at her, my bottom lip started to tremble and before I knew it I was in tears. 'What *have* they done to you. Tell me, I'll stop it,' she said. What had happened was that one of the reps at my first week-long training session had put the make on me

Grace Hartman at the Nova Scotia Division Convention in 1982. "With Marg Martel and my new Cape Breton shawl."

saying, 'You might as well sleep with me because I'm going to tell everyone that you did anyway.' I told him in that case I'd tell everyone he couldn't get it up. But it bothered me; I felt like a sex object. When I'd finished, Grace leaned over and patted my knee and said, 'Oh, Cynthia, if I'd fucked all the men that said they'd fucked Grace Hartman I'd be in a frigging wheelchair.' I burst out laughing and she handed me a kleenex. She took something that was really crushing me and with humour and affection allowed me to laugh at her, sharing a personal experience ... but for Grace, who looked like everybody's grandmother, to use those words!" There are stories of Grace cutting down men twice her size without raising a finger, stories about her tart tongue and cutting riposte, but the reality is subtly different, for Grace rarely raised her voice. Her assistant, Ed McAllister, admitted he could never tell when she was furious with him. "She was very gentle by nature and when angry she sounded exactly the same. Her demeanour, her voice and inflection were constant."

Considering who Grace Hartman was, and where Canadian society was in the late seventies, it seems obvious that she would be constrained as a leader. As she said, she expected that. She also expected she would have to invent her own political tactic and write her own rules of behaviour. Above all, her style of leadership was marked by reserve, though this too is at odds with the image. On the podium she could tongue-lash governments and employers with the best of them; her affect in public was strong, eloquent and informed. In the office and at meetings, where she had to train herself to cope with the culture of male prerogative at close quarters, she tended to be retiring rather than combative. You might call it the art of not reacting – not reacting to the slights or sexist attitudes or the emotional outbursts. This reticence, however, should not be equated with weakness, which is the way traditional union culture would picture it. Yet in some way this stoicism of hers, this strategic retreat in response to resistance, the silence in the face of confrontation, was puzzling to many. Curiously passive, like the kid in the schoolyard who lets the class bully berate her even though she's bigger (and, yes, one wonders what everyone else in the playground was doing on occasions like the CLC executive meeting when the men ganged up on Grace and no one said boo). Grace Hartman was a politician who'd made it to the top in the cut and thrust world of labour politics, and it is mere cliché to expect our hero to vanquish her opponents with a dramatic flourish. When you consider her character, however, passive resistance at the right moment was an excellent strategy. As Harry Greene says of her, "She was smart enough not to stop locomotives bare-handed."

In much the same way, Grace Hartman's politics were paradoxical. She was a left-winger all her life but she didn't conform to expectations. She wasn't particularly radical by nature, and she could be inconsistent. Her connection with the Communist Party is part of the enigma, for while she came out of that world understanding Marxism, she was not an ideologue. Though she was often accused of being a Communist, she was rarely thought to be peddling an agenda. Still, there is something in her approach akin to old-style political discipline, a strategy which thought in terms of decades and of winning wars, not necessarily battles. Whatever the philosophic derivation, Hartman was pragmatic. She knew what she wanted and she was willing to wait. She did not believe she had come to lead the CLC or the labour movement into a new feminist dawn, and she probably doubted it was the time to lead a public sector revolt either. In any case, she felt her main strength was in bridging things: genders, generations and, in the early years, NUPE and NUPSE. Hers was a nurturing role, though not a typical one, and one which traded more on the skills of strategic planning and conflict resolution than tactical combat.

As a feminist she was equally non-doctrinaire. Within CUPE her objective was to pull women into unions and into union activism by drawing on what they had in common and, most important, what they could *do* in common. She wasn't trying to convert or confront other women, just to challenge them to work together using the union as the vehicle of their own self-determination. That was the strategy and it bespoke moderation. While analysis and policies concerning women and gender politics could be radical – and were, for the time – the language was not. What strikes you on rereading the early debates on women's issues, at the 1971 CUPE convention for example, is how defensive the arguments were. Grace was starting from nowhere, representing a small and unorganized minority in the union membership, without a basis of shared understanding on which such policies could be set. She and her allies were intent on building a movement within the union, which meant in solidarity with men. Their appeal had to elicit people's sense of fair play and commitment to the union. "We just want to make sure that women have the same skills and abilities to participate in the union as you do". was the pitch. Safe and non-threatening. In doing this she was building on her own experience as, for most of her life, most of her politics had been done with men – not an uncommon practice for women pioneering in male preserves. Her most important political advisor and confidant was undoubtedly her husband, Joe Hartman.

Gil Levine's intellectual support was also critical to her work over the years, particularly with the women's movement of the sixties. His research and analysis was original and ahead of its time, and Hartman felt that, without it, CUPE could not have spoken with authority. For eight years she worked in close proximity with Kealey Cummings, who was national secretary treasurer during her term as president. "In the beginning we were affected by the NUPE/NUPSE camp thing which took a very long time to wash out," Cummings recalls. "But then we had worked together in the early sixties before the merger, putting together the constitution of the [Toronto] district council and on committees at the OFL." Perhaps because of this the two eventually established a friendship in office. The animosity and political rancour didn't carry over as it had with Stan Little; Hartman and Cummings were able to operate in consort with each other as national officers of the union with a level of co-operation and mutual trust.

Then too, Hartman always had male executive assistants (following Ralph Maillet and Ed McAllister, Murray Whepler and Don Cott worked with her briefly) who had influence mainly because they had daily access to her others hadn't, and partly because there was only one of them at a time. (Nowadays a president in Hartman's position has several advisors.) McAllister wrote a lot of her speeches and drafted memos, and Hartman relied heavily on his advice about media events (he steered her away from debates) and public statements, although she regularly doctored texts before delivering them. She also worked closely with men in PR and communications, Norm Simon and Fred Tabachnick mainly, who prepared press statements and articles in her name. Hartman was evidently a leader able to share authority as well as responsibility, an ability which, once again, was appreciated by some and impugned by others. Hartman was unquestionably an enigma to some people, her leadership style ill-understood in the context.

Like any leader, Grace Hartman had her fans and her detractors, but she was phenomenal in having been so rarely opposed at the polls. Over twenty-five years she won every election she contested for executive office, and was frequently acclaimed. Popular as a politician, she truly enjoyed meeting the membership, liked going to conventions and talking to people, especially one on one. She danced at the banquets and drank scotch with women on the national women's task force until the hotel bar closed. What she liked least about the job was being an employer, and she loathed having to negotiate with staff. Among the reminiscences of her contemporaries there is a recurring description from the men she worked closely with, to whom she appeared as a willow bending to the opinion of the last person she spoke with. Paste their comments together and Grace Hartman vanishes behind the various claims of authorship of her ideas and style. The truth is, Grace Hartman was neither the creation of some man or men, nor was she a self-taught invention. She knew her limitations; she was a consensus-seeker, a true democrat who indulged everyone's opinions and allowed herself to be persuaded to take actions and directions which she might initially have opposed. Sometimes that got her into trouble, sometimes she waited too long to act. But many people, women especially, appreciated that caution and flexibility.

As the union grows so does the office of president, and it is axiomatic that the occupant tends to become removed from the membership. She leads a different life from most of her members, and earns a better salary, which is an old labour political story and one which generates a familiar ethical debate. It is a challenge for any leader to remain in touch with a movement and maintain some perspective on events, and Grace Hartman struggled with it. Through it all she kept her door open. Most of the time, that is, but there were periods, particularly in her last term, when people felt the door was not open, that she was being "handled by the guys." These were times when she was, in fact, often out of the country, representing Canadian public sector workers at Public Service International conferences.

Most people saw Grace Hartman as a traditional trade unionist, neither bureaucrat nor expert, an unrepentant democrat, a modest and decent person. She was a woman other women liked to work for; a leader who habitually encouraged workers to reach beyond their jobs, to grow with their work. If labour historians and journalists said that she made her mark as a woman but not as an innovative leader in the movement because she lacked clout within the inner councils of labour, they weren't exactly wrong. Other commentators lamented the behemoth CUPE had become and the "self-inflicted paralysis" of its structure, pointing out that Hartman was part of a superstructure designed to exist rather than co-ordinate or lead. So claimed John Deverell in his infamous "Paper Tiger" article published in the Toronto *Star* following the 1981 convention. He took the view that more real power was vested with the regional directors than the national officers of CUPE, and pointed to the great conundrum of the union's existence – the imbalance of power between elected officers and staff in a situation where there are only two full-time elected officers and a huge staff barred from running for office. Deverell interpreted this as a force for conformity within the union, protecting incumbent politicians from the challenge of well-informed and talented competition. What is certainly true is that the prohibition, far from easing tensions between senior staff and senior officers over the years, seems to have exacerbated them. There was no cure for the fact that old timers like Lofty MacMillan, Gil Levine and Pat O'Keeffe felt as attached to "their union" as Grace Hartman did, and believed in their own vision just as fiercely.

Grace Hartman's union career is a study of good fortune and masterful timing. She came into the movement just as CUPE was forming and public sector workers were establishing themselves as a political force. The public service in Canada was itself undergoing fundamental change and unprecedented expansion. Her accession to leadership coincided with the rise of modern feminism, and with a period of political ferment and cultural activism in the country generally. She took over the presidency of CUPE at a moment when the status of women was on the national agenda because of Interna-

tional Women's Year, and in the midst of an economic crisis. Overnight she became a national figure, and over the next eight years was
repeatedly called upon, as no CUPE president since, to comment
on the affairs of the day: Jean Chrétien's budgets, changes in the
Health Act and Unemployment Insurance, and the Québec referen-
dum of 1980. As she spoke, she gave voice to women's issues and
legitimacy to the feminist perspective in a way that no one in the
labour movement had been able to before. She took the voice and
presence of working-class women into places where they had never
been heard or felt before, into cabinet rooms and council chambers,
onto the national news and into public debates. In the sixties and
the seventies, however, she was more than a debater; she was part
of the ferment and the activism around nationalism and feminism
in Canada. Waxing a bit sentimental in a 1981 Toronto *Sun* column
about Hartman's jailing, Laura Sabia wrote, "I remember some
fifteen years ago when women in Canada were beginning to assert
themselves and demand a royal commission on the Status of
Women, that Grace Hartman stood as women's staunchest ally.
Those of us leading the fray seeking solidarity with women's organizations across Canada will never forget this fantastic women when
she quietly announced that we had the total support of CUPE. It
was a great morale booster ... When Prime Minister Pearson turned
us down and we threatened to march a million women to Ottawa,
it was Grace Hartman and strong women like her who stood together, defied government and badgered the politicians into appointing a royal commission."

Grace Hartman's last term as president of CUPE was probably
her easiest. It was the one term when she allowed herself the
luxury of concentrating her efforts on projects important to her.
Within CUPE she oversaw the emergence of the National Task
Force on Women, which had its first meeting in May 1983 in

Québec City at the time of the CLC Women's Conference. An equal opportunities officer had been hired, and at the CUPE convention in Toronto that autumn the national executive board presented delegates with *CUPE Women: Survival in Crisis*, a strategy to assist women workers in the economic crisis. It stressed the shorter work-week, part-time work, re-training and affirmative action as areas for action. Finally the idea of "Implementation Committees," born at the 1971 convention, was coming to fruition. That year Grace commissioned a commemorative scarf for International Women's Day and sent it around to women politicians, activists and public figures with CUPE's greetings. Myrna Phillips, the MLA from Wolseley in Winnipeg, wrote back, "I wore it on the IWD march from the University of Winnipeg to the Legislative Building. You'll be pleased to know that we have progressed from shivering on the windy steps of the Legislature to being received by the Premier and two cabinet ministers ... The struggle continues from the inside!" Kay Macpherson wrote: "Who else but a union with a woman president would think of a scarf! I'll wear it year-round with pride and hope." Jan Tennant wore hers on Global Television as she read the national news.

This was the period when Grace began to take on some serious work with Public Service International (PSI), the co-ordinating body for public sector unions, headquartered in Geneva. After she became CUPE's secretary treasurer in 1967 she attended PSI conventions with Stan Little as part of a two- or three-person delegation from Canada. In 1975 she was elected to the PSI executive, the first woman in the organization's history, and in 1981 she became a vice-president. She had attended the first "Women in Public Services" conference organized by PSI in Stockholm in 1970, where she reported that "in spite of the large and increasing number of women employed in industry and in the public sector, women are playing a secondary role in trade unions in Canada. We have a long uphill fight, not only to win responsibility from the men who dominate unions, but to instill confidence in the women so that they can assume greater authority." In the early eighties she chaired PSI's Women's Committee, and the steering committee set up to plan the second "Women in Public Services" conference held in New York in 1984. She was also chairperson of that conference. In the seventies and early eighties, when a great deal was happening in Latin America, PSI formed an Inter-American Committee which Hartman chaired until 1985. As a result of all this committee work she found herself attending meetings of other international bodies, such as the International Labour Organization (ILO) and the International Confederation of Free Trade Unions (ICFTU), on PSI's behalf. These conferences and meetings were slow, plodding and pompous, and Hartman was dubious at first. "I mean, everybody gets up and congratulates the chairman for being elected chairman for the session, which takes up a lot of time. Even so, I think PSI is an important organization. We lodged complaints on two or three occasions with the ILO, as did NUPGE, and while the governments involved didn't jump to the ILO's decree, I do think it matters when a government is called publicly to account in an international forum, and found guilty of violating standards it has itself agreed to follow."

It was PSI's work in the Third World in defence of workers' rights which attracted Hartman. "A lot of education work was being done, and assistance offered to unions dealing with repressive legislation, or re-establishing themselves after the fall of a dictatorship. We had a number of seminars in Latin America [in the early eighties], and in a very short time I found I was accepted to chair meetings, which was rather unusual, I think. My Spanish is as limited as my French, and these were very male-oriented societies." She conducted women's seminars in Kenya, Mauritius, Singapore and Bermuda as well, and helped organize the first Inter-American Women's Seminar in Mexico in 1986. When her PSI term had expired in 1984, new CUPE president Jeff Rose asked Hartman to stay on, which she agreed to do, remaining active on the Women's Committee until 1989. By that time she was seventy years old and had acquired the aura of an elder in the public sector world. She had, of course, been chairing meetings like these since the mid-sixties, and she had been active in women's groups since she joined Canadian Girls In Training at Epworth United Church when she was a teenager. She was in her element and she felt it was important for CUPE, a well-established union in an affluent country, to make a contribution. "I always felt we shouldn't turn our backs on countries that needed our help." This meant monetary help, staff support and for some years, Grace Hartman's own time and energy.

There was always politics, of course. PSI work had a way of reflecting on positions taken by the CLC over Canadian foreign policy. There were dust-ups at executive council. "Yes, there were accusations that some people within the Congress were at best supporting right-wing social democratic forces, and at worst had ties to the CIA," Hartman told labour historian Wayne Roberts in 1989. "A number of times policy papers proposed by staff were shredded by guys like Bob White. That happened over El Salvador and Nicaragua and Chile. The debate was over questions like which were the 'real' unions. PSI was not a left-wing organization, that's for sure, but its positions were pretty good. I do remember, though, a long period when the Congress's positions were not considered favourably in international circles I travelled in."

They say a good feminist never retires, she just joins more committees. In Grace's case, the work she was doing as a trade unionist flowed over into her retirement years, overlapping with new activities. She returned to her roots and familiar causes: peace, the women's movement, the arts. She joined the Voice of Women, reconnecting with women she had known in the forties. Mildred Ryerson and Lil Greene were delighted to see her in VOW; Grace was happy to be back with small groups and small budgets again. She picked up where she left off in 1954, raising money, going to demonstrations, chairing the administrative committee, and generally helping out. "Grace appeared at ease and relaxed throughout our noisy and rather chaotic meetings, to which she often came laden with muffins and her famous knitting. She had a rare gift – she listened, seldom made judgments, and often had suggestions which led to peaceful and positive solutions," recalled Kay Macpherson. She became active on NAC's Survival Committee in these years too, and was president of VOW from 1988 until she died in 1993. With a free trade agreement between Canada and the United States looming, she joined the Council of Canadians and was elected to its first board in 1985, the same year she accepted an appointment to the Ontario Press Council. She thoroughly enjoyed both jobs: the first building a grassroots citizens' organization; the second adjudicating public complaints against the daily newspapers in the province. All the while she continued to attend women's conferences in the labour movement.

It was a good time for Grace. She was back in Toronto, Joe was retired and able to travel with her on PSI business, and she was plain Citizen Hartman again. She put time into all sorts of community events and debates, and branched out into new fields, labour arts being one. She was part of a group that lobbied the Ontario Arts Council to institute a program of funding for art projects in the workplace, and she worked for several years with a committee planning a labour museum. She enjoyed and supported Canadian theatre, read Canadian authors (Margaret Laurence was one of a group of Canadians who had taken out an ad in the *Globe and Mail* to express concern about Grace Hartman's incarceration) and joined with another group of trade unionists, feminists, writers and teachers who came together to support a local independent bookstore. There were many musical events and book launchings at the SCM Book Room which Grace and Joe participated in, and projects such as one dubbed "The Local Library" which was undertaken with the Ontario Public Service Employees Union (OPSEU). This involved packaging a small library of fifty books selected as "classics" by a group of activists and scholars associated with the Book Room, and designed for OPSEU locals to display and circulate. The launch organized by the Book Room for local members and their children was a huge "Carnivale Bien-Adios," full of music, dancing, theatrics

and a parade of authors in costume led by Grace Hartman, resplen-
dent in the breeding plumage of the Canadian Loon.

The night of Joe and Grace Hartman's fiftieth wedding anniversary, friends and relatives gathered at the Firefighters Hall in
Willowdale for a buffet and dancing. The Dunview crowd was there,
ready for some square dancing, along with union friends, Voice of
Women friends, NDP and Council of Canadians friends, old and
new. Warren Hartman planned and designed the event, right down
to the colour scheme of the balloons in gold, jade green, rust and
purple to match Grace's dress. Everybody was there, all the strands
of his parents' lives drawn together. Grace and Joe danced a bit of
the "Dip and Dive" until Grace's knees grew weak and Sybil Bellmore took over so she could sit a spell. Retirement hadn't been kind
to Grace. Her body seemed to have a will of its own, waiting until
she had some leisure time to break down. Arthritis settled brutally
in her knees and eventually forced an operation on one. Within a
year of leaving CUPE, cancer flared up again and she had a second
mastectomy. Cancer had continued to bedevil the Fulcher clan: after
Grace's bout in the late forties there were Edna's five miscarriages
and death at thirty-seven in 1963; Velma was almost sixty when she
died in 1980; and Rae, like Grace, survived breast cancer when she
was in her thirties. In the eighties, when women began talking about
breast cancer, Grace spoke out about hers, but through most of her
union career she kept it out of her public life. Very few would have
even suspected, given the robust health she was in most of the time.
She brimmed with life and energy, hardly missing a single meeting
in thirty years. At one point during her retirement she spent time in
Ireland, trying to piece together her family background in an effort
to track the pattern of the disease. When Bob developed kidney
cancer in 1987 it was devastating. "Telling Grace was the toughest
thing I've ever had to do. They tell me I've recovered now, but Grace

felt she was responsible and she cried at the thought of the legacy she had given me."

Like any mother, Grace Hartman worried that her notoriety might create problems for her sons. At nineteen and twenty-five they were all but grown up and on their own when she started in full time with CUPE. Warren had gone into the arts after leaving school at sixteen, finding his métier in costume and stage design, ending up with the Canadian Opera Company before taking a teaching position in the theatre department at Brock University. Bob's interests lay in the direction of autos and mechanics, and he eventually set up his own towing company. Although there was an assumption in the family that Warren took after Grace and Bob after Joe, it was Grace who would go off to the car races with her younger son. Some years later, when he joined the West Carleton volunteer fire department and began competing in vehicle rescue, Grace and Joe both turned up at his first world competition in Port Perry. (And Grace later presented each member of the team with a plaque worked in petit-point.)

For the most part Grace's job did not impinge on their lives, but then came the day Warren, who was becoming politically active in the gay rights movement, felt compelled to disclose his sexual orientation. He had been waiting for the perfect opening, mindful of the disclosures being made in other quarters, by the RCMP in particular. It had occurred to him that someone could just as easily and spuriously use his gayness to embarrass Grace. If she was going to hear about it, it had better be from him. Early in 1978, American singer and orange juice publicist Anita Bryant showed up in Canada to lead a "Christian Liberation Crusade" in defence of the family, heterosexuality and the missionary position. She had been invited by Ken Campbell of the People's Church, a leader of right-wing, anti-abortion forces in Canada. At the time, a heated public debate was underway about the protection of gays and lesbians by the Human Rights Code, and Bryant's tour was aimed at blocking the legislation. "We were having dinner and talking about the demonstration being planned and Grace said something about feeling she

Even after retirement, Grace Hartman, CUPE president emeritus, continued to attend conventions with her ubiquitous knitting.

ought to go. I was thinking 'If I miss this moment there'll never be another one like it.' I said something about people needing that support, that I needed it because I was gay too. Grace's response was, 'Yes dear, we've always known. Would you please pass the peas.' She'd known the way a mother knows, but had never brought it up. For ten years she'd been happy to think of my first lover as a roommate." Over the next six months Warren watched Grace sort it all through, arriving at a place where she too took pride in gay pride.

The family helped Grace get through tough times as well. It was Bob Hartman who set Grace straight one night when she returned home from Ottawa, bushed and beaten by the current crisis. "This is too much," she declared. "I'm quitting." "You can't," retorted young Bob. "The family decided you would do this job, and the family will decide when you quit." Recounting that story, Grace would always chuckle, "Give them a little democracy and see what happens." But the fact behind the story was the little community which was the Hartman family, its political sensibility and abiding concern for the welfare of people. Her family was the ballast in Grace Hartman's life; never was there doubt about their support or their commitment to her cause with the union. They would joke about her being bossy and tell her she couldn't be president of CUPE at home, but they took pleasure in her success and always came out to convention.

Ask people who knew and worked with Grace Hartman how she managed, and sooner or later they get around to her marriage with Joe Hartman. It's an historical commonplace that behind this or that great man lurks a greater woman, the unassuming "little woman" in the background whose self-sacrifice makes the whole thing work. But this is not a matter of role reversal or of the difficulties of keeping a long-distance relationship going for sixteen years; it is about the way Joe was there for Grace, his loyalty and genuine concern for what she was doing. "I was always more interested in her union than my own," he says. But that interest was discreet, his presence kept at a distance. She never talked much about Joe publicly, except to say that he was one husband who talked equality and practised it. Her sister Rae asked Grace one day why she and Joe were so successful, because Rae's own marriage wasn't. Grace told her, "Rae, when I see Joe walk up the street my heart still flips." They'd been married thirty years when she said that. Whatever the secret ingredient, Grace and Joe

Hartman had a marriage that worked and a love that lasted. People, and women especially, recognized that and thought of it as remarkable if not unique. There were the usual stresses and strains of separation, but it had its positive aspects, such as the opportunity it gave Grace to pitch in when her grandson needed a grandmother. But they both felt the loneliness, and indulged in hobbies to keep it company. They took up rock collecting one summer, which turned into serious lapidary and jewelry making for Joe. Grace kept on with her needlework, the two of them producing a flow of gifts and mementos presented to scores of colleagues and friends over the years.

Grace Hartman was a "giver" – generous with her compassion, her amazing energy and her talents as an organizer and conciliator. Her legacy is the memories people have of this generosity, and it includes the obvious self-sacrifice of going to jail as well as the good humour in being willing to dress up as a loon. Her subtler gifts were probably less appreciated by the recipients but no less important – some of the union barons who discovered, just in time, that the world was readier for female leadership than they were. Her personal friends have the one-of-a-kind sweaters she knit for them; the rank-and-file membership of her union have the example of her genuine admiration for them and the heroic work they do. Her successors in the leadership of the labour movement have her to thank for the timely way in which Canada's largest public sector union took up the cause of women. And all Canadians can be grateful to her for the value she attached to active citizenship and the commitment she demonstrated all her life to the creation of a better, fairer world.

Afterword

by Judy Darcy, President,
Canadian Union of Public Employees

Shades of Grace

G race Hartman walked where no woman in Canada had walked before. When Grace was elected president of CUPE in 1975, it wasn't a *glass* ceiling she had to break through. The ceiling was made of iron.

The 1975 CUPE convention was the second I'd attended, and I remember how excited we all were at the prospect of electing a woman president. Grace Hartman was more progressive than many of the labour leaders of the day. She had repeatedly spoken out about public employees' rights, about peace, about women's issues. She was known to trade unionists and feminists alike, and respected as the pioneer she was. But even though we considered her election a milestone, I don't think those of us who were young activists at the time truly understood its magnitude. To be both the first woman leader of a national union and to be arguing for women's equality at that time was swimming upstream Big Time. I know I didn't *fully* understand it until 1991, when I was privileged to be elected CUPE president and walked in her shoes.

In my early years in CUPE, Grace was a person I saw mostly at conventions. My main experience of her was from my place at the "con" mikes on the floor as I agitated about the need for a fightback plan or to go faster on equality issues; making her life miserable, I'm sure, while she was up at the front trying to chair the convention.

Grace and I had the opportunity to reminisce about this and many other CUPE events and people four days before she died, when I was able to spend a last few precious hours with her. It was just weeks after the 1993 CUPE convention – my first as chair. "Did you bring down the gavel on some delegates, Judy, the way I used to have to bring it down on you?" she asked.

During my time with her, I kept thinking about how much of CUPE's history had touched this woman's life – how much she meant to us, to where we are today, and what CUPE meant to her.

After reading her biography, I am more convinced than ever of the importance of making sure that working people learn about the labour movement's rich history. Workers need to know about the battles our foremothers and forefathers waged to win the workplace and broader social rights that many take for granted today. They need to know how they got these rights in the first place. Grace would surely have wanted this to be one of the main messages of her story.

Grace's greatest achievement, without a doubt, was the trail she blazed for women. Not with rhetoric or with fiery speeches necessarily, but with quiet determination and firm resolve. Grace was starting from nowhere. Very few women held positions on local union executives, or on any other union committees for that matter. And women's committees? Unheard of! Equality issues, such as women's economic status and the ghettoization of women's work, were a tough sell at union conventions, let alone in society as a whole.

Grace set about to change all that. She believed in "beating them at their own game," and would tell new women activists that to succeed in pushing equality issues to the front of the agenda, they had to learn how the union worked inside out, and become adept at rules of order at conventions. Otherwise they could expect frustration as well as defeat.

I think we forget, too, that many CUPE locals had had little experience with women workers to that point. The union's initial organizing efforts were mainly in the all-male outside municipal and utilities sectors. It was later that CUPE stepped up its organizing in sectors where large numbers of women worked – school boards, hospitals, nursing homes, inside municipal, libraries, universities, social services and childcare – so that today the membership is almost 60 percent women. It was even later, towards the end of Grace's tenure and beyond, that women started to be elected to local union executives, committees and the national executive board in growing numbers, sometimes reaching or exceeding the 50 percent mark. And when I was elected president and Geraldine McGuire secretary treasurer of CUPE in 1991, the fact that it was barely an issue that the two top jobs in the union would be held by women spoke volumes about how far our union had come.

Despite these major achievements, my own experience and that of other union women has not been without obstacles. We certainly encountered overt discrimination in our early days as activists. When it occurs now, discrimination is usually far more subtle yet every bit as damaging. Moreover, the tremendous difficulties of trying to balance work, family and union responsibilities that Grace and her generation of women activists faced, remain today, even though women are more accepted and supported in leadership and activist roles.

Our struggles for equality have taken different forms than those carried on during Grace's period, but I feel that they are as critical today as they were then. To be sure, she cheered us on in all of them. She saw our fight to put pay equity on the bargaining agenda (and then actually get it negotiated), as well as on the legislative agendas of governments, as a huge step to equality. She knew that it was important for us to show the connections between the different manifestations of discrimination; between sexism, racism, or dis-crimination against lesbians and gay men or people with disabilities. She understood the social and economic benefits that the fight for universal childcare, and better pay and working conditions for child-care workers, would produce if we won. While we've made inroads in some of these areas, I think it's obvious that victory is still outside our reach, especially now that right-wing governments are putting everything we've accomplished up for grabs. And it is sobering that current statistics point to an *increasing* number of women being pushed into poverty through cuts to social assistance, unemployment, and conversion of full-time jobs to part time.

Grace would be outraged to see the backlash against equality that has exploded on the social and economic scene. As well, she would be angry and troubled by the campaign to undo years of struggles for workers' rights, not to mention the attack that is putting the very existence of the public sector in jeopardy.

When Grace first came into contact with the labour movement, Canadian workers were organizing as never before in the industrial and manufacturing sectors. These workers and their unions waged historic strikes to secure basic rights, such as the right to union representation, as well as fair pay and working conditions.

I don't think most people are aware that in the fifties, sixties and seventies, public sector unions had to cover the same ground and wage the same battles. But as Grace's biography shows, governments did not hand union recognition and the right to strike on a silver platter to public sector workers. Quite the opposite. The workers had to fight tooth and nail for them, and for basic respect and a decent standard of living. In some sectors and jurisdictions they defied the law to defend themselves against injustice. Many public service workers still do not have the fundamental right to strike. These trials by fire showed workers that the union was their only way of taking control over their working lives; without it they were vulnerable to the whims and agendas of employers and governments.

The public sector was still growing in size and influence when Grace came into the CUPE presidency. By 1975 the union had emerged as a national voice for public sector workers and social issues. In the ensuing years the union championed economic and workplace justice for public sector employees as both a basic right for workers and an essential ingredient in maintaining high-quality public services. Throughout her career, Grace spoke passionately and with tremendous pride about the role of public employees, and about how the public sector and the programs and services it delivers – such as universal health care and education, to name just two – form the fabric of our society.

All the same, there was a good deal of bad press about public employees, accompanied by the usual bad jokes about bloated bureaucracies. No mention was made of the valuable and vital work public employees perform, or about their poverty wages in some sectors.

Today the jokes have been replaced by sweeping denunciations and a strategy to dismantle our social programs and all but wipe out the public sector. Free collective bargaining has been legislated away in many provinces, and informal wage controls exist in most others. Employers are forcing workers to make pay and benefit concessions or else get out of the way so a private contractor can come in to do the job for less. There is a major shift from full-time to part-time and casual work, the growth of a huge pool of low-paid labour and an ever-widening gap in incomes. More and more workers are forced to compete against each other for jobs in the race to the bottom.

Equally frightening is how employers, the media and politicians are trying to marginalize unions, just as they are trying to marginalize the public sector. Nowadays it has become commonplace, for example, for employers to try going around the union to appeal to the members as individuals, to imply that the union is getting in the way and that we could all be "one big happy family" without it. Those who promote this image are, of course, the same ones who've caused untold grief to this happy family by throwing people out of work and reducing wages and benefits in the name of deficit reduction.

Still, in this climate many union members *have* come to look at their union as a third party. Large numbers of workers in both the private and public sectors don't see themselves as part of the working class and are unsure where their interests lie. We are divided –

between younger and older, part time and full time, employed and jobless, public and private, activists and non-activists, those who see the struggle for equality as the struggle for fairness for all workers, and those who don't see it as their struggle. We are all anxious about the future and many of us feel that we've lost control of our lives.

I believe the challenge facing a union like CUPE is to find a way to rebuild a shared sense of purpose among the members and other workers by fostering basic union values in the membership. As Grace would say, we need to put the You in Union. We need the support of *all* workers to fight back effectively. Like the public sector itself, unions are about *collective* purpose and *collective* solutions, not everyone fending for herself or himself.

Reading the life of Grace Hartman, and through it the story of CUPE, provides inspiration to follow the example of our working parents and grandparents who built the union member by member, workplace by workplace, community by community. Building solidarity in this way means renewing efforts to communicate face-to-face with the members. It means showing we have to stand together in bad times as well as good. It means returning to our roots of social unionism. It means emphasizing the importance of political action and being involved in the life of our communities. It means staying true to the principle of democratic decision-making by the members on *all* the issues affecting them, every step of the way.

Grace was proud of the richness of membership democracy in CUPE, a democracy little understood – and often attacked – by those outside. She was a leader with profound respect for the right of members to make their own decisions. This was reflected in her strong support of local union autonomy, as well as the special relationship she had with members of our CUPE family in Québec. She and CUPE as a whole had recognized Québec's right to self-determination and CUPE Québec's "distinct" status within the union long before politicians dared utter those words.

The day that I was leaving for CUPE's 1993 national convention in Vancouver, Grace called to tell me she was seriously ill and would not be attending. We cried together. She was heartbroken that she would not be able to see old friends and speak to the delegates from the front of the convention one last time.

I told her that if she couldn't come to the convention, we would find a way to bring it to her. And so we gave convention delegates the opportunity to send a personal videotaped message to Grace. The afternoon of the taping there was a long line of delegates waiting their turn to tell Grace what she meant to them. Young, old, black, white, women, men, those who knew her and those whom she had never met – all sent heartfelt messages which she viewed a few days later as she sat in her living room. She told me afterwards that the tape had moved her deeply.

When I saw Grace for the last time, she asked me if I would say some words at her memorial service. I agreed gladly, of course. When I asked what she was proudest of, she didn't dwell on the headlines but on personal stories which spoke volumes about her. About flying out to a retirement party for a secretary in the CUPE Edmonton office, and how that decided a young man who had been undecided until then to accept a staff rep's job. "That's the kind of union I want to work for, where the national president flies across the country for a secretary's retirement," he told her.

Everyone who knew Grace has special memories of her for the big things she did, and the little ones. I will never forget the royal blue and white hand-knitted booties she sent me in 1984 for my new little baby boy. I will never forget the image of Grace walking between two buildings with a jail guard as CUPE members kept a daily vigil, with roses, outside the jail.

I'm not a poet, but I ended off my remembrance of Grace at the memorial service with a piece I had written about my last moments with her. It said in part:

> *The taxi came so soon, it seemed.*
> *Grace was tired. It was time to go.*
> *I cradled her soft thin cheeks in my hands.*
> *We held close. I couldn't let go.*

I wanted to ask her so many more things,
to learn so much more, and to hear
of her hopes and her dreams,
her disappointments, her fears.
Because I walk on the road Grace cleared.

In many ways, Grace helped clear a path for all of us. She knew that our journey would be long and hard. She saw the union as the vehicle to progress along that road. She saw the union as a community of working people organizing for themselves and each other – and for their communities – in the interest of equality and social change. If she had lived to see her biography published, I'm sure she would have dedicated it to this ideal.

NOTES

1. The Early Years

Irving Abella, *The Canadian Labour Movement 1902-1960* (Ottawa: Canadian Historical Society, Booklet #28, 1975).

Merrily Weisbord, *The Strangest Dream* (Montréal: Véhicule Press, 1994).

2. Local 373 and the Township of North York

Craig Heron, *The Canadian Labour Movement: A Short History* (Toronto: Lorimer, 1989).

3. Sister Hartman and Women's Liberation

Ruth Frager, "Women Workers and the Canadian Labour Movement 1870-1940" in *Union Sisters*, eds. Linda Briskin and Lynda Yanz (Toronto: The Women's Press, 1983).

Erna Paris, "The Education of Madeleine Parent," in *Her Own Woman: Profiles of Ten Canadian Women* (Toronto: Macmillan, 1975).

Wayne Roberts, *Honest Womanhood: Feminism, Femininity and Class Consciousness among Toronto Working Women 1893-1914* (Toronto: New Hogtown Press, 1976).

Joan Sangster, *Dreams of Equality: Women on the Canadian Left 1920-1950* (Toronto: McClelland & Stewart, 1989).

4. The Secretary Takes National Office

Gloria Montero, *We Stood Together: First-hand Accounts of Dramatic Events in Canada's Labour Past* (Toronto: Lorimer, 1979).

Robert Laxer, *Canada's Unions* (Toronto: Lorimer, 1976).

Gwen Matheson, ed. *Women in the Canadian Mosaic* (Toronto: Peter Martin Associates, 1976).

5. Leading Canada's Largest Union

Leo Panitch and Cy Gonick, "Wage Controls," *Canadian Dimension*, vol. 11, no. 1, February 1976.

Jerry White, *Hospital Strike: Women, Unions and Public Sector Conflict* (Toronto: Thompson Educational Publishing, 1989).

INDEX